*Twayne's English Authors Series*

EDITOR OF THIS VOLUME

Kinley E. Roby

*Northeastern University*

*L. P. Hartley*

TEAS 232

# L. P. HARTLEY

## By EDWARD T. JONES
*York College of Pennsylvania*

**TWAYNE PUBLISHERS**
A DIVISION OF G. K. HALL & CO., BOSTON

Copyright © 1978 by G. K. Hall & Co.

Published in 1978 by Twayne Publishers,
A Division of G. K. Hall & Co.
All Rights Reserved

Printed on permanent/durable acid-free paper and bound
in the United States of America

*First Printing*

Frontispiece photo of L. P. Hartley
courtesy of Hamish Hamilton, Ltd.

Library of Congress Cataloging in Publication Data
Jones, Edward Trostle.
L. P. Hartley.

(Twayne's English authors series ; TEAS 232)
Bibliography
Includes index.
1.   Hartley, Leslie Poles—Criticism and
interpretation.
PR6015.A6723Z72   1978       823'.9'12       78-4564
ISBN 0-8057-6703-7

To my parents

# Contents

# About the Author

Edward T. Jones is Associate Professor of English at York College of Pennsylvania, York, Pennsylvania, where he has taught since 1971. A graduate of Juniata College in his native Pennsylvania, he took his M.A. and Ph.D. at the University of Maryland. He has pursued additional study at the Bread Loaf School of English and the University of Grenoble in France. In 1973 he participated in a Summer Seminar at the University of Virginia sponsored by the National Endowment for the Humanities. He also taught at the University of Maryland and Central College, Pella, Iowa. His areas of specialization include Renaissance and contemporary literature as well as inter-cultural studies of the relationship between literature and the other arts and media. He has addressed regional and national conventions of the Modern Language Association of America and contributed articles to a variety of periodicals and journals. At present he is collaborating in editing a critical volume on approaches to the study of literature in relationship to the other arts. Professor Jones is a frequent discussant for community theatrical productions. He resides in York, Pennsylvania, with his wife and two daughters.

# Preface

The purpose of this critical study of L. P. Hartley's fiction is to examine the substantial canon, for the first time in its entirety, of an attractive and distinctive minor master of twentieth-century British prose fiction. Never a widely popular novelist, Hartley is the kind of writer whom enthusiastic readers perennially "discover" in libraries, small and large, throughout Britain and the United States, readers who then seek to introduce the pleasures of such readership to their friends. In that regard, Hartley shares both the aura and fate of a number of modern British novelists with their quasi-coterie status and reputation.

With some of these authors he shares more than a similar fate of neglect. There is a measure of resemblance, for example, between Ivy Compton-Burnett's novels of family life and some of Hartley's novels, although the attendant horror is far greater in the former. Likewise, Angus Wilson and Hartley share a similar moral rigor and recognition of good and evil together with a penchant for using nineteenth-century and twentieth-century narrative techniques. More recondently, a shared Forsterian tone links Hartley's novels with those of his less well-known (at least in the United States) friends—L. H. Myers, C. H. B. Kitchin, and, more recently, Francis King. An Anglicized Proustian common denominator coupled with social comment and satire might be summoned to link Hartley with Anthony Powell. On the other hand, the anti-utopian novels of Aldous Huxley and George Orwell suggest connections with Hartley's *Facial Justice*. Then, too, Hartley's delineation of external surfaces and his depiction of limited awareness are reminiscent, respectively and / or in tandem, of Elizabeth Bowen and Graham Greene. But infinite regress looms before further imputed tendencies. Suffice it to say, Hartley fits comfortably into twentieth-century British fiction while preserving his own distinctive voice.

My reading of L. P. Hartley is indebted to earlier interpreters, especially the two previous book-length studies of selected works, Peter Bien's *L. P. Hartley* and Anne Mulkeen's *Wild Thyme, Winter Lightning: The Symbolic Novels of L. P. Hartley*. Both these previous studies began as doctoral dissertations, and Hartley's reputation among American academicians remains high. With the aim of being neither too far out nor too in-depth, the present study observes Hartley's fiction in its totality by letting the Hartleian imagination speak for itself as often as possible, supported and extended by critical comment and analysis. Thus, while acknowledging that quotation is often an unsatisfactory method for critical analysis, I have included fairly extensive quotations from L. P. Hartley in order to suggest something of the quality of his books which, unfortunately, are not readily available in the United States. Even the paperback edition of Hartley's popular *The Go-Between* has recently gone out of print in this country. In rather leisurely passages, Hartley's style and sensibility are shown to best advantage, often without the necessity of a critical gloss. Of course, excerpts cannot substitute for the experience of the book itself, but perhaps some of the delight of whole works can be adumbrated through selected parts.

Rather than through observance of strict chronology, the following pages examine Hartley's canon according to thematic, generic, and structural groupings of individual works in the hope thereby of illuminating underlying conceptual unities which contribute to the creation of an *oeuvre*. This book is divided into eleven chapters. Chapter 1, which very briefly treats Hartley's life, attempts to set the biographical background for an interpretation of his fiction. Chapter 2 offers some suggestions for defining the Hartleian novel. Chapter 3 looks at Hartley's work in the short story. Chapters 4 through 9 discuss Hartley's novels. Chapter 10 considers Hartley's single volume of literary criticism, *The Novelist's Responsibility*, as a reflection of his tastes and concerns. Chapter 11 assesses his contribution to and place in British fiction of the twentieth century.

To many I owe a debt of gratitude for helping to make this book possible. My earliest debts are to my graduate professors at the University of Maryland: George A. Panichas who first introduced me to L. P. Hartley and Charles C. Mish whose love of early and recent fiction together with his generosity in making what must have seemed like permanent loans of books helped me considerably. I am especially grateful to Mr. Roger Machell of Hamish Hamilton Ltd. for numerous favors. Miss Norah Hartley has also been most kind and helpful. At various times in preparing this study, I have been aided and encouraged by correspondence with Professors Harvey Curtis Webster and Walter Allen, and, above all, Mr. Francis King, all of whom were friends of the late L. P. Hartley. Like Marianne Moore I recognize that acknowledgments may incriminate rather than honor; therefore, responsibility for errors in the book is, of course, wholly mine.

To a few I owe a special debt of gratitude. Ms. Joan Fortney, my former student and continued friend, assisted me when I most needed it. Former colleagues, Dr. Peg Cruikshank and Professor Robert O'Dell extended themselves most graciously on my behalf. Dr. Richard P. Batteiger, my very supportive department chairman at York College of Pennsylvania, helped me in numerous ways, including securing from the college administration a teaching load reduction for me which helped me to complete the study. My colleagues have been extremely kind, and I thank them collectively, with a personal aside of appreciation to Professors Van R. Baker, James L. Morrison, Jr., and Philip J. Avillo, Jr.

Finally, I must thank my father-in-law, Al Liebergott, for turning our basement into a study for me and playroom for the children; my wife, Ruth, for patient endurance and the gift of an IBM electric typewriter; and our daughters, Miranda and Vanessa, for diverting me by bringing something of their playroom into my study.

For permission to quote from the works of L. P. Hartley, I am indebted to the executors of the estate of the late L. P. Hartley and to Hamish Hamilton, Ltd. For permission to quote from the *Eustace and Hilda* trilogy, originally published by Putnam, I am grateful to The Bodley Head, Ltd.

EDWARD TROSTLE JONES

*York College of Pennsylvania*
*York, Pennsylvania*

# Chronology

1895    Leslie Poles Hartley, born at Whittlesea, a small town in the Cambridgeshire fens, December 30. Second of three children born to H. B. Hartley and Mary Elizabeth Thompson Hartley.

1896 - 1909    Lived at the family home, Fletton Tower, near Peterborough. Frequently visited his mother's farm home, Crawford House, Crowland in Lincolnshire.

1910    Entered Harrow School, Middlesex.

1915    Leaf Scholar, Harrow School; matriculated on 19 October at Balliol College, Oxford University.

1916 - 1918    Enlisted April, 1916 in The Great War and served as Second Lieutenant in the Norfolk Regiment; invalided out of military service in September, 1918.

1919 - 1921    Returned to Balliol for the Michaelmas Term; named Williams Exhibitioner and took his B.A. Degree 1 December 1921. Passed his Final examination in Modern History and was placed in the Second Class Honours.

1922    Remained at Balliol for a full academic year after his Finals but did not begin work toward a higher degree; first visited Venice.

1924    First volume of short stories, *Night Fears*, published.

1925    Novella, *Simonetta Perkins*, published.

1932    Second volume of short stories, *The Killing Bottle*, published.

1933 - 1939    Regularly visited Venice for April, May, and June and returned for October and November; visits suspended by outbreak of the Second World War.

1944    *The Shrimp and the Anemone*, begun twenty years earlier, published, the first volume of the eventual *Eustace and Hilda* trilogy.

1946    *The Sixth Heaven*, the second volume of the trilogy, published.

1947    *Eustace and Hilda*, the third volume of the trilogy, published.

1948    Awarded the James Tait Black Memorial Prize for *Eustace and Hilda*. Mother died at the age of eighty-five. Third volume of short stories, *The Traveling Grave*, published.

1949    *The Boat* published.

1951    *My Fellow Devils* published.

1953    *The Go-Between* published and awarded the W. H. Heinemann Foundation Prize of the Royal Society of Literature.

1954    Father died at the age of ninety-four. Fourth volume of short stories, *The White Wand*, published.

1955    *A Perfect Woman* published.

1956    Appointed Commander of the British Empire.

1957    *The Hireling* published.

1960    *Facial Justice* published.

1961    Fifth volume of short stories, *Two for the River*, published. Served actively during decade of the sixties in the English section of PEN and the Society of Authors.

1964    Clark Lecturer, Trinity College, Cambridge. *The Brickfield* published.

1966    *The Betrayal* published.

1967    *The Novelist's Responsibility: Lectures and Essays* published.

1968    *The Collected Short Stories of L. P. Hartley* and *Poor Clare* published.

1969    *The Love-Adept* published.

1970    *My Sisters' Keeper* published.

1971    *The Harness Room* and *Mrs. Carteret Receives*, sixth volume of short stories, published.

1972    Named Companion of Literature by the Royal Society of Literature. *The Collections* published. Died, of heart failure, London, December 13.

1973    *The Will and the Way* and *The Complete Short Stories of L. P. Hartley* published posthumously.

CHAPTER 1

# L. P. Hartley:
# The Man in Brief

LESLIE Poles Hartley, christened in honor of Sir Leslie Stephen, whom his parents admired and whose fame was not yet eclipsed by his more famous daughter, Virginia Woolf, was born 30 December 1895 at Whittlesea, a small town in the Cambridgeshire fens, and died in London, 13 December 1972. L. P. Hartley was brought up at the family home, Fletton Tower, described by novelist C. H. B. Kitchin and a "gothick castle,"[1] near the cathedral-city of Peterborough. Perhaps proximity to the Peterborough Cathedral brought Hartley *fils* from his father's Wesleyan Methodist faith to the Church of England. His father, H. B. Hartley, was a solicitor who practiced in Peterborough but retired from law early in life to assume chairmanship and direction of what became a very successful brickworks from which the family derived a considerable fortune. In later years L. P. Hartley, who confessed to feelings of snobbery, experienced some embarrassment about the family's success in "trade." His mother, Mary Elizabeth Thompson, was the eldest daughter of William James Thompson, Farmer of Crawford House, Crowland, Lincolnshire.

L. P. Hartley was the middle child and only son in a family of three offspring. An older sister, Enid, and the younger Norah completed the family, which appears to have been a loving and tightly knit unit. Hartley's friend, Paul Bloomfield, comments affectionately on Hartley's parents, whom he calls a remarkable pair:

Mr. Hartley was delightful. By profession a solicitor, he was by nature a grave, kindly, highly literate gentleman like some amiable philosophising character in a discursive book by Anatole France—only I soon recognised that he had a fibre that those others tended to lack. Of his wife, it has been written that "she was one of those small, at first sight, helpless-looking women who can do almost anything except, for long, disguise their enormous force of character." But I may as well be frank and confess that it was I who wrote it. . . . Her minute-to-minute proud solicitude for Leslie was something it did not enter her head to conceal.[2]

Of his father, Hartley himself wrote, "My father did not believe in sending his children to boarding school early; he was a man of culture, and at least half of my education was due to him."[3]

L. P. Hartley was an intensely private man, secured with an independent income sufficient to permit such privacy; but the relationship between his life and art can be explored briefly, though speculatively, on the basis of relatively few received biographical facts. His long life, long despite a sickly childhood, seems rather uneventful. His participation in imagination appears greater than his pursuit of active doing, a circumstance which likewise holds true for many of his protagonists. What Millicent Bell has written of Henry James is apposite for Hartley as well:

Literature gave him a way of both doing and being as nothing else might have, and the result was supremely contenting. It was, after all, an indwelling self-exploration so intense as to seem a mode of action; it was doing at its most motionless and invisible, on the other hand, a thing so entirely of the mind that one might forget that it was a way of interacting with other human beings.[4]

Hartley's work, then, embodies the man more completely than narration of events from his life could probably do, once beyond the anecdotal level. He was a cultivated amateur musician, a collector of art, and, above all, a man of letters who possessed affinities with his namesake, Sir Leslie Stephen. His supposed isolation of spirit undoubtedly contributed to the perfection of his metier, for Hartley was serious about his literary work.

Educated at Harrow School and Balliol College, Oxford, Hartley's formal education was impeccably that of the English gentleman or at the very least the English haut bourgeoise. He expressed, late in life to a friend, regret that his "school" had not been Eton. While friends and observers of Hartley have frequently noted that he looked at the world throughout his life with widening infant's eyes, Paul Bloomfield remarks on the impression the sixteen-year-old Hartley made at Harrow where he seemed civilized beyond his years:

What an ineffaceable impression he [Hartley] made, as a boy in Townsend Warner's form, with his air of falling in courteously with the manners and customs of the primitive society that Warner occasionally reminded us that school was! Leslie had no need to be reminded, and neither for that matter had I. But I was a more agitated sort than he, and to me his singular outward calm, his look at once benevolent and penetrating ("my stalled-ox expression" he once called it was a self-disparagement that has never been a pose), yes, and his credit in the eyes of the fierce Warner who treated him—and quite right, I respectfully thought—as an equal . . . to me all this was, how shall I put it, very *encouraging*.

(*Adam International Review*, 5)

The late distinguished classicist, C. M. Bowra, himself at a later date an Oxford don, offers similar testimony regarding Hartley at Balliol College; of particular interest is the reference to Hartley's nearly cultivated disadvantage with his tutors which subsequent Hartleian Oxonians presumably inherit from their creator:

Leslie Hartley at Balliol seemed much more nature than most of us. He had a winning smile, a quiet, humorous detachment, a keen observation of life, and already wrote with an unusual skill. He waged a quiet war with the dons of Balliol who did not appreciate his full merits and felt that he should work harder. Actually he worked quite hard, but did not make a parade of it. He was well abreast with modern literature and knew about T. S. Eliot and the Sitwells, but his chief personal claim was his gift for intimacy and understanding. He treated literature as part of life and wove its themes into his private relations. Leslie's series of distinguished novels still bear the imprint of his personality at this time, with its humour, its scepticism, and its sudden, scintillating moments of anger or delight.[5]

Hartley's years at Balliol were interrupted by the First World War. He served as a second lieutenant in the Norfolk Regiment, but because of a weak heart he was discharged without seeing action in France. Much later by way of confirming his own patrimony in what R. H. Tawney once called the "generation of illusion" Hartley wrote, "The First World War shook one's belief in the essential goodness of humanity—the belief that all's for the best in the best of all possible world that, with many conspicuous exceptions, had dominated Victorian thought."[6] Following the war Hartley returned to Oxford and received a Second Honours Degree at Balliol in 1921.

Now Hartley's moral and artistic life began, as Henry James might have described it, with a private income and an empty engagement book. From 1923 until the middle forties he was an indefatigable reviewer of fiction for such periodicals as the *Spectator*, *Saturday Review*, *Week-end Review*, *Sketch*, *Observer*, and *Time and Tide.* J. W. Lambert acknowledged this facet of Hartley's writing career in his tribute at the time of the novelist's death:

Between the wars, no reviewer of fiction, I dare say, did more than Hartley to accustom readers outside the rockpools of the literary world to those delicacies of perception which gradually invaded, and ultimately enfeebled, the novel in the assorted wakes of Henry James and Virginia Woolf. From Venice or from his house by the Avon in Bath, he led unadventurous readers down unfamiliar paths with demure charm and inflexible civility.[7]

The Second World War curtailed his yearly sojourns in Venice, but by the end of the war he was publishing the volumes which comprise the trilogy known as *Eustace and Hilda* (1944 - 47). Without having to earn a livelihood by writing, yet demonstrating a desire to be psychologically employed as a man of letters, Hartley used his reviewing and writing of occasional short stories in the nineteen-twenties and thirties as a means of acquiring leisurely readiness for his later novels. At age forty-nine he finally published the first installment of the eventual trilogy, *The Shrimp and the Anemone.* Thereafter, despite some dry periods, Hartley's productivity was nearly prolific: seventeen novels, six volumes of short stories, a book of criticism, with more than half of these appearing in the last decade of his life.

Paul Bloomfield again offers an insight into Hartley's *modus vivendi,* even as a young man, which may partly explain the long interval between publication of his first collection of short stories, *Night Fears* (1924), and the highly regarded novella, *Simonetta Perkins* (1925), and the efflorescence of his maturity:

[Hartley's] attentiveness was integral both with his congenital make-up of a born writer, who attends because it is part of his function to be observant, and with the to-some-extent phlegmatic temperament of a young man not pressed for money and semi-conscious, perhaps, that he had inherited the gene of longevity; he could bide his time. His mother lived to a ripe age, his father died at well over ninety while in the middle of rereading Hardy's *The Woodlanders.* (*Adam International Review,* 6)

Hartley took his literary career seriously in his own distinct fashion and with his own special diffidence. Brought up as he claims he was on the theories of John Stuart Mill concerning man's moral responsibilities, Hartley shuns for himself and his characters sybaritic indulgence. He is a novelist of civilization rather than of the private self, although he usually shows the limits of civility in the individual sensibility or the urbane and cultivated intelligence. Matters of keeping faith with social codes and the manners of society are frequent Hartley concerns. At a fairly advanced age, in explaining the origin of one of his obsessive mature themes, i.e., the state's devaluation of the individual, Hartley wrote,

> I was brought up on the theories of John Stuart Mill to believe that the state is the great enemy because it takes man's moral responsibility out of his hands and imposes its decisions on him, which have come to be accepted as fatalistically as if they were laws of God—more so, indeed, for they have thrived on the decline of the belief in God as the supreme lawgiver, to whom man is responsible for his acts and who is the only keeper of his conscience. The laws of God depend on faith; the laws of the state depend on fact: In the material and to some extent in the moral sphere, the state can make you do what it likes, whereas God cannot; the state has usurped the kingdom, the power, and the glory. The individual has been devalued: He takes his orders from the state. ("Three Wars," p. 255)

It is to the family as the repository of civilized values that Hartley turns rather than to the state. He takes the traditional view that people are born with the capacity for good and evil, to make the best use of their talents or to waste them; and that upon one's early upbringing, especially those standards and that self-discipline with which children are brought up at home and later at school, much of the individual's whole future depends. What is termed in this study the "bourgeois paradigm" for family living figures prominently in Hartley's fiction as a touchstone for individual and social excellence. On the other hand, the biographical fact that not one of the three Hartley children ever married or assumed familial responsibilities of their own cannot be ignored. Without speculating at all on the possible effect of parental design on the adult sexual lives of the Hartley children, it can be noted that Hartley did justice to the darker tangles of family life; and family relationships in Hartley sometimes appear covertly as sexual battlegrounds. Indeed, as commentators have remarked, correctly I think, Hartley's family relationships in his fiction occasionally have much in common with those in Ivy Compton-Burnett's without perhaps her gleeful cruelty.

Hartley worked to pattern his life with moral probity. Similarly, his elder sister, Enid, served for many years as a Justice of the Peace and was, according to her brother, inured to all human frailties.

Norah Hartley, the younger sister, became a well-known breeder of deer-hounds and through that activity possibly participated more directly in the cycle of life and generation than did either her brother or sister. Privileged as they were in their own family, the Hartley children were apparently unwilling to risk disillusionment through marital and familial relationships of their own. But, of course, L. P. Hartley had his art; and while remaining a bachelor in life, he set up housekeeping and portrayed a version of conjugality often enough in his house of fiction.

As if always somewhat suspicious of instinct and spontaneity, Hartley usually portrays passion, particularly adult sexual passion, as an invitation to disaster. Few mature relationships in Hartley prove conducive to long-life and extended happiness. Not surprisingly, then, Hartley writes best and most distinctively about the adolescent's discovery of submerged sexual tension during the transition out of childhood innocence which yields awareness, if not often the experience, of adult possibilities. Hartley expertly captures a turning point in childhood when an awakening appreciation of human relationships is first experienced, frequently with an acceptance rather than a judgment of someone loved.

Sexuality as a component of adult characterization presents difficulties for Hartley, and a certain ambiguity on such matters is pervasive in his work. Whether this attribute has its source in Hartley's biography can only be conjectured. His friend, Francis King, whose own candor is on public record, has assessed L. P. Hartley's reticence most decorously and sympathetically:

Had he been a man less scrupulous about not offending convention or shocking his friends, there is no doubt that, like E. M. Forster's, his books would have been very different. But the tension set up between what he wanted to say and what he felt was sayable by a man of his position and age may, I suspect, have helped to generate the extraordinary electric energy that powers his finest works. Late in his career he began to be more explicit; but even over "The Harness Room" he worried aloud in my presence whether this or that friend might not be shocked and disgusted by it. ("Sweet, Cosy, and Tough: On L. P. Hartley," *Sunday Telegraph*, December 17, 1972)

On the other hand, like Henry James whose very art often depended on ambiguity, Hartley's fiction needed the indirection he espoused in his interplay between society and the individual on most private matters. Biographically, Hartley's own sense of alienation from the social mainstream may be attributable to nothing more than the fact of his never marrying.

Hartley's social position and cultural achievement were buttressed by his being awarded some of England's highest literary honors and prizes, including the James Tait Black Memorial Prize for the most outstanding book published in 1947—*Eustace and Hilda,* and the Heinemann Foundation Prize of the Royal Society of Literature in 1954 upon publication of *The Go-Between* (1953). He served as head of the English section of the International Association of Poets, Playwrights, Editors, Essayists, and Novelists (P.E.N.); and for several years he was a member of the management committee of the Society of Authors. In 1956 L. P. Hartley was appointed Commander of the British Empire. Early in 1972, the last year of his life, Hartley was made a Companion of Literature by the Royal Society of Literature, an honor restricted to ten living British authors.

At his London flat in Rutland Gate and in his country house near Bath on the Avon River, where he often rowed, Hartley was judged a most companionable host. Like other members of the British upper class he spent a great deal of time entertaining or being entertained and frequently traveled abroad. It would be a mistake, however, to suppose therefore that Hartley was somehow frivolous in the manner of Evelyn Waugh's effete characters. On the contrary, Hartley's often tenacious hold on life and his instinct for self-preservation have been remarked upon, as in the following reminiscence, again from Francis King:

"What a sweet, cosy old man!" a woman writer once exclaimed of [Hartley] to me at their first meeting. Certainly he was sweet and cosy—the most charming and considerate of hosts, the most helpful of friends; but it was not the sweetness and cosiness but a formidable intelligence and toughness that gave his novels their touch of genius. (*Sunday Telegraph,* December 17, 1972)

The avuncular Hartley, despite the outward appearance of cosy comfortableness, sought out the darker underside of things imaginatively or vicariously through the experience of others. Through his ever-changing assembly of servants, for example, he appears to have extended his knowledge about human relationships of many kinds. According to J. W. Lambert, Hartley's West Country home was "rich with oriental carpets on floors and walls and ballustrades, and permeated, as often as not, by the presence of those sinister servants who seemed to haunt his life as well as his books" (*The Sunday Times*, December 17, 1972). Indeed, as Francis King suggests, Hartley may have deliberately cultivated a degree of chaos in his otherwise seemingly tranquil life by his very choice of servants. Sometimes their lack of references provided for him the major impetus to hire them. If at times one or another of these employees, themselves somewhat confused about their status as friend or servant in the Hartley household, took advantage of their employer's generosity by running up debts on his account, Hartley would patiently forbear for awhile, and then suddenly a new advertisement for service personnel would appear in the *Times*. As Hartley aged the realities of life in the social and political structure of the modern welfare state failed to win his approval. He deplored the loss of personal responsibility and individual accountability (especially the self-centered trivilization of care and concern for others), but these conditions of modern life provided material for the novelist as the works beginning with *Facial Justice* witness. Hartley the moralist persisted in reaffirming authority to the past and forecasting obligation to the future.

Hartley's increasing severity toward the outside world sometimes approached the blackly comic as, for example, in his proposal once (perhaps with Hawthornesque mordancy) that convicted criminals be visibly branded as a means of reducing the rising crime rate. While such a perspective may confirm Hartley's naïveté as a thinker on the social and political problems of twentieth-century England, he forcefully recognized the more insidious trends at work within his culture which attacked and undermined the traditions he valued. Occasionally Hartley sounds a note of regret or special pleading which implies that he may be deluding himself into thinking he could somehow relive the past. At the end of his writing career and his life, Hartley seems to have sought through his fiction a poignant, if somewhat puerile, emotional identification with something like happy endings, even as his experience, intelligence, and toughness would not quite let him fake them.

The aging Hartley, who probably drank too much, a trait often ascribed to his writer characters in the later short stories, and whose heart trouble worsened as the years passed, remains in the decade of the sixties a survivor in control of life. Between his fiction and the newfound worldliness of modern British life Hartley struck out toward a kind of balance, which, if not actually often achieved, still has its heroic aspect. Like his characters, Hartley strives to please more than to astonish and to charm rather than to stir passion. He was saddened at the generally poor responses, critically and commercially, to his last books; and he regretted his inability to secure an American publisher for them. Yet for all of his very real "English" reserve, Hartley the novelist in his last five years takes a few risks against his customary sense of order. Considering his slow start in writing extended fiction, his last prolific period constitutes, for him, an uninhibited "letting-go." Perhaps he worried less at the end, ironically akin to the spirit of the permissive times he so often disdained and deplored, about what other people thought. Or rather as a slight novel like *The Collections* attests, Hartley steadfastly defined his life by the vast historical context in which Englishmen live, which prevented him from panicking when, in his opinion, things went wrong with modern times.

Appropriately the literary achievement of L. P. Hartley should eclipse the life. The man, like many of his protagonists, succumbed finally to heart disease. But the weak heart which had removed him shortly before the Armistice from the First World War had withstood seventy-six years. At the time of his death his chief bequest was to his younger sister, Norah Hartley. Some people who knew of Hartley's familiarity with the precarious financial state of English PEN found their hopes frustrated. No legacy to that beleaguered organization was forthcoming from provision in Hartley's will. Hartley, however, was true to his own patrimony. His developed sense of what is done or is not done paid unashamedly its last tribute to his family. What else could be expected from a loving son and a devoted brother? The integrity and disciplined relationships of family and class endure for L. P. Hartley even in death. To be sure, his conduct has its parallels in his fiction, confirming once again that life imitates art. Hartley was one of the last gentleman-writers, as Richard Jones has remarked, "with a sensibility schooled at a time when a limited number of people could spend a great deal of time being complex about very little."[8]

However far this sensibility is from contemporary American life and temperament, Hartley's books usually are, as the English say, a "good read," and it is easy to be held and affected by the intelligence, skill, wit, and moral conviction that make Hartley's fiction emotionally all of a piece. At their finest, Hartley's narratives address themselves to what is worth preserving in human life.

CHAPTER 2

# Toward Definition
# of the Hartleian Novel

## I    The Major Influences: Hawthorne, James, Emily Brontë

CONTEMPORARY critics and literary historians who have
noticed and analyzed at any length the work of L. P. Hartley
tend broadly to divide into two camps regarding his artistic ancestry
and identity in twentieth-century British prose fiction: they see him
either as a Jamesian realist or as a latter-day Hawthornian
romancer. Good and persuasive cases have been made for both
these designations, supported by Hartley's own acknowledgment of
this dual influence.[1] In this writer's opinion the influence of
Hawthorne in Hartley's fiction may have been filtered through
Henry James; that is, while Hartley may have considered himself a
moralist in the Hawthornian sense, he wrote more like James.
Indeed, Hartley's nostalgia for innocence (and even immaturity of
the pre-1914 variety) together with his frequent use of symbols (this
latter fact often used to link him to Hawthorne) would seem to ally
him credibly with an Edwardian aesthetic, which Richard Ellmann
thinks can include writers as diverse as James, Conrad, Forster,
Lawrence, and Galsworthy with their penchant for external symbols
and thematic centers.[2] Some years ago, Kenneth Allsop referred to
Hartley as a "marooned Edwardian,"[3] but the more recent revival
of interest in and sympathy for the Edwardians may have removed
some of the patronizing stigma of that remark.
   Perhaps less restrictive than the Edwardian label is Lord David
Cecil's suggestion that Hartley writes in "the classical mode,"
wherein the novelist starts with a pattern imposed by situation, "to
discover some means of imposing an orderly pattern on reality
without making his picture of it unconvincing."[4] Cecil finds this
mode extending from Jane Austen, George Eliot, and Henry James

to their twentieth-century successors, E. M. Forster, Elizabeth Bowen, and L. P. Hartley; all of which may indicate little more than that Hartley inherited nearly a two-century-old moral tradition in the novel. Furthermore, Hartley demonstrates comprehensive knowledge of the art of both the English and American novel which he subtly calls upon in his own fiction. Hartley's range, then, of possible influences is sufficiently large that specific claims of indebtedness become suspect, beyond the recognition that as a novelist Hartley was quite familiar with past achievements in the genre. Early and late, for example, Hartley frequently uses epistolary devices—from *Simonetta Perkins* to *The Will and the Way*, respectively his first novella and posthumously published novel—and he never forgets Samuel Richardson's feelings about the advantage of writing letters "to the moment," on undecided events. As inquiry into human behavior Hartley's fiction avails itself not only of the epistolary form with which Richardson pioneered the genre of the novel but also more recent narrative techniques like the interior monologue.

Because Hartley is a novelist to whom epistemology is important, as it was also for Henry James, his characters are often overwhelmed by the distracting obligation to assume a role in the external world when they scarcely know who or what to be to themselves in their private consciousness. Hartley's characters are likely to distort external reality by means of some consoling fantasy or strategy designed to make a difficult truth palatable or to keep the truth at bay a little longer. What characters actually must confront, as opposed to what they dream or fantasize seeing reveals Hartley's contrast of consciousness and unconsciousness, innocence and experience, and, perhaps most central to the Hartleian games of apprehension, as James Hall felicitously calls them,[5] winners and losers. But, of course, in the twentieth century not only is a convenient scorecard unavailable but a moral standard also eludes the novelist who, like Hartley, looks back to Victorian novelists with some envy; for "they were partisans in the moral sphere: they distinguished sheep from goats."[6]

Hartley's characters often resemble Hawthorne's Miles Coverdale (in *The Blithedale Romance*) whom Henry James describes as having a great deal in common with his creator:

Coverdale is a picture of the contemplative, observant, analytical nature, nursing its fancies, and yet, thanks to an element of strong good sense, not bringing them up to be spoiled children; having little at stake in life, at any given moment, and yet indulging in imagination, in a good many adventures; a portrait of a man, in a word, whose passions are slender, whose imagination is active, and whose happiness lies not in doing, but in perceiving—half a poet, half a critic, and all a spectator.[7]

To be sure, the foregoing supplies a common denominator appropriate to Hawthorne, James, and Hartley characters as well as to the three novelists themselves. When Hartley breaks out of this dominant mold in his fiction, he seems most largely indebted to another of his favorite authors, Emily Brontë, whose influence upon the Hartleian novel may be somewhat subliminal, or at least indirect through her twentieth-century descendant, D. H. Lawrence.

Unlike Lawrence and Emily Brontë, Hartley as a novelist appears more disposed to work out his narrative and its moral implications within the context of traditional society. But insofar as he assumes, from time to time, a prophetic strain, Hartley shares with Emily Brontë an imaginative vision of the interanimation of the earthly and divine sphere, as he probes the world beyond the one we think we know to determine whether people have the imagination to conceive of life as more than the bodies it is written on.

Hartley, moreover, demonstrates further influence of Emily Brontë in his tendency to explore cruelty and perversity, especially the potential dread implicit in impossible connections and completions—between man and woman, brother and sister, and persons of the same sex. Like Emily Brontë, Hartley seems very close to the regressive and "normal" cruelty of childhood, and even more like her, he exhibits a measure of exhilaration from such proximity despite the flawed choices and emotional failures which come out of the nursery.

## II  *Psychological Approaches to Hartley's Novels*

Although Hartley was unusually reluctant to identify a coherent psychological makeup for his characters (*pace,* his continual denial throughout his life that he was familiar with Freudian formulations except in the most general and casual way as currents of twentieth-century opinion), his critics have fewer scruples about such coordinates and influences in his novels. Like Freud, certainly, Hartley shows the near impossibility of outliving one's childhood or the recognition that by mid-adolescence most people know what they are and spend their remaining years reconciling themselves to that knowledge. James Hall, for example, describes characterization in Hartley as "repeated neurotic pattern" (Hall, p. 112):

> More than most people, though, [Hartley's] characters cannot be anybody but themselves. They have worked to be exactly what they are, have made persistent efforts to fit in with some going ideal of conduct, and have established a clear social status. The timid writer [in *The Boat*], the suburban housewife [in *A Perfect Woman*], and the energetic social worker [in *My Fellow Devils*] seem in the beginning, the commonest of stereotypes, and mean to be just that. But a perverse desire to violate these carefully built images of themselves takes hold of them. They want, at the same time, a life so habitual as to create no emotional stress and a life different from this one they know how to live. (Hall, p. 113)

It is a considerable psychoanalytic leap from James Hall's view of attempted character change in Hartley's fiction as a matter of perverse desire or Freudian neurosis to Anne Mulkeen's reading of Hartleian characterization and plotting according to Jungian monomyth:

> And so the individual search for salvation, for meaning, is the core of, the key to, the Hartley cosmos. The search takes place amid the seemingly opaque properties and petty events of contemporary urban and suburban life—except that always an imaginative eye within the story (usually the protagonist's own) gives us a vision of these landscapes and homes and clothes and pleasures as the stuff of dreams and Golden Ages, of gods and demons, heavens and hells. . . . Hartley's stories build upon (often play upon) the age-old archetypal patterns discerned by Jung in dream, romance, fairy-tale, religious rite—the monomyth of heroic quest, ordeal, death and rebirth. (Mulkeen, pp. 156 - 157)

If a psychoanalytic model is desirable for Hartley (which it probably is not), perhaps a better source than either Freud or Jung is Erik Erikson whose popularization of the life-cycle displays an imaginative faculty which is closer to that of a good novelist than to the usual received image of a psychiatric clinician. In particular, Hartley's fiction considered as studies of human character from youth to old age parallels the last three stages of the famous Eriksonian life-cycle, especially the crises often attendant upon the challenge and dynamics of change—the crisis of Identity, the crisis of Generativity, and the crisis of Integrity.[8] While, generally, these crises occur in youth, middle age, and old age respectively, they can overlap as they do in Hartley's fiction, although the predominating crisis is usually commensurate to the chronological age of the protagonist as described by Erikson's hypothesis of the life-cycle. Thus, the so-called identity crisis, which is never very far out of range in any Hartley novel, rules supreme in the novels of remembered adolescence like *The Go-Between* and *The Brickfield* where Hartley examines the consciousness of a young person trying to discover who he is apart from what others believe or wish him to be. Erikson's use of the word, *crisis*, connotes, of course, not so much catastrophe as a time of both increased vulnerability and heightened potential for change—connotations which are wholly consistent with Hartley's portrayal of adolescence.

Erikson's crisis of generativity, a crisis of conscience as opposed to consciousness, is by definition an adult dilemma in which people of some maturity wonder what moral influence they have had on others—for good or ill. In one way or another, most of Hartley's adult protagonists from *The Boat* onward face the generativity crisis in exercising their freedom and choice, often more vicariously than directly, under the guise of Hartley's favorite go-between role. For example, the aged Leo in *The Go-Between* partly fulfills his neglected generativity in helping to reconcile a member of a younger generation to the problematic future, and Leadbitter in *The Hireling* performs the same service for Lady Franklin.

Because Hartley likes to reflect upon youth from the perspective of old age, his dual articulation of time frequently incorporates a concern with fate and necessity, characteristics of old age (Erikson's integrity crisis), with the identity crisis of remembered youth. Or in later novels with aged protagonists, Hartley develops the constituents of a final resolved integrity crisis as an heroic, if last, will and testament. Erikson's statement on integrity deserves quotation for its applicability to Hartley:

It is the ego's accrued assurance of its proclivity for order and meaning. It is a post-narcissistic love of the human ego—not of the self—as an experience which conveys some world order and spiritual sense, no matter how dearly paid for. It is the acceptance of one's one and only life cycle as something that had to be and that, by necessity, permitted of no substitutions. . . . It is a comradeship with the ordering ways of distant times and different pursuits, as expressed in the simple products and sayings of such times and pursuits. Although aware of the relativity of all the various life styles which have given meaning to human striving, the possessor of in-

tegrity is ready to defend the dignity of his own life style against all
physical and economic threats.

(Childhood and Society, p. 232)

Not only is Erikson's summation of integrity relevant to Hartley's
last novels like *The Collections* and *The Will and the Way* where
the accumulated possessions of a lifetime materially embody for his
characters the dignity of their life style and their place in one seg-
ment of history, but it also is a possible way of viewing the more
sharply crystallized end toward which Hartley's children in other
novels embark. According to Hartley (and to Erikson) childhood is
the place where the adult's particular virtues and vices slowly but
with increasing clarity develop and make themselves felt.
Therefore, the child is less father of the man than the beginning of
the man *qua* man himself—a notion which is very close to Erikson's
epigenetic viewpoint of the life cycle. Admittedly, Hartley's adults
have considerable difficulty deciding to whom—if anyone—they
may give whatever sense of identity, generativity, or integrity they
have achieved. Generativity, for instance, is always in danger of
yielding to its opposite state, stagnation, when Hartley's middle-
aged or prematurely middle-aged adults succumb to self-
centeredness. Yet Hartley's fiction remains true to his engagement
with the sequence of generations and his faith in a process of
growth in which the past is not left behind but endures, shapes, and
finally is assimilated into the present: time future is, indeed, contained in time past. In Hartley the immaturity of youthful illusion
gives way to the absolute and terrifying realism of maturity and integrity, relatively independent of individual fate, as styles of adaptation become increasingly significant for survival. Living, as his
protagonists often sadly discover, involves losing people and learn-
ing to love new people.

Despite the greater congeniality of the Eriksonian life cycle to
Hartley, as opposed to a Freudian or Jungian formulation, the
novelist's conception of stages on life's way may finally have more
in common with Kierkegaard than with Erikson—a progression in
Christian understanding. However well psychology accounts for
anxiety, it is less adequate in describing the operation of faith which
Hartley intimates should replace anxiety. Perhaps the only species
of psychoanalysis which Hartley could wholeheartedly embrace
would be what William J. Bouwsma terms "the Christian form of
psychoanalysis,"[9] derived from the method of Augustine's

*Confessions:* retracing through God's presence and with His help
the whole course of a life with the aim of recovering the health of
faith. Nevertheless, faith, as a function of man's dependence on
God, has often been repudiated by mankind in his historical existence, and no more so than in the twentieth century. By
acknowledging this latter fact, Hartley is careful not to substitute in
place of faith some more recent panacea like psychoanalysis. He
cannot merely represent in his fiction what modern people do
without hinting at the relationship these actions have to the principles and purposes, considered eschatologically, of human existence. While this concern may not necessarily culminate in a
resurgence or even assertion of faith, it does confirm Hartley as a
moralist, an epithet the novelist proudly accepted. Virtue, while less
than faith, is a partial answer to sin and demonstrates, as Hartley
would wish, that for the novelist something matters.

Caught between the weight of the past and the fear of the future,
Hartley's go- and in-between characters reluctantly find the capacity for growth. Once more Bouwsma's conception of Christian
adulthood appears apt:

> . . . the worst state of man is not so much sinfulness (for sins can be
> forgiven) as the cessation of growth, arrested development, remaining fixed
> at any point in life. In these terms just as adulthood requires growth, its op-
> posite—what might be called the Christian conception of immaturity—is
> the refusal to grow, the inability to cope with an open and indeterminate
> future (that is, the future itself), in effect the rejection of life as a process.
> (Bouwsma, p. 87)

If Western civilization lacks a concept of the whole of life, in contrast to the civilizations of the East, as Erikson has argued, Hartley,
the diffident Christian,[10] qualifies his characters' nostalgia for the
only reality they can be sure of—the past—by offering at least
through implication the wholeness of the saving work of Christ
whereby all believers insofar as they are growing in Christ are,
irrespective of chronological disparity, "equally becoming
adults—or equally becoming children" (Bouwsma, p. 87).

Hartley's characterizations of a curiously detached lovingness
follow from his conception of humanity as explained by Lord David
Cecil: "Man, as seen by Mr. Hartley, is born with a soul that instinctively desires virtue and happiness. But some original sin in
himself and the nature of things is at work to thwart his strivings

toward them and brings them, more often than not to disaster—a disaster he accepts as largely deserved."[11]

### III  *Hartley, Sir Thomas Browne, the Great and True Amphibian: Emblems and Dualities*

Hartley doubtlesssly identified himself and his characters with Sir Thomas Browne's great and true amphibian, man, who lives in a divided and distinguished world, allied both to the visible and invisible realms. Paul Bloomfield reports that at Hartley's Balliol College digs the future novelist invited friends to put it about "that we met for the purpose of reading Sir Thomas Browne, a rich edition of whose works in three volumes, one of them (opened at random) was always in prominent position during our sessions" (Bloomfield, "L.P.H.: Short Note on a Great Subject," p. 5). Despite the facetiousness, this Brownian emblem helps to account for the range of dualities present in Hartley's art and thought, as he negotiates amphibiously between the residual romancer's sea of enchantment and the novelist's land of reality, always aware—unlike his characters—which hemisphere he resides in at any given moment. He imitates Browne in seeing that artists must appeal to the senses, showing substantial things in order to shadow forth abstract concepts best expressed through analogy and symbolism. Skeptical of man's ability to find the truth, Hartley manipulates between the world he lives in and the world he imagines—perhaps a little like J. R. R. Tolkien 's "Primary World" and "Secondary World" retrieving via the novel the institution of dreaming in significant form, yet qualifying it with a measure of self-mockery that can be seen as novelistic in the English tradition of the comic novel.

Hartley is able to integrate within one volume and from novel to novel a variety of fictive modes from romance to realism including the *Bildungsroman,* naturalistic and psychological analysis, and studies of manners, all channeled toward felicity of formal design. Generic transformations within the novel form are easier for Hartley to manage than the transfigured lives which the submerged romancer in him would like to envisage, even as the novelist recognizes the essential impossibility of such character transfiguration. Because Hartley never loses sight of man's final possession, the meaningful potential of existence, his characters are fully realized in their novelistic identities without sacrifice of what might be termed their romance "entity," to borrow from Gertrude Stein's distinction (later picked up by Saul Bellow) between identity which one has and entity, an almost impersonal power, which one is (or could be). Accordingly, character itself in Hartley sometimes partakes of a subtle cultural cohesion different from and greater than the consistencies of psychological realism, as the author looks toward the romance and its promise of an upward journey toward recovery of a myth to replace reality. Hartley's characters alternate between wishfulfillment and anxiety over things as they are. Northrop Frye's formulation in *The Secular Scripture* of the vision in romance suggests the basis of its appeal to Hartley even as the realist in him prevents complete acceptance of that vision:

> But a man lives in two worlds, the world of nature and the world of art that he is trying to build out of nature. The world of art, of human culture and civilization, is a creative process informed by a vision. The focus of this vision is indicated by the polarizing in romance between the world we want and the world we don't want. The process goes on in the actual world, but the vision which informs it is clear of that world, and must be kept unspotted from it.[12]

Perhaps the social snobbery of romance appeals to Hartley as a means of salvaging standards of moral conduct—of keeping his ideal world unsullied, but the ultimate freedom of romance is denied by his chosen genre, the novel. Hartley's frequent adoption of symbolism, for example, while not always the most credible part of his novels, brings an element of the romance to his mode of telling.

Alternately attracted by and repelled by the world of nature, Hartley draws toward the world of art where one is able to believe both what is and what is not. One of Hartley's sustaining tenets is an insistence on the individuality of people and even of things. In particular, Hartley displays no sympathy for the idea of a collective society. He writes as if he believes civilization still exists and is worth protecting. He does not exhibit the bitter line of hostility to civilization and culture which sometimes has been assumed to be the characteristic element of modern literature. Rather, Hartley's novels provide powerful reinforcement of a particular class structure and of a social structure adapted to support it. Money, position, legacies, favorite art objects, performances of music, and the like serve to define character in Hartley, even as he takes some pains to insure that bourgeois privilege and highly developed cultural interests do not entirely separate his characters humanly from people without them. While fully conscious of the social, psychological, and moral dislocations of the twentieth century which have disrupted civilization and cast doubt on its existence and continuance, Hartley seems to hold the Jamesian notion that it takes an endless amount of history to make even a little tradition, an endless amount of tradition to make even a little taste, and an endless amount of taste, by the same token, to make even a little tranquility.

Hartley's fundamentally favorable reading of traditional bourgeois values, of course, is not something new in English fiction; it extends backward in time to before Jane Austen and continues, if in a somewhat diminished and ironic form, in the modern English social history offered by Anthony Powell. What Hartley especially celebrates in his characters' lives is their essentially private mode of life, which itself is a distinctly bourgeois legacy as historian John Lukacs explains:

> We are approaching a social situation where the most envied, and most admired people will be those who can afford privacy, not merely financially but culturally speaking, by which I mean people who have inherited or acquired a largely private way of life, who are able to live by themselves with their families, who are not entirely dependent upon the standardized and mechanical features of mass society and of mass culture, of mass entertainment and of mass leisure. [13]

Throughout his career Hartley subscribed to John Stuart Mill's belief that the individual will works to oppose the drab parade that utilitarianism, public opinion, and indiscriminate equalizing makes of human lives. At the same time, Hartley's characters are not mere accumulations of individualist impulses; nor does consciousness replace character in his fiction, although his characters are conspicuously subjects of their own history and not the objects of social structures. Perhaps because his characters both need and hate society, they are capable, as John Bayley submits in defense of the kind of art which bourgeois society nurtures, of loving it:

> Only bourgeois society can thus, so far as one can see, produce the balance. A totally "committed" society, if such a thing were possible, would have no use for the novel of character and no proper understanding of how it works. From the point of view of the "character" novel, society may be—indeed must be—mad; but we are compelled to live in it and make the best of it. [14]

In contrast to the Bloomsbury writers whose highly individualist morality remained principally subjectivist and aesthetic, Hartley as a moralist is closer to a transcendentalist position, since he touches on universal matters in his novels—addressing timeless questions of alienation, responsibility, and the soul's distant prospects for redemption. With his cool, yet compassionate and lucid prose style, a concise phrase or two can sustain amazement, exaltation, and disapproval; yet his longer periods unite the moral and the aesthetic as well as the individual impulse with the social. Like his exemplar, Sir Thomas Browne, who, seeking neither compromise nor neutrality, actively defended the Anglican Cathedral in Norwich against volatile seventeenth-century dissenters threatening to destroy it, the cathedral-loving L. P. Hartley took his stand on behalf of cultural traditions and moral values, both of which inform his fiction and preserve its continuity with the literary past. Part of the pleasure of reading Hartley novels is discovering the allusive texture of his conception of the genre in which he works to make art give meaning to life, all without excessive bookishness.

From the beginning of his rather delayed start as a novelist, Hartley seemed the finished, consummate craftsman who paid his debt to his predecessors by the originality of his invention and sensibility derived from them. He remains a minor master, one of these rare artists who has something to say about culture and civilization and who can express serious thoughts with ingratiating humor and poignant candor. Neither novelists nor his protagonists are readily drawn into the mainstream of contemporary life, a reluctance which exerts its own special appeal; but Hartley succeeds with stylish inventiveness to implicate his aloof characters in novelistic cause-and-effect relationships that have the power to attract, touch, and finally haunt readers who share his literate (and literary) sensibility together with his toughness.

CHAPTER 3

# L. P. Hartley and Short Fiction

HARTLEY'S earliest successes in imaginative literature were with short stories, beginning with his first volume, *Night Fears* (1924); and his interest in this genre continued throughout his life, with additional volumes appearing at regular intervals: *The Killing Bottle* (1932), *The Travelling Grave* (1951), *The White Wand* (1954), *Two for the River* (1961), and *Mrs. Carteret Receives* (1971). *The Collected Stories of L. P. Hartley* appeared in 1968, and a revised volume including the stories from *Mrs. Carteret Receives* appeared posthumously in 1973 under the title, *The Complete Short Stories of L. P. Hartley*, which is the edition used here.[1]

By far the largest number of these stories is in the Gothic mode which Hartley derived from his beloved forbears, Poe, Hawthorne, James, and the Brontës. Hartley's point presumably was to write the kind of story that these great predecessors might have written had they lived in the twentieth century. If Hartley demonstrates that he occasionally possesses what T. S. Eliot called in Hawthorne, "the ghost sense," in a larger measure his tales of the supernatural are examples of craft rather than art, an *amusette*, as Henry James rather erroneously termed the deceptive child's play of his own *The Turn of the Screw*.

Admittedly some other commentators have regarded these productions more highly, as manifestations of Hartley's genius rather than of his powers to mimic his favorite antecedents. Lord David Cecil, for example, asserts,

> Mr. Hartley's moral preoccupations also have their place in his tales of terror. His ghosts are never inexplicable elementals, but the spirit of vengeance or manifestations of spiritual evil. This moral element in his tales gives them a disturbing seriousness not to be found in the ordinary ghost story. Like those of Henry James and Walter De LaMare, they are parables of their authors' profounder beliefs. ("Introduction to *The Collected Short Stories* of L. P. Hartley," 1968, *The Complete Short Stories*, p. viii)

One's approach to the Hartley canon may well determine the thematic emphasis and evaluation accorded the short stories. Thus Anne Mary Mulkeen, who sees as the center of Hartley's art his exploitation of new artistic forms to reveal and illuminate the spiritual crisis in contemporary civilization, finds that his "ghost stories give us intimations of the apocalyptic universe which moves in the background of his novels." In her view of Hartley, "the visible world we live in is surrounded by, in touch with a greater and more frightening invisible one of spirits, forces, connections, and consequences." (Mulkeen, p. 26)

## I   Crosscurrents between Short Stories and Novels

Students of Hartley's fiction should be grateful to Miss Mulkeen and to Paul Bloomfield before her (in his Hartley monograph for the British Council's Writers and Their Work series) for initiating the pleasure of making and marking connections between the short stories and the novels, a task which earlier interpreters had not attempted. These crosscurrents may be as casual as a shared image or symbolic description or the germ of a theme begun in a short story and amplified in a novel.

An example of a shared image or metaphor in "The Island" from the earliest collection, *Night Fears,* appears when Mrs. Santander's island is described "as some crustacean, swallowed by an ill-turned starfish, but unassimilated." (p. 210) Another image derived from marine biology comes to the mind of someone familiar with Hartley's canon—the shrimp and the anemone of the *Eustace and Hilda* trilogy, the first volume of which was probably begun about the same time as "The Island." Although the Santanders in this story have constructed their island home without sharp angles and edges—an architectural feature which Hartley will return to in *Facial Justice*—their marriage develops its own "edges" as Mrs. Santander in her husband's absence takes on a series of lovers. To the narrator, the latest, if least, of the lovers, Mr. Santander explains how he acquired his torn fingernail, "a jagged rent revealing the quick, moist and gelatinous." (p. 221) The description again suggests a similar slimy, sea provenance. Santander's injury was incurred in the act of strangling his wife. He, in turn, kills himself by leaping sixty feet onto the rocks below, and the primordial ooze reclaims a sophisticated specimen. Meanwhile, the corpse of Mrs. Santander remains in its place in the easy chair.

The genesis of *Poor Clare* (1968) would seem to be two stories from *The White Wand* collection, "Witheling End" and "Up the Garden Path." In the former story, Oswald Clayton signals the end of a friendship by inviting guests to spend a weekend with him at his home in Witheling End. The narrator of the story assumes he has been given the *coup de grâce* as a result of his weekend visit; but a mutual friend, a painter named Ponting, explains the basis of Oswald's dilemma, which he succeeded in extracting from him in the course of another weekend visit:

> He said it made him nervous and shy, looking after people in his own house, especially when he felt he had got on their nerves. He did everything he could, he went out of his way to give them a jolly time; but it was killing work, he said, like trying to warm up an icicle; they just moped and drooped and dripped. What he really meant was, they were like warmed-up death. But he didn't blame them; he said it was all his fault. Then we laughed over the whole affair. (pp. 343 - 344)

The air cleared, "Witheling End" closes with reconciliation and friendships intact as Ponting whistles for Oswald to join him and the narrator upstairs in the latter's flat.

"Up the Garden Path," on the other hand, catches the tragic tone and the insuperable misunderstanding and betrayal of friendship which characterizes *Poor Clare*. The story examines a love triangle which pits a man of aesthetic sensibility against a callous realist for the affections of a woman named, ironically, Constantia. Christopher Fenton, away in Rome, asks his barrister friend, Ernest Gretton, to visit his country home and at a designated hour to inspect his beloved garden as if through the eyes of his absent host. Yielding to his friend's request, Ernest journeys to New Forest and discovers Constantia already there with the same commission. Christopher's absence being almost more potent than his presence, Constantia refuses to submit to Ernest's suggestion that since they have been put into the position of an illicit couple, they should accept the challenge. Ernest ruminates with distaste on what Christopher's flowers represent:

> The flowers, I felt, represented that part of Christopher with which I was least in sympathy; his instinct to substitute for life something that was apart from life—something that would prettify it, aromatize it, falsify it, enervate and finally destroy it. (p. 420)

Hartley exposes a contest of wills played out against an alternating sinister Hawthornian garden and a Lawrentian garden of pastoral fulfillment, the backdrop emblematic of Hartley's recurring ambivalence toward his literary predecessors. Ernest insists that Christopher has kept Constantia trapped in the unreality of what he terms a "eunuch's paradise" (p. 422), thereby denying himself and Constantia the opportunity to become man and wife. When the time comes for the couple to view the garden according to their promise to Christopher, Ernest manages to lock Constantia in the house and then proceeds to fall asleep outside her door until the sound of a shot wakes him. He finds her uninjured, and silently they repair to the garden to follow the promenades outlined for them in Christopher's letters. Their absent host, in the shadow of a towering rhododendron bush, is found shot:

> Something or someone—perhaps Christopher, perhaps Constantia in the shock of her discovery, had shaken the bush, for the body was covered with rose-pink petals, and his forehead, his damaged forehead, was adrift with them. Even the revolver in his hand had petals on it, softening its steely gleam. But for that, and for something in his attitude that suggested he was defying Nature, not obeying her, one might have supposed that he had fallen asleep under his own flowers. (p. 427)

In his final letter dated Sunday 4:30, Christopher explains that he had meant to join his two friends at the garden-party, but their tardiness in keeping their promise has led him to alternative action, suicide. "Was it too much to ask, that you should keep your promise to me, or too little? All my life I have been asking myself this question, in one form or another, and perhaps this is the only answer. Bless you, my children, be happy—Christopher." (p. 427) The benediction anticipatory also of the ending of *Facial Justice* renders impossible Christopher's injunction to happiness. As in *Poor Clare*, Constantia is unable to forgive either herself or Ernest for having failed their friend; and after the inquest, Ernest reports they never met again.

Seen from Ernest's point of view, Christopher was a failure who deserved to die because he was unable to come to terms with life; but "Up the Garden Path" is more complex (or at least more equivocal) than Ernest's interpretation of events in the story. Christopher is a lover of beauty, and as his garden shows, a careful cultivator of art. But the artist needs appreciators of his handiwork—an audience. His art, however, is too remote from human life to be intelligible to realists like Ernest. Men of action scarcely ever credit their counterparts who cultivate imagination and sensibility with anything more than sentimentality. Ernest assumes Christopher must have some ulterior motive which, in fact, he probably does not have. However, Christopher's innocence and in-genuousness hold danger both for himself and others in a corrupt world; his suicide note tacitly acknowledges the guilt which accompanies innocence, especially when one indulges in the typically Hartleian go-between role of experiencing life vicariously through friends.

Less covertly, Hartley in the same collection, explores the relationship of the literary artist to his life and work which prefigures *The Love-Adept.* In "A Rewarding Experience," writer Henry Tarrant is unable to write a short story he has been commissioned to produce. Despite precedents like *The Golden Bowl,* Tarrant cannot write any longer about objects nor can he evoke Nature in the manner of Hardy or Conrad. While he had written often in the past about the human race, nothing new on the species stirs his consciousness. Hartley's description of Tarrant and his dilemma approaches droll self-reference, even self-parody:

Harry Tarrant was a bachelor and fiction-writing had confirmed him in the single state. The more he wrote about human beings the less he wanted to have anything to do with them. He got them where he wanted them, and that was outside. Outside, they obeyed the rules—his rules. Critics had remarked on his aloofness, but it was perfectly in order for an artist to be aloof. (p. 379)

Later, he reminisces that he had kept "illness at bay, the war at bay, marriage at bay: he had kept life itself at bay. Only art had he welcomed; and now art had gone back on him." (p. 379)

Into this life comes a lady and her dog who bring, much to Tarrant's relief, blood and dirt into his fastidious house and too well-ordered rooms. On a walk he encounters a dog-fight; separating the two dogs and returning a pet to its mistress, Tarrant sustains a bloody hand. The woman is solicitous about him and accompanies him to his home. Proud of the evidence of his own blood shed in defense of another, even a spaniel, Tarrant enjoys the nursing attention given his hand by his new acquaintance. The spaniel, understandably nervous after his ordeal, wets the rug, but Tarrant is inexplicably happier because his house has now been fouled and blood-stained, although he cannot articulate his feelings to the woman who elects to leave without the sherry he has offered. But once outside the lady and her spaniel discover again their original attacker. Triumphantly Henry Tarrant shuts his gate, exclaiming, "Now you simply *must* come back." (p. 381) The implied consequence is that the writer will find his art less desiccated because of this renewed contact with life.

A less fortunate portrait of the artist is on display in "W.S." In this story Hartley examines the relationship between the author and his creation, somewhat along the lines of epistemological hide and seek. Walter Streeter keeps getting postcards from a "W.S." who, sounding like a critic, accuses him of moral ambiguity and spiritual drifting in his character delineation. When "W.S." finally appears in the "flesh," he turns out to be the one completely evil character Streeter created in his youth before he graduated to "ambiguity." Streeter realizes that his characters are largely projections of himself or else diametric opposites to him. Hartley once more includes some amusing self-reference. "W.S.", for example, sends Streeter postcards showing towers of famous cathedrals because the author, like Hartley himself, is known to admire cathedrals. However, the ominous tone is more reminiscent of cathedrals in M. R. James perhaps than in L. P. Hartley. The character goes by the eponym, William Stainsforth, and he claims his author made him a scapegoat, unloading all his self-dislike on a helpless character. The author is given one chance to soften his portrayal of Stainsforth. All Streeter must do is find one virtue with which he ever credited his character—"just one kind thought—just one redeeming feature." (p. 390) Faced with a moral and aesthetic choice, Streeter tries desperately to think of something or to fabricate something within the two minutes alloted him, but his moral rigor and the cause of goodness prevent him from asserting good where there is only evil. Of necessity he submits to the literally iron hand of his character, and he is strangled mercilessly. Streeter has come face to face with his own unpardonable sin, and he deals with it without extenuation or ambiguity. "W.S." is a disturbing fable, given Hartley's usual component of "realistic" plausibility, of the artist submitting to the perilous limitations of his own former creations—the identification turns inward without sympathy, and with fatal results.

Hartley offers a range of statements in the short stories on the uses and value of possessions and art objects, a perennial theme in his fiction and the subject of *The Collections* (1972). Three stories, in particular, illuminate his somewhat ambivalent feelings about objects and possessions.

"Two for the River," the title story of another collection, is a very beguiling tale, narrated in first-person by Mr. Minchin, a bachelor writer who debates with himself the advisability of selling his river home to a young couple:

> My beautiful things! They had seemed so once, when one by one I had collected them: but how seldom had the glow of acquisition lasted from one side of the counter to the other! How soon one took them all for granted! Whereas the possessions of the mind!—It was the onset of old age, no doubt: once I hadn't felt that way. Nor would a young couple coming fresh to a place, with eyes and hearts alive to pretty things, feel that way either. (p. 469)

The *genius loci* of his house accuses Mr. Minchin of fickleness; as the writer once had fallen in love with the house, now he was transferring his affections to the young couple—" 'Their youth shall be my youth, their happiness my happiness, their children my children, their future mine!' Yes, grey-haired Mr. Minchin, you thought you could renew yourself in them, and lead vicariously the life you never led!'' (p. 471) Paradise Paddock seems ill-suited to the sounds of squalling children whose din will forever drown out the voice of the house. Mr. Minchin himself fears that the house will be altered, broken up into flats, and that he will be left homeless.

His interior monologue is interrupted by the sounds of a swan attack on the river. The Marchmonts, the house-hunting couple, have taken their canoe on the river to give Mr. Minchin time to reach his decision about selling his house. Although he has decided to sell, Minchin's announcement is stifled by the couple's story of how they were attacked on the river. Marchmont has destroyed the male swan with his canoe paddle, and thus saved his wife from drowning, when the swan had jumped on her back. Wanting no more swansongs, the honeymooning Marchmonts decide Paradise Paddock is not for them. In gratitude for his hospitality, they offer Minchin their canoe, and he accepts. The canoe signifies the true ownership of the river and the house.

Minchin apostrophizes the river, claiming it has let him down. But, in truth, it has saved him through the intervention of the swans. He spies the female swan anxiously seeking her fallen mate and thinks, "She never had to call him before, . . . and now he will not hear her." (p. 476) Minchin's identity with the house and river are once more indivisible; he is his own *genius loci:*

There was nothing more to wait for; the air was turning cool; I had an irrational feeling that my clothes were wet. Stiffly I got up and climbed back to the house—my house, for it was mine after all: the swan had saved it for me. A moment's doubt remained: would the switch work? It did, and showed me what was still my own. (p. 476)

Hartley's "Two for the River" embodies his best manner, method, and tone. The interior monologues and dream narrations succeed in penetrating beyond consciousness into the privacy of the interior self which Hartley values and seeks methods to explore. In his evocation of the house and the swans used as symbolic reminders of Mr. Minchin, Hartley resembles the late Elizabeth Bowen. The outer, external world becomes a character itself as well as the symbol of the narrator's inner self. Hartley's animation of inert matter clarifies the special human relationship with the universe of objects, often with both affection and some chagrin, as in the instance of Mr. Minchin. The undertone of self-deprecation and the pathos he feels for the bereft swan make Minchin even more ingratiating.

Inanimate objects, though aesthetically satisfying, are not always held by Hartley in such high esteem apart from the human value affixed to them. In "The Price of the Absolute," for example, Timothy Carswell goes off with his over-priced Celadon Vase utterly elated because he feels he is the possessor (having been told so by the salesman) of Absolute Beauty incarnate. Lord David Cecil thinks that Hartley is endorsing art over life in the following description of the art object:

Suddenly he stopped, for on a shelf above his head was a vase that arrested his attention as sharply as if it had spoken to him. Who can describe perfection? I shall not attempt to, nor even indicate the colour; for, like a pearl, the vase had its own colour, which floated on its surface more lightly than morning mist hangs on a river. . . .
"Turn on the light!" commanded the proprietor. So illuminated, the vase shone as if brightness had been poured over it. It might have been floating in its own essence, so insubstantial did it look. Through layer on layer of soft transparency you seemed to see right into the heart of the vase. (pp. ix - x)

Cecil notes of the foregoing: "This passage is memorable not only for the light it throws on Mr. Hartley's beliefs, but also as an example of his art in its beautiful best; the precise and exquisite expression of an exquisitely refined sensibility." (p. x)

But in the context of the story Carswell's faith in his art object is largely vitiated, although he does not admit this fact to himself, by his overhearing the salesman deliver a similar endorsement to another customer about another *objet d'art*. To Carswell, his vase may well be *sui generis*, but Hartley has dramatized the situational absurdity of purchasing Absolute Beauty in the marketplace. If art is absolute, life remains distressingly relative, and survival requires continual attention. The inherent comedy of the claim, "The Price of the Absolute," surely is the best incarnation in the story.

The ultimate *reductio ad absurdum* of any claim regarding the superiority of art over life is sketched in "Mr. Blandfoot's Picture," where all the fashionable ladies in Settlemarsh contrive to get a glimpse of Mr. Blandfoot's reputed masterpiece. The redoubtable Mrs. Marling succeeds in getting Mr. Blandfoot to accept an invitation to her salon to exhibit his picture. She discovers to her shame that the picture is tattooed on her guest's chest. Social snobbery and the pretension to elegance are of little avail before such an exhibition. Poor Blandfoot collapses in the middle of his display, to be revived shortly. The Lawrentian Blandfoot thrusts his physicality into the rarefied atmosphere of the drawing-room, to rebuke through his own selfhood the Settlemarsh culture vultures. The Jamesian Hartley again shows another visage (or a bared chest), and Lawrentian life takes precedent over disembodied art.

Lastly, the resources of deliberate fantasy wherein the settings are enchanted or imaginary and the plots point to magical themes of an archetypal life-giving quality appear in Hartley prior to his adult fantasy, *Facial Justice* (1960) in "Conrad and the Dragon" and "The Crossways." Conrad is a most unlikely dragon-slayer, as might be expected in a fairytale devised by L. P. Hartley. His older brother has died earlier in a futile attempt to free the Princess Hermione from the dragon, and since then Conrad's indifference to the Princess "had deepened into positive dislike." Yet the only way to get at the dragon is to utter words of love about the Princess:

[Conrad] could not bring himself to say he loved her, even without meaning it. So he set himself to devise a form of words which would sound to the greedy, stupid Dragon sufficiently like praise, but to him, the speaker, would mean something quite different. (p. 204)

His novel approach to the dragon is successful; and he slays the beast only to discover, as does the kingdom to its horror, that the Princess and the dragon are one and the same. His address to the dragon is a masterpiece of equivocation:

But when I remember what you have done for me: rescued me from the dull round of woodland life; raised me from obscurity into fame; transformed me from a dreamer into a warrior, an idler into a hunter of Dragons; deigned to make yourself the limit of my hopes and the end of my endeavors—I have no words to thank you, and I cannot love you more than I do now!

The conquering hero is transformed instantly into a social pariah, paralleling somewhat the duality of the Princess herself. Conrad is given the opportunity tc leave the country, in secret. With Charlotte, his deceased brother's sweetheart, Conrad makes his way to a Republic where the couple marry and live happily ever after.

The import of "Conrad and the Dragon" is appropriately mysterious. At one level it provides a nightmare projection of the nascent sexual fears that Hartleian men frequently manifest toward women. Or possibly it is a parable of the dragons women become, because their lovers and admirers will them to be so, a variation on Hartley's perverse teleology where the promised adult end is frustrated by the inner child. When Hartley turns again to a wildly imaginative fable in *Facial Justice*, he wisely concentrates his moral vision on political rather than sexual issues; but, in passing, "Conrad and the Dragon" compels attention as much for what it does not say as what it does.

"The Crossways" fulfills the expectations for an ideal fairy-tale by suggesting the conditions necessary for a happy marriage; therefore it serves as a harbinger of Hartley's happy-ending novels like *My Sisters' Keeper* (1970). Lucindra, a stranger in a strange land, marries the strong and handsome woodsman, Michael, whose only blemish is an enormous scar from a previous encounter with a bear. A peddler from her native country one day entices Lucindra with stories of the road to the Land of Heart's Desire, which is to be found at the Crossways deep in the forest. In time, Lucindra leaves her husband and two typically Hartleian children, Olga and Peter, in search of her heart's desire. Finally, despite their father's warning, the children penetrate the forest, and they find Lucindra injured in a ditch by the Crossways. But all the road signs are blank. When Michael appears, he insists he has been unkind to his wife, for she must have the freedom to go where she likes. With this reaffirmation of her free will, she desires only to return home. Dependent now on her husband to carry her, Lucindra expresses the renewed love she feels for all her family. The signpost suddenly becomes clear. The Land of Heart's Desire is the homeward path they must follow. This parable of wedded love is a little too clear; the blond dreamer Lucindra takes the realist woodsman Michael hereafter to love and to cherish. The supernaturally unclosed world of fairy-tale loses something in translation to the more problematic and realistic milieu of the novel, as the deceptively sanguine L. P. Hartley at this juncture fully understands. The trembling balance which D. H. Lawrence saw as the necessary play of opposites requires not a fairy-tale but another genre—the novel.

## II  *Hartley and the Uncanny: Ghosts, Evil, and Punishment*

The macabre tales in Hartley's *Complete Short Stories* represent explorations in fantasy different in kind from the near allegories of "Conrad and the Dragon" and "The Crossways." Hartley here concerns himself less with right and wrong, as he does in the novels, than with evil and its effects. His conception of the horror story seems closely allied to H. P. Lovecraft's definition:

The true weird tale has something more than secret murder, bloody bones, or a sheeted form clanking chains according to rule. A certain atmosphere of breathless and unexplainable dread of outer, unknown forces must be present; and there must be a hint, expressed with a seriousness and portentousness becoming its subject, of that most terrible conception of the human brain—a malign and particular suspension or defeat of those fixed laws of Nature which are our only safeguard against the assaults of chaos and the daemons of unplumbed space.[2]

And insofar as can be determined, his intended effect upon the reader likewise suggests Lovecraft's standard:

The one test of the really weird is simply this—whether or not there be excited in the reader a profound sense of dread, and of contact with unknown spheres and powers; a subtle attitude of awed listening, as if for the beating of black wings or the scratching of outside shapes and entities on the known universe's utmost rim. And of course, the more completely and unifiedly a story conveys this atmosphere, the better it is as a work of art in a given medium. (Lovecraft, p. 16)

Withal, though, Hartley's climaxes in these stories are often predictable, and strangely flat, because they have not been made to matter very much. When Hartley attaches fear to what Freud calls the "uncanny," i.e., "nothing else than a hidden, familiar thing that has undergone repression and then emerged from it,"[3] his

macabre stories can be genuinely chilling as in "Night Fears" and
"A Visitor from Down Under." Otherwise, fear becomes merely
decorative.

In "Night Fears," a newly-hired nightwatchman who has been
fabricating incidents of trial and stress to impress his wife finds himself sharing his brazier with a stranger. In conversation with the
stranger the watchman articulates the anxiety-producing circumstances of his life, as the stranger, Iago-like, stimulates his most submerged fears—of his wife's fidelity, the loss of his children's affection, the real possibility of his own mental breakdown as a result of
his inability to sleep during the day. In desperation, the watchman
pulls a knife and, in turn, is murdered with it. And the stranger
steps over the dead body, disappearing into a blind alley with only a
track of dark, irregular footprints left behind. The watchman's
previous fictions of peril and threats have become gruesome reality
for him. The imagination, of course, has the power to terrify
without any external correlative. The watchman could be a victim
of his own dark mind. But there was a stranger, uncannily not feeling the cold which grips and finally destroys the watchman.

The tell-tale icicle on the window-sill in "A Visitor from Down
Under," a "thin claw of ice curved like a Chinaman's nail, with a
bit of flesh sticking to it" (p. 73), similarly makes palpably real the
visitation of the ghost which carries off Mr. Rumbold, who back in
Australia had killed Mr. James Hagberd. Rubold had been forwarn-
ed that vengeance was imminent, when he listened to a children's
program on the radio where innocent rhymes suddenly were
transformed into ominous threats from beyond the grave.

Hartley is fond of symbolic retributions as the villain in "The
Travelling Grave" is trapped by his own trick coffin which he would
have used on his guest; or symbolic substitution as in "Feet
Foremost" where the curse and ghost of Low Threshold Hall spare
the ailing Antony, preferring the recently crashed aviator. Thus the
apparition is subject to its own law: "to abandon her Victim and
seeking another tenement enter into it and transfer her vengeance,
should its path be crossed by a Body yet nearer Dissolution. . . ."
(p. 142) Both retribution and substitution figure dramatically in
"The Killing Bottle" where the would-be victim, Jimmy Rintoul,
amateur lepidopterist, survives the plot of Rollo Verdew against
him. Rollo's brother, the insane Randolph, takes homicidal action
against people and animals who are unnecessarily cruel to living
things. When Jimmy appears at Verdew Castle with his killing bot-

tle of cyanide to collect butterflies and moths, Rollo has a perfect set-up to contrive murder. Once Randolph is arrested for killing Jimmy, the family estate and fortune will devolve to Rollo.

At Randolph's insistence Jimmy Rintoul gives a demonstration of how the killing bottle works, using as victim the rather unworthy Large Tortoiseshell butterfly. Randolph expresses disappointment that the bottle is not larger, possibly large enough to admit a man. Hartley's description of the butterfly's death is appropriately grisly and lends ironic suspense in the context of the story:

> Alas, alas, for the experiment in humane slaughter! The butterfly must have been stronger than it looked; the power of the killing bottle had no doubt declined with frequent usage. Up and down, round and round flew the butterfly; its frantic flutterings could be heard through the thick walls of its glass prison. It clung to the cotton-wool, pressed itself into corners, its straining, delicate tongue coiling and uncoiling in the effort to suck in a breath of living air. Now it was weakening. It fell from the cotton-wool and lay with its back on the plaster slab. It jolted itself up and down and, when strength for this movement failed, it clawed the air with its thin legs as though pedalling an imaginary bicycle. Suddenly, with a violent spasm, it gave birth to a thick cluster of yellowish eggs. Its body twitched once or twice and at last lay still. (p. 251)

The last fillip to the foregoing comes when Rintoul blithely tells Randolph that this particular butterfly is not a parasite of any flower or vegetable, because it is too scarce to be a pest but is fond of gardens and frequented places, a rather sociable specimen like a robin.

Predictably, with what he considers a patent betrayal of natural piety having been committed, Randolph murderously takes after Jimmy Rintoul. The latter manages with great effort to escape, only to find vengeance fall upon Rollo, who is unable to remonstrate against the intent of his crazed brother. Once more abrogation of the age-old sanction to protect one's guest results in disaster for the villainous host.

In the best and most provocative of these horror stories, Hartley seems to be saying that man, the sick animal, bears within him an appetite for evil, revenge, and retribution which is inexorable. The more familiar masochism of Hartley's novels is transformed here in to something closer to sadism. Hartley can be not only cold to life but actively punishing to it. Of course, the figure in Hartley's carpet may well be a Rorschach inkblot of considerable psychological unpleasantness. As a character observes in "Podolo," "We loved her and so we had to kill her." (p. 79) Admittedly, this statement is made in a dream sequence, yet for that very reason its relevance might be greater than a waking insight. Perhaps Hartley is using the horror story as a kind of little theatre of submerged passions, transforming hidden desires for punishment into freedom, play, and pleasure. Playfully Hartley presents the ubiquity of guilt and corruption in tales of elegant literary spookery through the implication that everyone is latently a killer.

Two stories from Hartley's last collection, *Mrs. Carteret Receives*, record that the wages of thievery is death, as typically Hartleian protagonists devise ingenious retributions for theft. In "Paradise Paddock," Marcus Foster very much wants to have his turquoise-colored beetle, possibly an Egyptian scarab, stolen. A friend who has traveled extensively in the Near East informs him the object may be cursed. As no person is wholly innocent in Hartley, perhaps no object is either. Because a series of fairly trivial misfortunes have befallen members of the household at Paradise Paddock, credence is lent to the friend's warning about the scarab's potential evil. Marcus, consequently, removes the beetle from the drawer and places it on the mantel to see what will happen. Mrs. Crumble, his daily help, shortly confesses she has accidently knocked the insect off the mantel and, according to her, it broke into dozens of unmendable pieces. Greatly relieved to be rid of the jinx on his house, Marcus learns from his factotum, Henry, that Mrs. Crumble slipped the scarab into her bag. The unfortunate Mrs. Crumble becomes mortally ill; and upon her death, her daughter comes to return the scarab to its rightful owner, as requested by her dying mother:

> For once Marcus was able to make up his mind quickly. Never, never would he accept, above all from a dead woman's hand, a gift which had given his subconscious mind, however misguided it might be, so much anxiety. (p. 689)

Expressing desire it may bring the child luck, Marcus forces the scarab upon her. Later, when the friend who had originally alerted him to the potential danger of the art object returns for a visit, Marcus proudly tells him the evil has been exorcised from Paradise Paddock. He jokingly relates that the local people refer to his home as the House of Death. As the two men take an evening stroll after dinner, Marcus's friend catches his foot on the curb and falls headlong. He sustains a broken leg:

Writhing a little, he turned his screwed face towards the street-lamp overhead, which invested it with a yellowish pallor and gasped, between broken breaths, 'Thank you for only breaking my leg—you might have killed me. Did no one ever tell you you had the Evil Eye?' (p. 691)

Vivian Vosper, yet another Hartleian bachelor living alone in a small mews house in "a burglarious part of London," devises a clever retaliatory scheme against thieves in "Please Do Not Touch":

> He survived, however, and he hadn't lost much of value for he hadn't much of value to lose; chiefly the drinks he kept on the sideboard, to which the thieves had liberally helped themselves, before relieving themselves, as is the habit of burglars, all over his sitting room floor. With the help of his daily help . . . he cleared up the mess; but the material stink of it, no less than the indescribable smell of violation that any burglary brings, remained with him for several days. (p. 723)

He breaks out a bottle of Amontillado sherry and doctors the wine with potassium cyanide left over from his youthful days of butterfly and moth collecting. He reflects on his lack of malice toward the poor creatures which he as a naturalist used to collect as opposed to the very real animus he feels against the burglars who have "robbed him and beaten him and pinioned him as if he were a moth on a stretching-board." (p. 725)

Rationalizing about his diabolical scheme, Vivian Vosper notes that experts now claim violence is inherent in human nature and that any retaliation he might take would merely illustrate the well-known law of every action having an equal and consequent reaction. Still his fundamental decency triumphs, and he resolves to empty the poisonous bottles down the drain in the morning with a measure of precaution taken for that evening:

> Having written on a stick-on label, in the largest capital letters, 'PLEASE DO NOT TOUCH' he affixed it to the sherry bottle, which he placed in a prominent position on his drink-table so that neither by day nor night could its warning notice be ignored. (p. 726)

The following morning, Ethel, his daily help, reports that more rats have infiltrated his home, and Vivian decides to set the poisoned sherry as bait for them. This extermination maneuver works surprisingly well; his solution to the rat problem becomes the envy of his mews' neighbors. Meanwhile, Vivian takes additional precautions against future burglaries by installing ornamental iron

over his front door and lower windows. Hartley at this point includes special comment on one of his favorite topics in the later
novels—the fact that the permissive society often places the victim
in the wrong: "Permissiveness was the pass-word to today's society;
and little as he agreed with it he felt slightly guilty for trying to
stand in its way." (p. 732)

Despite the laws of probability, Vivian Vosper finds burglary
striking again, but this time he discovers one of the three burglars
dead in his sitting-room, looking like a butterfly on a stretching-
board. To Vivian's shock, he perceives the deceased burglar to have
been an acquaintance he had met at parties. During the subsequent
police investigation, the possibility that the burglars were there as a
result of a homosexual invitation is subtly intimated: "You'd be surprised, Mr. Vosper, if you knew how many men living alone as you
do, complain of burglars who aren't really burglars, but burglars by
invitation, so to speak." (p. 735)

"Please Do Not Touch" depicts a world in which anything can
happen, and seemingly innocent things are threats, including casual
acquaintances and bottles of sherry. Distinctions and priorities
become ever more elusive. Vivian Vosper, however, finds his new
emotion, revenge, enthralling. While revenge may stand as the
historical fallout of a violent age, it gives him a renewed sense of
ironic union with his fellows:

> Revenge, revenge. It was an emotion as old as jealousy, from which it so
> often sprang. It was a classic emotion, coeval with the human race, and to
> profess oneself to be free of it was as dehumanizing, almost as much, and
> perhaps more, as if one professed oneself to be free of love—of which, as of
> jealousy, it was an offspring. (pp. 736 - 737)

Thus, with the disappearance of the original cyanide sherry taken
by the police as evidence, Vivian repairs to the basement for another bottle of sherry in which he mixes a portion of cyanide neglected by the police. He puts his warning on the bottle in red ink
this time; and cautiously sniffing the almond-breathing perfume,
"he had a sensation of ineffable, blissful sweetness." (p. 738)

At once humorous and frightening, "Please Do Not Touch" dis-
tills Hartley's special variety of macabre comedy and displays his
mastery of emotional rhythm in short fiction. The story illustrates
Hartley's endorsement of Bacon's sentiment that revenge is a kind
of wild justice, an idea which propels a number of the short stories.
Moreover, "Please Do Not Touch" confirms Hartley's understanding of the Poesque principle that the short, highly unified literary

work is ideal as a vehicle for producing a pronounced emotional effect. This story is probably the best achieved tale in *Mrs. Carteret Receives*, proving that the elderly Hartley has not lost his "touch."

Unfortunately, Hartley exhibits the greatest tendency to repeat himself in the stories of terror and the supernatural, which appear sometimes more than twice-told. While some repetition may be inevitable in works which depend on similar plot devices, Hartley's imagination does seem to fail him when he ascribes virtually the same unfulfilled goals to thirty-three-year old Jimmy Rintoul in "The Killing Bottle" and seventy-year old Henry Kitson in "Pains and Pleasures": to play the Moonlight Sonata quite perfectly, climb the Matterhorn, read the *Critique of Pure Reason*, in the case of Rintoul, and write a book that would be classic, in the instance of Kitson. Otherwise, the recurring wet footprints, *Doppelgängers*, masks, and games of hide-and-seek proliferating in Hartley's stories with slight variation from one to another have some charm even in their predictability. As James Hall has noted about the evolution of Hartley's novelistic technique from his suspense stories, human relations in the novels are seen "as absurdly dangerous games of hide-and-seek, though he no longer deals in mystery." (Hall, pp. 111 - 112) What is supernaturally explicable in the tales of terror becomes ironically more oblique in the presumed reality of the novels where revenants are generally excluded. The writer of horror stories can reduce both evil and adversaries to size by stylizing the situation to suit his abstract purposes. Supernaturalism gives the writer the means of controlling reality, if not necessarily understanding it, for magic deals in feints, ambiguities, distractions, and illusions.

### III  *Studies in Human Psychology and Domestic Relations*

Among the more interesting stories are those in which Hartley examines imaginatively the by-ways of human psychology. An especially incisive portrayal of a Hartleian fearful self is found in "A Tonic," a tenderly destructive vignette of hypochondriacal Mr. Amber's visit to the specialist who inexorably confirms the patient's worst suspicions:

> "I read about diseases for pleasure!" said Mr. Amber simply. "But of course it is hard when you have so many of the symptoms, not to feel that you must have at any rate one or two of the diseases." (p. 322)

Mr. Amber's heart is, indeed, badly damaged, as Sir Sigismund

Keen discovers during the examination which he is able to conduct only after his patient has fainted. No disguising of symptoms and requests for a tonic can obviate the painful future for Amber.

In a related vein, the first-person protagonist of "A Summons" awakened shortly after midnight lets his morbid imagination roam as he listens to a bluebottle fly in his room:

> Flies have a *flair* for putrefaction; what had brought this one to my bed-side, what strange prescience had inspired its sharp, virulent rushes and brought that note of deadly exultation into its buzz? It had been all I could do to keep the creature off my face. Now it was biding its time, but my ears were apprehensive for the renewal of its message of mortality, its monotonous *memento mori*. That spray of virginia creeper, too, had apparently given up its desultory, stealthy, importunate attack upon the window. . . . I seemed to see its shrivelled, upturned leaves, its pathetic, strained curve of a creature that curls up to die. . . . (p. 315)

Indulging in these associations, he refuses to answer the summons of his little sister in the next room who hitherto has informed him she has recurring dreams about being murdered, doubtless inspired by vivid recitals of his own thoughts and dreams:

> For my sister knew, or would know now at any rate, that I was a heavy sleeper; and if she referred to the matter at breakfast I would use a little pious dissimulation—children are so easily put off. Probably she would be ashamed to mention it. After all it wasn't my fault; I couldn't direct people's dreams; at her age, too, I slept like a top. Dreaming about murders . . . not very nice in a child. I would have to talk to her alone about it some time. (p. 317)

Such self-righteousness coupled with surprising lack of self-knowledge produces a wry character sketch.

"Someone in the Lift" relates a grisly Oedipal accident at Christmastime. The Maldons with their son, Peter, are spending Christmas at Brompton Court Hotel. Peter is fascinated by the hotel lift which he imagines has an occupant who disappears as soon as the elevator comes to rest. Peter's mother tells him to ask his father whether someone is truly there each time, but the son hesitates to risk his father's ridicule:

> Like all well-regulated modern fathers, Mr. Maldon was aware of the danger of offending a son of tender years: the psychological results might be regrettable. But Freud or no Freud, fathers are still fathers, and sometimes when Peter irritated him Mr. Maldon would let fly. Although he

was fond of him, Peter's private vision of his father was of someone more authoritative and awe-inspiring than a stranger, seeing them together, would have guessed. (p. 478)

When his father is with him, Peter never sees the figure in the lift. Hence Peter theorizes that the "someone" in the lift must be his father.

Two days before Christmas Day the lift breaks down, and Peter is forbidden to touch the button during the period of repair. On Christmas Eve, however, as he waits for the appearance of Father-Christmas whom he knows is really his father, he surreptitiously pushes the button and activates the lift:

The lift was coming up from below, not down from above, and there was something wrong with its roof—a jagged hole that let the light through. But the figure was there in its accustomed corner, and this time it hadn't disappeared, it was still there, he could see it through the mazy criss-cross of the bars, a figure in a red robe with white fur edges, and wearing a red cowl on its head: his father, Father Christmas, Daddy in the lift. But why didn't he look at Peter, and why was his white beard streaked with red? (p. 481)

The final image in the story is of toys covered with blood at the feet of Peter's father, "red as the jag of lightning that tore through his brain. . . ." (p. 481) Although Peter never manifested any conscious desire to harm his father, circumstances have contrived to bring the unconscious Freudian struggle to hideous reality. "Someone in the Lift" and "The Waits," in which ghostly carolers turn assailants, introduce psychological terror to the silent night of Christmas Eve.

Another story illuminating father-son relationships and jealousies is "The Pylon." Laurie identifies himself with a large electrical transformer symbolized by a great steel pylon:

One day his short, plump body would shoot upwards, tall and straight as the pylon was; one day his mind, that was so dense in some ways, and so full of darkness, would fine down to an aery structure that let the light in everywhere and hardly cast a shadow. He would be the bearer of an electric current, thousands of volts strong, bringing light and power to countless homes.

The pylon, then, had served him as a symbol of angelic strength. But in other moods it stood for something different, this grey-white skeleton. In meaner moods, rebellious moods, destructive moods, he had but to look at it to realize how remote it was from everything that grew, that took its

nourishment from the earth and was conditioned by this common limitation. It was self-sufficient, it owed nothing to anyone. (pp. 611 - 612)

The adult masculine presence of Laurie's father produces additional
ambivalence for his son, threatening, in particular, the child's imaginative identification with the pylon. The father who is delighted
when the pylon is dismantled contrasts with the son who at that
point feels he has lost some standard by which to measure himself.
Subsequently Laurie has a bad dream where the pylon becomes
equated with his father and both frustrate his desires. At the end of
the story a bigger and better pylon is about to be erected, the
father's denial to the contrary; but Laurie finds himself overwhelmed by his own violent and discordant emotions regarding the
pylon, his father, and himself. The Freudian bruise which the father
hoped not to inflict seems only too patent.

In "Per Far l'Amore" a father in Venice between the wars worries
about his daughter's too ready availability to young men who buzz
around Annette like the omnipresent August mosquitoes Mr.
Elkington equally deplores. A party is organized where guests may
find respite from the heat and mosquitoes in tent of netting. Here
they may indulge their fancy—for conversation, cards, even for mis-
anthropy, and especially per far l'amore, for making love. In one of
the latter the misanthropic father discovers his young daughter
strangled with the tent's scarlet fork-tailed pennon. Hartley once
more suggests the pain and mortal risk implicit in love and passion
when the wild blood is stirring.

A number of Hartley's last stories and some of the earlier ones
concern the relationship of master to servant and vice versa. In most
of them the Hartleian employer is desperately trying to keep
domestics happy, because the servant, having learned well the tasks
of his trade, has acquired a mastery over the immediate environment that his employer usually lacks. Hartley adroitly develops with
humor and some pathos contemporary stresses which put strain on
the historic master-servant relationship. He delineates especially
well the servant's power over his master, born of the latter's
dependency upon the person who competently deals with the trivial
details of daily life.

In "The Prayer," for example, Anthony Easterfield loses his expert chauffeur, because Copperthwaite's ambition has always been
to drive a Roland-Rex, which an American employer makes
available to him. Easterfield's aging, temperamental automobile
offers no contest against the Roland-Rex. Indeed, Anthony had

previously prayed that Copperthwaite might be granted the gift of a Roland-Rex motor-car, but his prayer's answer proves disadvantageous to the original petitioner who then is without a chauffeur. But before long Copperthwaite writes to his former employer, asking to be rehired:

> Never take a servant back again was the advice of our forebears. The word "servant" was now out of date, it was archaic; it could never be used in polite or impolite society. A "servant" was "staff": even one "servant" was "staff". One envisaged a bundle of staves, of fasces (infamous word) once used as a symbol of their office by Roman Lictors, and then by Mussolini.
>
> Copperthwaite a staff? The staff of life? Thinking of the dreary days and weeks that had passed since his departure, thinking of his forerunners, so much less helpful and hopeful than he, looking to the future, which seemed to hold in store nothing more alluring than an Old People's Home, Anthony began to think more favourably of Copperthwaite's return. (p. 676)

Easterfield fears that the returning Copperthwaite might become even more bossy than he had been previously, deciding "for Anthony many small problems of food, wine, and so on, that Anthony had been too tired, or too old, or too uninterested, to decide for himself." (p. 676) The chauffeur informs his old employer of the reason for his return to him: he found the Roland-Rex such a perfect car that he had nothing to do. With Easterfield and his car, Copperthwaite explains, "I *am* the car, sir." (p. 682) The story closes with the chauffeur asking his employer to say a big prayer for the car, and Anthony Easterfield speculates that an answer to his own prayer has perhaps been given to the mutual satisfaction of both himself and Copperthwaite.

In "Fall in at the Double," like "The Prayer" included in Hartley's last collection, *Mrs. Carteret Receives,* Philip Osgood finds himself haunted in his West Country house by ghosts from the Army occupation of the dwelling during the Second World War. He discovers beneath the coat of thick paint on his bedroom door that Lieut.-Col. Alexander McCreeth had formerly occupied the room, which the officer had marked *private.* His factotum, Alfred, claims to be psychic and familiar with poltergeists, and he relates to his employer what he has learned about the house's past history at the local pub. The men of Col. McCreeth's command staged an incident during which their commander was drowned at the weir below the house. The Colonel was purportedly checking on a suspicious

person, possibly a German spy, whom his men claimed was down by
the river.

A few nights later Philip awakes to knocking on his bedroom door
and hears the thrice-given order, "Fall in at the double." As if seiz-
ed by an irresistible compulsion, Philip obligingly falls in and
follows the apparitions to the riverside where he sees re-enacted the
original plot against McCreeth. The Colonel, however, directs his
mutinous men to transfer their hate to his double, Philip:

Their strong hands were round him and Philip, hardly struggling, felt
himself being hoisted over the garden wall, to where, a few feet below, he
could see his own face mirrored in the water.
"Let's get rid of the bastard!" (p. 666)

The psychic Alfred intervenes to save his employer from the fates:

"A hot bath, a hot bottle, a whisky perhaps, and then bed for you, sir.
And don't pay any attention to that lot, they're up to no good." (p. 667)

The story celebrates the faithful servant who fully anticipates and
meets the needs of his employer, to a truly life-saving extent.

In "Pains and Pleasures" the well-ordered miniaturized universe
of Henry Kitson and his general factotum, "Bill," who cleaned his
cottage, cooked his meals, and drove his car, is disrupted by the
behavior of Kitson's old tomcat, Ginger. Objecting to his ritual
banishment from the house at night, Ginger claws and bites
whoever performs this task. When the cat is permitted to spend the
night comfortably inside, his forgotten house-training results in a
mess each morning for Bill to clean up. Henry Kitson feels guilty
about subjecting Bill to this ordeal, especially out of fear that he
must choose between the cat and his employee. Bill suggests
providing Ginger with a box of sawdust for bathroom purposes, but
the cat prefers to use its new box for a bed. When Bill finally gives
notice of his imminent departure, saying he will look for a job
where there are no animals, Kitson offers to clean up any future
messes. Bill explains rather that he minds putting the cat out at
night:

"It isn't his scratching and mauling I mind, it's when he purrs and tries
to pretend I'm doing him a kindness. I'm not that tender-hearted, but I
know what it's like to spend a night in the open," the ex-policeman added.
(p. 720)

Shortly thereafter Ginger dies, and Bill elects, much to Kitson's delight, to remain with his old employer. The "master" is temporarily disturbed at the end of the story when the cutlets which Bill offers for lunch sound like "catlets," but as Bill accepts a drink from his employer, their mutual dependency and affection are shown to be secure. The story may be trivial, yet its tribute to Bill seems genuine and heartfelt, although like Hartley himself Kitson has difficulty thinking about others without serving his own psychological needs:

> With the advent of Bill, "a soundless calm", in Emily Brontë's words, descended on Henry. Domestic troubles were over; nothing to resent; nothing to fight against; no sense of Sisyphus bearing an unbearable weight uphill. No grievance at all. Had he lived by his grievances, was a question that Henry sometimes asked himself. Had his resistance to them, his instinct to fight back and assert himself and show what he was made of, somehow strengthened his hold on life and prolonged it? (p. 714)

In the highly personal genre of the short story, Hartley sometimes reveals more about himself, as the foregoing suggests, than he does elsewhere in his fiction. Little broken bits of the author's life and habits of mind help to substantiate some rather negligible stories like "Pains and Pleasures" with that imaginative reality which, when applied to Hartley's subjective self, seems intuitively and emotionally right. The fifty stories of *The Complete Short Stories* vary considerably in quality. This chapter has sought to focus on the representative majority of Hartley's better stories where his contrived manipulation of plots and the general sameness of characterization are yet somewhat redeemed by intuitive perceptions which, at their best, transcend authorial wishfulness, a besetting vice in Hartley's short stories. His evocation of feeling is usually richer than his assertion of strangeness and mystery. Hence the supernatural tales seem appreciably less significant than those stories where Hartley looks more attentively at character interaction and the inner life of his characters. On these latter occasions, he invests characters with his own special brand of self-knowledge—that which is carried along, sometimes acted well upon, but knowledge which, in general, issues no clarion call to action. Hartley masters such knowledge as a clue to being with quiet grace and occasionally lyric intensity. Understandably, Hartley achieves his most convincing character portrayals with people, like Henry Kitson, who most resemble their author.

While Hartley's short stories manifest the restrictiveness and limitations which are equally a part of his longer, more sustained narratives, the further narrowness of the short story genre itself points up, to a greater disadvantage than the novels, the limitation inherent in the author's viewpoint and preoccupations. Nevertheless, any claim for excellence in Hartley's short fiction must rest with these restrictive character sketches and not, I suspect, in the more wildly imaginative Gothic tales which appear unduly derivative. In variations on the Hartleian personae the short fiction holds its interest and authenticity. These short stories are best seen, according to Anne Mulkeen's suggestion, as studies, sketches, experiments for the larger canvasses of the novels (Mulkeen, p. 17). The cumulative effect of *The Complete Short Stories* is that the quantitative largess of the collection far outstrips its qualitative richness; such a result may be the price of completeness. Yet the sameness of Hartley's oeuvre in short fiction bespeaks a high level of consistency which should be respected and not ignored. Hartley's symbols and metaphors, situations and moral stringency in the short stories become ghosts which haunt, often to good effect, his larger fictions.

CHAPTER 4

# *Designated Heir:* Eustace
# and Hilda *Trilogy*

ESTABLISHING L. P. Hartley as an important novelist, the
*Eustace and Hilda* trilogy, which appeared between 1944 and
1947, was acclaimed almost immediately as a masterpiece of
modern fiction, and its reputation has been sustained. The three
novels, *The Shrimp and the Anemone* (1944), which Hartley began
twenty years earlier, *The Sixth Heaven* (1946), and *Eustace and
Hilda* (1947)[1]—the latter title in time standing for the entire
trilogy—trace the life of Eustace Cherrington and his sister, Hilda,
from the summers of 1905 and 1906, during Eustace's ninth and
tenth years and Hilda's early adolescence, through Eustace's years
at Oxford, to September 1920 and the death of Eustace. Hartley's
evocation of the Edwardian twilight and his portrayal of the passive
Eustace whose inability to make connections with the world outside
himself except through his own fantasy provide a pattern and a tone
which become characteristic of much of Hartley's subsequent fiction. In structure and theme, the trilogy is somewhat reminiscent of
George Eliot's *The Mill on the Floss* with Eustace like Maggie
Tulliver demonstrating almost pathological dependence on a sibling
and pursuing daydreams and fantasies which culminate in an imita-
tion of Christ.

Hartley's unifying symbol of the shrimp and the anemone appears as prologue to the trilogy and returns as epilogue. Eustace as a
youngster faces an early moral crisis. The sensitive and pliant boy
looks into a pond by the seaside and sees an anemone sucking life
out of a shrimp. He debates the morality of the question before
him: the shrimp is obviously dying, but the anemone has a need for
and a right to its dinner. "But while he debated the unswallowed
part of the shrimp grew perceptibly smaller." (*The Shrimp and the
Anemone*, p. 9) Lest he get his socks wet or in some other way dis-

59

please his peremptory older sister, Hilda, Eustace scruples against wading into the pond to rescue the shrimp. Instead he calls upon Hilda to take action which she impulsively does.

The children's intrusion into the balance of nature has disastrous results for the creatures they mean to preserve. The shrimp lies dead, and the anemone has been partially disembowelled by Hilda's interference. Without its digestive tract the anemone takes no interest when the shrimp is proffered to it; and Eustace, who initiated the drama, can only sob that he wishes they had left well enough alone. Hilda insists that something had to be done. Eustace, of course, is misled in supposing that the previous relationship between the shrimp and the anemone had been mutually satisfactory, although it probably had been ecologically sound. In a symbolic way Hartley introduces one of his principal themes throughout his fiction; namely, no matter how noble the intentions, there are always victims. Through intricate variation Hartley illustrates in the trilogy the correspondence between the shrimp and the anemone and Eustace and Hilda. Joseph Conrad's unprepossessing phrase, "squeeze the guts out of it," which Richard Ellmann finds emblematic of the way Edwardian writers bear down very hard on symbolic nuclei, seems especially apt, literally and figuratively, as a description of Hartley's symbol and method in *Eustace and Hilda*. ("Two Faces of Edward," *Golden Codgers*, p. 123)

## I   *The Fearful Self as Protagonist*

Eustace Cherrington is the prototype of the well-meaning but neurotic protagonists who inhabit Hartley's fiction. His actions, such as they are, for inaction comes easily to him, are dictated by women who surround and smother him. Their solicitude becomes emasculation. Although his mother died giving birth to his younger sister, Barbara, a host of women including Aunt Sarah, Hilda, and his old nurse, Minney, eagerly serve as maternal surrogates for Eustace at the family's modest seaside home in Anchorstone. In the first novel of the trilogy Eustace acquires yet another mother substitute through his friendship with Miss Fothergill, an infirm, very wealthy spinster whom the impressionable youngster befriends at Hilda's insistence despite the terror the old woman's appearance had earlier brought to him. In fact, to avoid meeting the invalid old woman in her bath-chair, Eustace openly rebels and embarks on a paper-chase with Nancy Steptoe, the only female character in the three novels who offers him the chance for a healthy experience and a non-subservient relationship. As is usually the case in Hartley, this single independent act results in Eustace's physical collapse. He is rescued by the knightly Richard Stavely, the scion of Anchorstone Hall. Eustace's veneration of the aristocracy, represented in his fantasies by Richard Stavely, leads to distortions in his own personality.

Never really recovering from the physical and emotional crisis of his pre-pubescent fling with Nancy Steptoe, Eustace becomes obedient to the wishes of Miss Fothergill, whom Nancy views as a witch, and repudiates his earlier, abortive will to independence. For his future self, this change is crucial:

> In an indoor atmosphere, prepared by affection and policed by money, youth's natural dislike of what is ugly and crippled and static had dropped away from Eustace. To find his most intimate satisfaction in giving satisfaction, to be pleased by pleasing, this was the lesson that Miss Fothergill had taught him. She did not mean to. She had tried not to. No woman, certainly no young woman, wishes a man she loves to be deficient in desire and indifferent to the call of experience. (*The Shrimp and the Anemone*, p. 133)

At her death, Miss Fothergill leaves Eustace a legacy of 18,000 pounds to secure economic independence for him, but he continues to see himself sacrificed for other people's happiness, at least in daydreams and fantasies. Before the west window of Frontisham Parish Church, the apotheosis of Eustace Cherrington into St. Eustace takes place as a reverie, thus beginning a tradition of the hagiolatry of martyrdom which exerts recurrent appeal to a number of fearful protagonists in L. P. Hartley:

> Pictures of saints and angels, red, blue, and yellow, pressed against and into him, bruising him, cutting him, spilling their colours over him. The pain was exquisite, but there was rapture in it, too. Another twitch, a final wriggle, and Eustace felt no more; he was immobilised, turned to stone. High and lifted up, he looked down from the church wall, perfect, preeminent, beyond criticism, not to be asked questions or to answer them, not to be added to or taken away from, but simply to be admired and worshipped by hundreds of visitors, many of them foreigners from Rome and elsewhere, coming miles to see him . . . Eustace, Eustace of Frontisham, Saint Eustace. (*The Shrimp and the Anemone*, p. 144)[2]

Because Aunt Sarah has withheld from him word of the legacy, when Craddock, the driver, mentions to Eustace on their return trip from Frontisham that he hears "we shall be losing you before long," the boy immediately assumes the worst, that he is going to die; for Miss Fothergill only a little while before had passed away. In truth, Craddock's reference is to Eustace's imminent departure to boarding school which the legacy makes possible. Back on the beach with Hilda, Eustace, under misapprehension of a death sentence, makes his bequests to his sister who screams that she will not permit him to die. She will keep him clear of the cliff's edge and take away his knife and ball of string so that he cannot do anything to harm himself. Hilda perceives her brother's unconscious death-wish and struggles to save him, as she earlier had tried to save the shrimp.

Dick Stavely and Nancy Steptoe appear on the beach and congratulate Eustace on his new fortune, reported at the inflated figure of 68,000 pounds. With customary largesse Eustace offers half of his fortune to Hilda, drawing on the sand a heart with an arrow through it, "Eustace to Hilda," with the amount of 34,000 pounds listed. The money which drips into a pile of gold from the tip of the arrow looks to Hilda more like blood than money. In the subsequent novels of the trilogy Hartley develops the symbolic meaning of love equated with money, even blood money. Brother and sister end *The Shrimp and the Anemone* playfully engaged in a three-legged race back to their home, a foreshadowing perhaps of the cripples to whom Hilda dedicates her strength and her brother's small fortune in *The Sixth Heaven*, the second volume of the trilogy.

The initial volume is doubtless the best of the trilogy judged according to Hartley's skill in bringing thematic and symbolic energies together to achieve overall unity. In some measure the subsequent novels must be viewed through the lens of *The Shrimp and the Anemone*. Hartley is especially skillful at portraying childhood, as, for example, the vivid evocation of Eustace's terror that he might go down the bathtub drain. On the other hand, Hartley's adults sometimes seem a trifle retrogressive, even immature. Perhaps, like Rilke, Hartley assumes that fate is not more than the gathered impressions of childhood.

## II   *The Sixth Heaven:*
### *The Difficulty of Telling Shrimp from Anemone*

*The Sixth Heaven* offers a curious triangular study of the catastrophic friendship of both Eustace and Hilda with Dick Stavely, who is described by a friend as "always either rescuing or giving

cause for rescue." At first, Hilda's interference in Eustace's life
seems far more obtrusive than his in hers. "St. Hilda" presides over
Highcross Hill, a rehabilitation home for cripples; she views her
clinic as an extension of Eustace whose money underwrites it. At
one point Hilda seeks to have the Master of St. Joseph's College,
Oxford reaffirm Eustace's scholarship which is in jeopardy because
his academic essays, while very agreeable, show little sign of
rigorous scholarly development:

> "In fact, that seems to be his policy in life—to make time pass agreeably,
> and not only for himself, but for a large—an increasingly large—number of
> people. The hour he spends with me is only an hour like the others. His
> work is a means to that end—he's too conscientious really to scamp it, but
> he never loses himself to it, he's too anxious to bring it out palatable and
> nicely served. Now that's not what we want here, especially from our
> scholars; we want good, hard, spade-work. This is a kitchen-garden, not a
> flower-garden." (*The Sixth Heaven*, p. 41)

Eustace as an Oxford undergraduate enlarges and refines the earlier
supreme attribute of his character—the capacity to render himself
agreeable. As a youngster he postponed thinking about his future
manhood; now a young man Eustace sees his submission to the
domination of others, especially Hilda whose influence extended
sufficiently for her to obtain a medical release for him during the
war, as a moral imperative—"he had subconsciously decided that
what he wanted was automatically wrong, and that to strike out for
himself was to infringe the Moral Law." (*The Sixth Heaven*, p. 74)

Despite Eustace's outwardly deferential temperament, his interior life of fantasy is rich in possibilities, in young manhood as it
was in youth. After becoming reacquainted with Dick Stavely who
has gained some renown as a minor T. E. Lawrence during the war
years in the Middle East, Eustace dedicates himself to winning
Hilda's assent to accompany him for a weekend with the Staveleys
at Anchorstone Hall. She persists in her reluctance, carried over
from *The Shrimp and the Anemone*, to become involved with the
gentry. Her brother, however, prevails over her better judgment.
Hilda remarks that he must look forward to seeing her sacrificed on
the social altar, and she remembers him as a little boy playing at being a tidal wave or earthquake or the Angel of Death: "You were
always destroying things—in your imagination, of course." (*The
Sixth Heaven*, p. 105)

Indeed, Eustace fantasizes about the coming together of Hilda and Dick Stavely in a romantic marriage, joining the Puritan angularity of Hilda, a dove rather like her namesake in Hawthorne's *The Marble Faun*, and the "sheer masculinity" and hedonistic derring-do of Dick Staveley. But Hilda, in truth, is seduced and abandoned by the knight-errant for whom her brother had such high hopes. When Hilda and Dick secretly take flight in an airplane, Eustace exults at the exit which he finds reminiscent of Bacchus and Ariadne.

Prior to the airplane ride at the Anchorstone Hall houseparty, which is the climax of *The Sixth Heaven*, the Dick-Hilda relationship is given a vivid symbolic correlative when Hilda's hands are badly bruised during a game of billiard-fives. This sequence offers a prefiguring of the events which bring misfortune in the final volume of the trilogy. While Eustace professes great concern for Hilda's hands, the "fact" of brutalization represented by them yields before his mind's imaginative transformation a fantasy version representing an idealized relationship between a knight and his maid.

Eustace's sleeping dreams, as opposed to his waking fantasies, are even more disturbing. One, in particular, concerns his futile struggle to locate Hilda's room at Anchorstone Hall. He imagines in his dream that he will be able to find her room by recognizing clothing which his sister impolitely would leave in the hall for the servants to care for. Eustace himself has recurrent visions of various solecisms regarding clothes and servants, as does Leo Colston, in fact, later in *The Go-Between*, which will show conclusively his own lack of gentlemanly breeding. Hilda in Eustace's dream vision has gone naked into the night, having left all her clothes by the bedroom door. Earlier in the novel she had been referred to as the Lady Godiva of Highcross Hill. When brother and sister arrive at the hall, Hilda is attired inappropriately in a scarlet gown selected by Eustace. By the end of *The Sixth Heaven* Hilda has become a version of the "scarlet woman," despite Eustace's distortion of her upon her return with Dick Staveley from their air junket, "clothed in more than her own clothes, clothed in the glory and radiance of Anchorstone Hall." (*The Sixth Heaven*, p. 198) Ironically, Eustace's dream is symbolically a more accurate rendering of the pilgrimage and actions which follow from it than his waking interpretation.

Prior to Dick Staveley's proposal of flight to Hilda, she and Eustace had planned to commemorate their youth and former selves by strolling on the beach together. Eustace who dreams of seeing his sister become through marriage inheritor of Anchorstone

Hall—a marriage made, as he supposes, in seventh, if not sixth, heaven—is more than happy to have Staveley interfere with their nostalgic walk on the beach. Thus, in his own way, Eustace intrudes himself as fantastic projector and manipulator as much into Hilda's life as she intervenes in his. Eustace's low dominance coupled with good intentions proves surprisingly troublesome for his sister before the trilogy ends.

III   *From Fantasy to Art:* Eustace and Hilda

In *Eustace and Hilda,* the third novel, which covers the period from 6 July 1920 to September of that year, Eustace is forced to recognize the true nature of his sister's affair with Dick Staveley without deception or even fantasy. Much of the action takes place in Venice, the drawing-room of Europe, as Henry James described it, where Hartley earlier found the setting for his novella, *Simonetta Perkins* (1925). The particular drawing-room where Eustace finds his appropriate milieu is Lady Nelly Staveley's. She is the aging grande dame of the Staveley family who assumes in the final novel of the trilogy something like the role of Dame Fortune, a suitable replacement for Miss Fothergill of *The Shrimp and the Anemone.* Hartley's young men often appear to be true connoisseurs of the superannuated. Lady Nelly's fifteenth-century *palazzo* pleases the northern Eustace because he finds it more Gothic than Baroque. Yet slowly during his sojourn in Venice he begins to absorb into his rather chilly being some Venetian sensuousness. Indeed, the city supplies the catalyst for him to take up writing. Parenthetically, gothic elements continue to exert great appeal not only to Eustace but also to his creator, L. P. Hartley. The submerged incest motif, for example, about which Peter Bien in his study of the author has much to say regarding Eustace and Hilda is related perhaps less psychodynamically to Freud than to its tradition in Gothic fiction.

Eustace assumes the popular Hartleian role of go-between for his sister and Staveley, apparently in the hope that in their union he will be able to consolidate the divided inclinations of his own character. A recent commentator has noted that Eustace as a character is beautifully done, "except that he should have been overtly homosexual—and Hilda is misogynously manipulated into a villainess."[3] The closest Hartley comes even to hinting such a thing about Eustace is in a letter from Stephen Hilliard, a would-be suitor to Hilda, which explains Hilda's plight and accuses her brother of complicity with the Staveleys:

Perhaps you will never get nearer to a love-affair than the thought of
your sister in Staveley's arms. And what a superb stroke of strategy then to
hurry away, leaving her with no one to turn to, no one to consult, no man, if
the expression fits.
For I could do nothing. But your vagueness is so misleading. Did you and
your protectress put your hands together? Was her ladyship in the plot?
Women of her type feel their time is being wasted unless they have their
finger in some sort of sexual pie. It's a compensation for their own failing
powers, the sort of thing they can refer to with elegant euphemisms and
choisi French past participles. (*Eustace and Hilda*, p. 193)

Admittedly, Eustace seems incapable of pursuing romantic love
on his own. In Venice he chances to meet Nancy Steptoe, now Mrs.
Alberic, her name possibly now hinting, at least to Eustace, of
associations with the evil dwarf in Wagner's *The Ring*, the victim of
an unfortunate marriage; and she offers him the opportunity for a
love-affair. Ruefully he concedes the impossibility of such a
relationship for him. Eustace has given up love in exchange for a
kind of power. He requests Nancy's address only because he wants
to send her a check in order to facilitate her comfortable return to
London. As usual, Eustace confuses money and love.

Hilda's relationship with Dick is equally disappointing, because
even though he apparently adored her, she could not take Staveley
as he was. Dick thereupon marries Mona, his old stand-by, and
Hilda, out of shock, suffers psychosomatic paralysis. Her puritanical
rigor applied to Dick's conduct suggests that she is as deluded about
reality as her brother, or at least as susceptible to fantasy projection.
Ironically the comforter of the infirm becomes paralyzed herself.

Before he learns through a series of letters, telegrams, and visitors
to Venice the true nature of his sister's status with Dick Staveley,
Eustace writes a novella, *Little Athens*, which portrays in idealized
fiction the happy marriage he foresees for Hilda and Dick, the union their real personalities deny them. Eustace foresees the gradual
interchange of Hilda's and Dick's good qualities, and in their issue
children whose temperament, unlike Eustace's, would not be at
odds with what they genuinely desired. Eustace is more fortunate
than his sister, because art liberates him, as fantasy separated from
artistic creation cannot. That an artifact, the novella, complements,
and eventually replaces Eustace's fantasy represents a triumph of
sorts, an externalizing of his imagination through art which leaves
him better able to face reality upon his return to England.

## IV    *Eustace Takes the Plunge*

Eustace's other normative action in Venice, which like the novella alters his outlook, is his participation in the Feast of the Redeemer, the *Redentore,* for which Lady Nelly had initially invited him to Venice. Abandoning his usual caution against getting wet, Eustace plunges into the cold Adriatic as is traditional at the conclusion of the Festival. In climax, the Feast yields the greatest image of sacrificial love consuming itself for others in the spectacular realization through fireworks of the iconic Christ crowned with thorns.

Throughout the trilogy Eustace seeks transcendence. Before the west window at St. Eustace's church in Frontisham he had momentarily experienced suspension of the corporeal. At Oxford he had gained some fame for a paper read to an intercollegiate society on "Some Nineteenth-Century Mystics," among whom was included Emily Brontë, a Hartley favorite. But at the Feast he engages himself totally:

> He never knew at what moment his dread of the ordeal left him, but suddenly like a ball that finds an incline and begins to roll, he found himself starting to undress. He could not join in the laughter and talking, but he could feel the common impulse—indeed, he could feel nothing else; it seemed to be the first time he had ever acted with his whole being.
> . . . It caught [the crowd's] breath, too, for at this hour of the morning even the Adriatic in July was not quite warm—not warm to bodies which in the past twenty-four hours had seen much service, both in work and play, and had eaten plentifully and fasted long, had loved and hated and felt indifferent and now, between jest and earnest, were putting all these experiences behind them while the friendly water of the ancient sea crept higher and higher up legs and thighs and stomachs, submerging warts and scars and birthmarks, omitting nothing from its intimate embrace, making free with the flesh that had been theirs so long. Perhaps more essentially, certainly more demonstrably, theirs than the minds which hovered and struggled kite-like in their wake. Scores of heads were now bobbing in the water, moving slowly towards the crescent sun; and among them, and indistinguishable from them, was Eustace's. (*Eustace and Hilda,* pp. 97-98)

His transcendence here culminates less in mysticism than in shared insouciance and later a measure of common sense, perhaps the most meaningful state of redemption for a sensitive young man. No longer need Eustace envy the boldness of Dick Staveley or secretly wish to emulate the rigorous moral principles of Hilda. He has found out how to be more at one with himself and others—toleration and acceptance being the chief legacy of his visit with Lady Nelly vis-à-vis the recalcitrant facts of reality and experience. He even attempts to recognize the reality of Hilda's seduction and betrayal. The exigencies of life back in England must be faced directly without fantasy. Symbolically, of course, Eustace's plunge is related to the earlier image of the shrimp and the anemone, but the naturalistic image of biological struggle gives place to the transcendent image of the Redeemer Christ.

## V   *The Shrimp as Hero*

Upon his return to England, Eustace finds the Cherrington household strangely retrograde. Minney is once more in the family employment, taking care of the invalid Hilda. Aunt Sarah again is offering homilies on the dangers of presuming beyond one's social and economic birthright as Hilda did with the Staveleys. Doctor Speedwell who cared for the young Eustace during his many upsets is again the attending physician. Unable to return to Oxford because of Hilda's condition, Eustace becomes his sister's keeper.

Notwithstanding the similarity between past and present convalescence back in the Norfolk seaside village of Eustace's youth, he devises a daring scheme to give Hilda the kind of mental and physical shock which gives the only hope for an instant cure. That he embarks on such a course of action indicates the change within him which took place in Venice. The plan is to push Hilda in the bath-chair to the very edge of a cliff before stopping its progress with the large granite chips Eustace carries in his pocket as a safeguard. The day of his perilous experiment affords Eustace a number of successes which reflect upon earlier incidents in the trilogy. During a visit to Anchorstone Hall he learns from Anne Staveley that, in the opinion of the family, her brother's behavior has been improved as a result of his relationship with Hilda (her rehabilitation skills extending to redemption?); moreover, in a letter from his Venetian acquaintance, Jasper Bentwich, Eustace learns that his novella has been accepted for publication. Robustly, Eustace has also powered his bicycle up the hill where as children he and Hilda had tobogganed. Last, he is delighted to discover Hilda attired in the blue Fortuny dress Lady Nelly had helped him select for his sister to wear on light-hearted occasions.

Yet overlooking the beach where he and Hilda had built their pond and watched the shrimp and the anemone, Eustace does not have the courage to fulfill his planned experiment. He turns the bath-chair toward the abyss, and then almost accidentally his fingers slip from the handle. The chair, moving by itself, is stopped by the falling Eustace who manages to pass his hands through the spokes. Once more in the act of mental and physical exertion, his reserves crumple. Hilda, however, serendipitously recovers her own powers sufficiently to attend to her fainting brother who finds himself the new occupant of the bath-chair, pushed home by a kindly stranger and for the last lap by Hilda herself.

The recovered Hilda takes charge of her brother again. She arises from her bath like a Puritan Venus, fresh from a symbolic baptism which parallels Eustace's Adriatic plunge, "A ritual bath, a lustral bath, a purification from the past, a preparation for the future. Eustace's tired limbs rejoiced with Hilda's, that were celebrating the recovery of their freedom." (*Eustace and Hilda*, p. 300) Hilda immediately orders Eustace to shave off his mustache, despite Minney's protestation that it makes him look more of a man. Hilda's recent experience with a *macho* male leads her to suggest that Eustace leave that sort of thing to other people—"There are quite enough men already." (*Eustace and Hilda*, p. 298) Delighted to find his sister exercising her former authority, Eustace agrees to remove the mustache. Hilda's response to the announcement of Eustace's future publication is equally undercutting:

"I shall read it with great interest," said Hilda. "But writing novels isn't a life's work. You'll have to do more than that, and better than that, if I am to be as proud of you as I want to be." (*Eustace and Hilda*, p. 296)

Nonetheless, brother and sister retire for the night exchanging through Hilda's initiative a "long embrace on the lips," and Eustace turns euphorically to letter-writing, informing friends and acquaintances of Hilda's deliverance.

Before drifting off to sleep, Eustace receives one last piece of good news; namely, the birth of his nephew, the son of Barbara and Jimmy Crankshaw. Because the baby resembles Eustace, he will be so christened. Uncle Eustace remonstrates that the name is unfit for a child, acceptable perhaps only for a saint. And inexorably Hartley views the mature Eustace *sub specie aeternitatis*.

Eustace dreams of his impending examinations at St. Joseph's where he will shortly return for the fall term. The single question concerns what he knows about the souls of the righteous. He answers with alacrity from the Apocrypha, yet, in dismay, he observes the words fill only half a page:

> But the souls of the righteous are in the hand of God, and there shall no torment touch them. In the sight of the unwise they seemed to die: and their departure is taken for misery, and their going from us to be utter destruction: but they are in peace. For though they be punished in the sight of men, yet is their hope full of immortality. And having been a little chastised, they shall be greatly rewarded: for God proved them, and found them worthy for Himself. (*Eustace and Hilda*, p. 308)

The ubiquitous, if not quite omniscient, Hilda assures him the highest authority (God the Father) has approved his answer. In jubilation three cheers are shouted for the triumphant Eustace.

Without transition another dream immediately takes the place of Eustace's academic trial; this one returns him to the beach of his childhood and the first novel of the trilogy. He goes off in search of Hilda and discovers once more the white plumrose anemone, stroking the water with its feelers but this time without a shrimp. Worried about the anemone's lack of food and unable to find a shrimp, Eustace wades into the water and offers his own finger to the hungry creature. Subconsciously thinking he will wake up, Eustace experiences the cold of the water and the still colder feel of the anemone's lips closing around his finger: "But the cold crept onwards and he did not wake." (*Eustace and Hilda*, p. 310) Thus ends Harley's trilogy with what Walter Allen has called, "the quietist, most subtle and therefore most shocking death in contemporary English fiction." (Allen, *The Modern Novel. . .*, p. 254) Perhaps, but death has been the not so far off divine event toward which the novel's symbolism and Hartley's characterization of Eustace through psychological reporting have been moving all along. Eustace has proved divisible by whom he loves, especially his sister. His death is not a matter of ending so much as of becoming—possibly even a saint.

## VI  *The Bourgeois Paradigm*

The promise of new life in the birth of the infant Eustace further mitigates the tragic effect of the trilogy's ending. In the marriage and fecundity of Eustace's younger sister emerges the bourgeois paradigm which few Hartleian protagonists actually opt for in their life-choices but which exerts the appeal of a paradigm or desideratum in most of the novels. Barbara's husband, engineer Jimmy Crankshaw, is described as a representative of "the Better Sort rather than the Finer Grain," nothing at all like a character in Henry James. (*The Sixth Heaven*, p. 53) The Jamesian Eustace, as he accompanies Barbara down the aisle on her wedding day, experiences the almost palpable exuberance from the Crankshaw side of the church as contrasted with the discreet reverence from the thin and effete ranks of the Cherrington relatives on the left side.

Often the vitality and recognition of the sense of reality which exists within a domestic relationship are engendered in a couple's decision to have a child of their own. Thus Hartley presents the new-born Eustace as a second chance for the deceased Eustace who aspired to sainthood out of the world. Within the interior reality of the bourgeois family as opposed to the interior fantasies of his late uncle, the infant Eustace may be able to grow up without the worst fears of his namesake to redeem the past and its failures. Their child a token of the childhoods they themselves had or remember, Barbara and Jimmy as new parents catching glimpses of themselves and Uncle Eustace in the infant can perhaps both love and forgive the world as rigorists like Hilda or fearful selves like Eustace could not.

Hartley does not sentimentalize parental instincts and responsibilities, but his portrayal of the Crankshaws as a family complements and completes the cycle of life in the trilogy. However much conjugal and familial relationships elude Eustace and Hilda, Hartley offers the bourgeois paradigm of the family here and in later novels as an attractive, though rather oblique, alternative to the lonely destinies of his isolated, fearful protagonists. While someone like Eustace yearns for release from the life-incapacitating quality of his own nature, imagining himself as martyr and saint, Barbara and Jimmy Crankshaw seem obliged, simply by the presence of their young son, to be somewhat better people than they otherwise might settle for being. In and through the family, love is equated with something visible, not left hidden as in Eustace's dreams. In *The Sixth Heaven* Jimmy Crankshaw proposes a puzzle and spells out the solution with matches—L,O,V,E. Similarly, L. P. Hartley spells out parental love, not particularly in any metaphoric sense, as possibly the most accessible and indispensable way to insure the growth of healthy human beings, because it is the only way to teach them to love themselves. Without that accomplishment, no one can survive long in the real world.

## VII   *The Novel as Hermetic Sphere*

The trilogy of the lives of Eustace and Hilda is a work of strict and delicate calculation, something like an hermetic sphere which Henry James considered the ideal shape for a novel, with a surface so intricately joined and highly polished that even the finest pinprick cannot be found on it. *Eustace and Hilda* is portentously multilayered not only in and of itself but as a model for the Hartley novels which follow. In the trilogy we may perceive the structural principle underlying Hartley's art, and his typical plot, character alignments, and imagery are explainable readily in terms of it.

That the structural principle Hartley embraces usually involves metaphor becoming symbol, as in the instance of the unifying shrimp and the anemone, may seem too closed and contrived for contemporary tastes. Yet to read the trilogy is to be made aware of how the simple symbols of shrimp and anemone in the first volume become the complex characters of Eustace and Hilda in the final book, the brother and sister at once more and less than the governing metaphor. Although in the state of nature life distinguishes the strong from the weak as exemplified by the shrimp and the anemone, its categories are not so absolute regarding human beings. The apparently weak Eustace whose grip as a youngster cannot pass the test of the Try-Your-Grip machine is schooled in the strength of dreams, as a crypto-artist must be. In this guise Eustace appears as Hartley's model of the writer as someone akin to Hawthorne's conception of the artist as "the conscious dreamer."[4] In Eustace's quiet death lie both epiphany and plangent closure of the trilogy's sacrificial theme that the expense of art is life.

Eustace's final legacy to his sister is her life. Miss Fothergill's bequest has permitted him to become a munificent shrimp, and his imagination in exercise of his generosity represents the "capital improvement" possible through art, even as his monetary worth may be diminished. Hartley's legatees never live in a dream world of financial power and tidy ledgers; they rather distribute their resources with inventive abandon, the economy of abundance characteristic of art if not of wealth. Eustace, perhaps like Hartley and his predecessor Hawthorne, is caught suspended between the claims of form (engendering art, fantasy, and metaphor) and reality embodying materiality, history, and death). Hartley hints at such polarities beautifully poised between gravity and comedy.

The death of Eustace represents his inevitable loss of control over reality even as Hilda resumes her life and its good works. Perhaps eventually she will marry the bright, young solicitor, Stephen Hilliard, who though less romantic than Dick Staveley would prove the better mate for her. Eustace acknowledges his sister's readiness for the future in contrast to his own love of nostalgia in a prophetic passage from *The Sixth Heaven*:

> At all costs one must go forward. Hilda had always known that. . . . She had never been afraid of big things. She had never shared his weakness for the motionless and the miniature and the embalmed; she never clung, as he did, to the forms of things after the spirit had gone out of them. . . . she did not like retracing her steps. She would not have wanted to look for a sea-anemone in a pool or stop outside the white gate of Cambo and try to recapture their feelings when last they stood there. (The *Sixth Heaven*, p. 199)

Hilda is left to mediate with a substantial world as must her nephew Eustace and all the survivors at Anchorstone, but the late fictionalizing Eustace has, by his death, left them free to act in their own behalf without the distortions which he had formerly imposed. Hartley's major fiction starting with this trilogy marks out his own rapprochement with issues similar to those Iris Murdoch delineates in "Against Dryness":

> We are not isolated free choosers, monarchs of all we survey, but benighted creatures sunk in a reality whose nature we are constantly and overwhelmingly tempted to deform by fantasy. Our current picture of freedom encourages a dream-like facility; whereas what we require is a renewed sense of the difficulty and complexity of the moral life and the opacity of persons. . . . Literature must always represent a battle between real people and images; and what it requires now is a much stronger and more complex conception of the former.[5]

But Hartley is disposed to sympathize with his fantasts, and hence his intellectual judgment against them, as in the case of Eustace, must be qualified by his emotional tolerance and even support for their projections, indicative of the author's residual faith in values and realities which transcend the here and now. Eschatologically, Eustace may be destined for sainthood; and the world which passed out of the hands of God into the hands of men, to borrow Rilke's assessment of post-World War I Europe, is no place for him. Hartley's machinery of plot, metaphor, dream, vision, and even geography brings the trilogy's psycho-moral problems to a solution of sorts through transcendence. In any event, Eustace and Hilda seem to escape the disillusionment experienced by George Eliot's "Brother and Sister":

> Till the dire years whose awful name is Change
> Had grasped our souls still yearning in divorce,
> And pitiless shaped them in two forms that range
> Two elements which sever their life's course
>
> But were another childhood-world my share,
> I would be born a little sister there.[6]

Hilda would still be born Eustace's big sister, and together brother and sister would attempt to abolish change. In no other novel does Hartley portray characters who work so relentlessly against change with the ironic result that the persons become the parable as the shrimp and the anemone merge into Eustace and Hilda. As a novel on the myth of arresting development, the *Eustace and Hilda* trilogy stands as L. P. Hartley's rather perverse *Peter Pan*. If audiences have been eating up Barrie's tale of innocence for years, in various media, Hartley gives his own special literalness to the act of eating in the *Eustace and Hilda* trilogy to surprisingly modern effect. The Walt Disney organization has not yet optioned Hartley's trilogy, but the BBC has produced a highly successful and popular radio drama from it. Hartley's gift of sneaking up on the darker meanings of myth is put to resonant purpose in the trilogy, and our concern as we read it, unlike *Peter Pan*, has to do emphatically with life as it is now in the twentieth century. A life is passing by, and yet is stayed by the hand of art.

# Risk-Taking and Withdrawals: The Comedy of Adult Misapprehension: The Boat, My Fellow Devils, A Perfect Woman

L P. HARTLEY'S first full-length novel with an adult protagonist, *The Boat* (1949)[1] is a long, perplexing, but entertaining, study of the serio-comic bind an adult can get himself into by misunderstanding his own and other people's motives and actions. What partakes of pathos in the child becomes more a matter of comedy when an adult who appears rather arrested in his development pursues willful fantasy; the artist again is the exception in his legitimate fantasy-fulfilling outlet. In each of the three novels to be considered in this chapter Hartley starts and finishes on the surface of a rather doubting, commonplace, even provincial situation; but along the way he throws shadows longer than those of the misled protagonists with his resonant and numinous comedy, the model of which can be found in *The Boat*.

Timothy Casson, a forty-nine year old English writer, devoted as was L. P. Hartley, to sculling, returns from an eighteen-year sojourn in Italy to take up what he hopes is a brief residence in Upton-on-Swirrel as of January 1940, to live out the war in comfort. Whatever else *The Boat* may be, it is an ingenious, distinctly Hartleian war novel, as Timothy precipitates his own private war with the gentry of the village, principally retired military officers, who view the river as a spawning ground for fish and off-limits to boats. As Hartley suggests in the incidents and symbols of his novel, wars have been fought over little more, and the microcosmic conflict at Upton mirrors in almost mock-epic fashion the larger violent world which was embarking on a period of unprecedented destructiveness. Perhaps to put it too baldly and frivolously, not only

Timothy Casson and the fishermen of Upton-on-Swirrel but
humanity and civilization itself were in the same "boat" in the early
1940's—at the very least trapped on a ship of fools; at worst on a
black ship to hell. It is this historical context which makes Timothy's
boat important in its own right, not exclusively as a symbolic index
to his mind, though it functions in that capacity as well.

## I   The Boat as Multivalent Symbol

Early in the novel when Timothy discovers that his neighbors'
fishing rights are inviolate and that he will not be allowed to use his
boat, he writes to his friend Tyro humorously minimizing his dilemma and frustration:

> My feelings about the boat are utterly disproportionate, I know; what
> *does* it matter (and in a European war!) whether I go for a row or not? And
> what a comedy, to take the house for boating, and then not to be able to
> boat! But of course I shall, as soon as I get in touch with Mrs. Lampard.
> (*Boat*, p. 21)

Timothy as an aging English Candide assumes that once he
petitions the ruling landholder (and his own landlady) Mrs. Lampard, special dispensation will be forthcoming. However, as a result
of accident, not malice or design, he is denied access to the lady; so
he becomes an injustice collector, ascribing dastardly intent to these
slights.

In its Gothic revival boat-house, replete with stain-glass windows
and a pointed roof (Hartley's cathedrals come to mind as normative
symbols). Timothy's boat seems absurdly to have become a surrogate deity. Mrs. Purbright, Timothy's chief supporter in the community, construes the boat as a way for her friend to praise God.
During another visit to the boat-house, Timothy enters into a fantasy of fairy-tale romance with strong sexual overtones in the
presence of his beloved, virginal boat:

> The lock turned stiffly and he had to push the door open; damp and
> leaves and cobwebs and disuse combined to keep him out; it was like break-
> ing into the palace of the Sleeping Beauty. The goddess slept in her soft
> narrow bed, transoms of coloured light falling on her. She did not seem to
> have changed; but raising her reverently by the rowlock, he detected on her
> polished flank a narrow ridge of green, and from the rudder wisps of water-
> weed were trailing like green hair. She has grown older, he thought sadly;

even here in her shrine she has not escaped decay. To rot away unused! (*Boat*, p. 276)

Apart from these personal associations, Timothy's boat takes on additional ideological significance as the struggle with the gentry increases and as he acquires new friends and supporters. Timothy arrives in Upton prepared to live with a Kantian kind of well-tempered affection; he writes to his three friends, Magda, Esther, Tyro, all somewhat involved in the war effort, insisting on "the right and duty of each human being to treat another as an end in himself, not as a flag or a coloured shirt or a sinner." (*Boat*, p. 57) He seeks initially to be the genial individual free of jealous, estranging "isms"; but after Timothy meets Vera Cross, a Communist, he increasingly sees the boat as a symbol of class struggle. He imagines how boating will liberate the poor and the oppressed, giving little children the opportunity for wholesome exercise and manly development, and letting young people enjoy the company of one another in romantic, poetic surroundings. From idyll Timothy progresses to his River Revolution, declaring war on his "enemies," lest he be guilty of another Munich:

Timothy grew even more indignant that the fishermen should escape censure and he not. It was sheer snobbery on the part of his solicitors to imply that fishing was a more reputable war-time pursuit than boating. Boating was a proletarian pastime; fly-fishing was a privilege of the rich; that explained their attitude. Almost for the first time Timothy felt himself warmly proletarian, a champion of the have-nots against the high-ups. (*Boat*, p. 67)

Much of the irony and moral force of *The Boat* develops from Hartley's examination of the process whereby the Kantian Timothy, the defender of individual sovereignty, is transformed into a politically motivated partisan and ideologist, humorously but lethally indicative of the war-mentality that assesses individuals not at all except as members of a particular camp. People are seen as means and never as ends as the categorical imperative would have it. And, of course, Hartley relates this change to the development of a distorting fantasy in which Timothy perverts his identity. Like most Hartley protagonists, Timothy wants to please and be pleased, but his totemist obsession with his boat alienates him from the constituency of the gentry he wishes to join. If rather jokingly Timothy early in the novel refers to his boat as the Argo, suggesting the motif

of a quest, by the time he launches the boat, an effort which requires nearly the whole length of a sizable novel, he truly believes
he is Jason, but more fleeced than triumphant. He loses his own
particular golden fleece, the blonde Vera whom he finally sees, in
reversal of traditional nineteenth-century symbolism, as his bad
angel. His two Egerias, Vera and Mrs. Purbright, both die as a
result of their struggle by the flood-swollen river where the latter
had gone to warn Timothy of the dangers of the Devil's Staircase.
Having constantly risked absurdity with the Argo before, Timothy
is left spread-eagled, clinging "to the struts of the rowlocks, while
the boat crashed from boulder to boulder." (*Boat*, p. 477)

The sexual consummation promised by Vera is never achieved,
and Timothy, recovered from the debacle with the Argo, looks back
upon his relationship with the two women in terms of the sacred,
self-sacrificing love of Mrs. Purbright and the profane, selfish love
of Vera. He trusts that his good angel, Mrs. Purbright, will be able
to obliterate the memory of Vera if at any subsequent time her
shade should obsess him. In his dream, though, he discovers the two
women inextricably bound together as not so blithe spirits in his unconscious mind.

## II    *The Imperative of Diversity:*
*Mrs. Purbright vs. Timothy*

Inasmuch as Timothy Casson can accept, if only in his dreams,
the duality of goodness with evil, his maturity has advanced immeasurably from his former ingenuousness. Timothy as a typically
disoriented modern man, guilty of partisan ideologies and misled by
fantasy-induced distortions, is in the process of partial recovery by
his acknowledgment of human needs and human diversity. Hartley
supplies through the character of Volumnia Purbright, the rector's
wife, another of his moral touchstones—women from an older
generation who serve as guides, benefactors, and savants to the
younger men of his fiction. Her name itself, if too conspicuously
symbolic, embodies her comprehensive sweetness and light; and as
a character she invites comparison with similar women in E. M.
Forster, as Peter Bien has noted, like Mrs. Moore in *A Passage to India* (Bien, pp. 148 - 149), or, perhaps better in Hartley's rural context with the seasonal allusions, Mrs. Wilcox in *Howard's End*.

Mrs. Purbright actively tries to live by the categorical imperative
Timothy professes but often violates; however, her greatest contrast

with him and many of the other characters in *The Boat* is her scrupulous avoidance of the attitudinizing which frequently causes Timothy to misunderstand and to be misunderstood. She is flexible because of her capacity for loving; he is obdurate out of pride and vacillating attractions and affections which are deficient in love. As Mrs. Purbright views Timothy, he shifts his loyalty and passions capriciously: from the boat to collecting china bowls; onward to the evacuated children who temporarily reside with him until their families "kidnap" them away again; then to his dog, Felix, who alienates the village, and back to the boat again.

She further detects in him a tendency to overvalue inanimate possessions simply because they have no will of their own apart from the possessor (a theme Hartley frequently explores in his last novels). On the other hand, the heterogeneity of art objects in Mrs. Purbright's drawing-room reflects her greatness of soul, aesthetically and, by implication through metaphor, socially and morally, as Hartley suggests in the following extended but highly evocative passage:

> Timothy looked up and saw all round him, clustered on tables, piled on cabinets, balanced precariously on brackets, glimmering from behind glass, the most heterogenous agglomeration of objects that he had ever beheld in any human habitation. Hanging from the ceiling, clinging to the walls, springing up in thickets from the floor, were spoils from the four corners of the world. Of all styles, shapes, sizes, colours and substances; of ebony, ivory, mother-of-pearl, silver, lacquer, china, tortoiseshell and lapis-lazuli, they solicited but did not clamour for attention. A League of Nations! But how much more decorative, how much more effectively creating unity out of diversity, than parallel assemblies at Geneva and the Hague! Mrs. Purbright's catholicity of taste had wrought a miracle. For what can be more selfish, more intolerant of each other's claims, than works of art? Here, towering in pyramids, or reaching outward in espalier formations, they each contributed their own quota of beauty to a collective beauty that was not their own. (*Boat*, p. 72)

Mrs. Purbright is equally hospitable to disparate ideas and diversified groups of people, because she cultivates the sympathy which understands otherness at the same time it is true to its own values. Timothy, in contrast, abstracts qualities from other people to exploit as absolutes according to his own schemes and thereby fails to credit the otherness which Mrs. Purbright so highly values. Even the misanthrope Tyro faults his "friend" Timothy on just this issue at the end of the novel—"He [Timothy] likes things raised to a higher power—some instinct of worship, I imagine—just as he likes people to be types of themselves." (*Boat*, p. 537)

Closely allied to her aesthetic, ethical, and social response to diversity is Mrs. Purbright's organic conception of the universe as alive and flowing. Timothy again represents the opposite impulses: he quite early and late has been nipped in the bud. He supposes he can regain a closeness to nature through his affair with Vera Cross, whom he imagines a child of nature; but it falls to Mrs. Purbright, as to Forster's Mrs. Wilcox, to intercede on behalf of life-values. Described often with references to seasonal changes in vegetation and pervasive garden images, these two women stand respectively in Hartley and Forster as distinctly English approximations of the Earth Mother. Moreover, in *The Boat*, Mrs. Purbright also assumes the Hartleian role of go-between to bring Timothy to reconciliation with his adversaries, real and imagined.

Timothy is finally entertained by the gentry, notwithstanding Mrs. Purbright's unsuccessful efforts to make peace between him and Colonel Harbord. The Colonel fortuitously has saved Timothy during the disastrous charade with the Argo, and the league of gentlemen welcome the erstwhile sailor to the Colonel's home, Lawnflete. In light of Hartley's symbolic associations of nature with Mrs. Purbright, Timothy's inordinate admiration of the Colonel's lawn is ironic. For while thinking such a treasure as Lawnflete might rival his boat, Timothy does not know that Mrs. Purbright, his feminine sustainer of life, lies dying as a result of her labors on his behalf. As he leaves the affair at Lawnflete, Timothy is doused with red paint from a trap set by his own supporters, the villagers and evacuees, who wished, presumably with Timothy's knowledge and approval, to disrupt the Colonel and his friends. Tyro refers to his friend as "Blood-boltered Timothy." (*Boat*, p. 510) Yet because of his meeting at Lawnflete and the Colonel's new-found esteem for his rowing-skills, the whole question of Timothy's status on the river is to be re-opened. The "blood" which has gone into the conflict seems to be only red paint except that Mrs. Purbright's real sacrifice has not been recognized.

Timothy changes sides whimsically; he never manifests the true magnanimity of Mrs. Purbright in his dealings with people. "But what *is* your point of view?" Tyro asks Timothy in disbelief:

Yesterday, or at the most two days ago, it excluded from salvation all the people we met last night [at Lawnflete]; you were ready to exterminate them, you know you were! Who put up the booby-trap, and for whom? You did, for them. And today, just because they butter you up they are your dearest friends, and, what is more shameful, you appear to approve of them on moral grounds. (*The Boat*, p. 516)

Timothy's loyalty is conditional upon the admiration he receives, which makes him appear rather narcissistic and self-serving, calling into question the strength of his ideological commitment.

### III  *In the Balance: Spontaneity, Calculation, Hypocrisy*

The peace-loving Timothy may indeed lack a point of view. He has been caught, often enough, in any number of surprisingly war-like situations at Upton—with the gentry, his own servants, and most inexplicably in his betrayal of Mrs. Lampard. In this last instance, Timothy has become infuriated because he has not received his anticipated invitation to the wedding of Désirée, Mrs. Lampard's daughter. He earlier had met Désirée accidentally and in conversation encouraged the young girl to marry. The wedding gift purchased, Timothy waits, in vain, for the invitation. Meanwhile on a long walk, he discovers stacks of discarded books contributed to a salvage drive, "a small selection of civilization's most precious and characteristic output, naked to the elements, uncared for, finished, waiting for the knacker's cart to come and convert them to bombs." (*The Boat*, p. 281)

The connection between the books and bombs becomes more sharply delineated as Timothy casually picks up some French books, bearing Mrs. Lampard's bookplate, and even some old railroad timetables. Moved by nostalgia, he looks up the departure time of the Orient Express from the Gare de Lyon for Venice in 1924. Suddenly a slip of paper falls out of the timetable with a brief note on it addressed to Mrs. Lampard from a Frenchman named Charleroi, informing her that "little Désirée is as much mine as yours." (*Boat*, p. 283) Timothy now understands the reasons for Mrs. Lampard's opposition to her daughter's marriage: the bridegroom is Désirée's half-brother. "Below him in the brittle October sunshine," as Hartley describes Timothy's thoughts, "lay Upton-on-Swirrel, much as it must appear to the pilot of a German bomber, carrying his lethal load. Should he drop it, or shouldn't he?" (*Boat*, p. 283) Timothy drops his own bomb by posting his discovery to Mrs. Lampard who subsequently goes insane. Although he does finally receive an invitation, the marriage is cancelled.

Perhaps the incipient Communist in him can rationalize his action by telling himself, as James Hall remarks, "that insanity and incest are at the heart of the established order." (Hall, p. 118)

Parodies of similar Hardyesque coincidences and bad timing recur throughout the novel, as Timothy, and not the Germans, brings the war to Upton. He becomes his own pocket dictator, mirroring the larger forces of totalitarianism in miniature. If he assumes some complicity in the disastrous events of *The Boat* and accepts Tyro's judgment of him as an ordinary sinner, Timothy at the end of the novel is asleep. He misses the milestone, but his somnolence is doubtless preferable to his earlier self-deception. Maybe a measure of hypocrisy serves as well as Tyro's insistence on always facing things, which Hartley partly mocks. The pattern of continuity in Timothy's character is based on contradiction, of balancing imbalances, of faithfulness to change which accounts for what Peter Bien sees as the tonal problem in *The Boat;* namely, how do the serious and the comic balance out? (Bien, p., 152) They do not balance out, of course, for it is Hartley's tonal virtuosity and contradiction which give *The Boat* its peculiarly modern thrust after the Edwardian scenes of the *Eustace and Hilda* trilogy. The symbols and metaphors inspire thoughtful laughter of the kind that undercuts solemnities but hints at the apocalypse. There are moments in *The Boat* when Hartley, retrospectively from the decade of the nineteen-seventies, appears almost to be a harbinger of writers like Günter Grass, Joseph Heller, or even Thomas Pynchon in his divided serio-comic tone. At least he has captured the absurdity of the microcosm which adumbrates the larger chaos.

That Timothy Casson anticipates joining the Censor's Office at the end of the novel, while testifying to his new-found respect for the war effort and public security as he departs forever from Upton, still evidences in his nature some of the old rigidity which few Hartley protagonists can ever be divested of. Yet perhaps he is better able to accept as inalienable both his own and other people's selfishness with tolerance and even generosity. L. P. Hartley's sly, satirical humanist style has seldom been put to better service than in *The Boat*, which is the progenitor of most of the subsequent novels with adults as protagonists. But nowhere else in the Hartley canon have characters and their action been more wittily and sympathetically perceived, with metaphor arising out of the plot; in the novels that follow Hartley reveals a tendency to deal more with a surface that is all conscious metaphor with the accompanying result that everything is so preconceived that the reader is left with little to discover or respond to. Hartley deals with the perennial problem of evil in *The Boat*, even as he and his protagonist appear farthest removed from it, celebrating finally the renewability of life.

IV   My Fellow Devils: *Standing Firm
Against the World and the Devil*

Hartley's neglected novel, *My Fellow Devils* (1951), which he esteemed rather highly, deserves reappraisal; it takes the categorical imperative of *The Boat* and elevates the moral tenets to a responsibility before God, a position even more perilous after the Second World War than in the midst of it. Margaret Pennefather, Hartley's adult protagonist, is an unmarried, twenty-eight year old magistrate, a rural Portia, who struggles to find a moral *modus vivendi* which does not succumb altogether to the relativist ethics of post-war Britain. She complicates her task and her identity immeasurably by marrying an unlikely suitor, Colum McInnes, a movie tough guy hero, in the tradition of Humphrey Bogart or the young Jean Gabin, whom audiences love in spite of or really because of his seemingly unregenerate nature. Caught in her marriage between illusion and reality, Margaret McInnes fills the vacuum of her life with a quest for God in the one Hartley novel where divinity enters explicitly and not incognito.

The setting of *My Fellow Devils* is the post-war wasteland Hartley increasingly evokes in his fiction; Margaret's father remembers with some special fondness, and in terms similar to those Hartley himself uses in *The Novelist's Responsibility*, the antebellum world when standards were still respected, even if they did not always prevail, before the onslaught of the atom bomb, concentration and labor camps, and increase in crimes of violence and juvenile delinquency. As a magistrate and social worker, Margaret is attempting to rectify the wrongs of the times. Her marriage to Colum McInnes is largely motivated by a comparable reformist desire to salvage the kind of criminal ne'er-do-well he usually portrays on the screen and, as she learns, in fact, actually is, stealing from himself and her for insurance money. Colum as an adult is closed in the dream world of films where childish feelings are given professional status.

A curious epistemological dilemma befalls Margaret as a member of the audience at a Colum McInnes film. Her response to his per-

formance is at odds with that of the audience. L. P. Hartley elsewhere finds the queue the mass formation of modern times; and *My
Fellow Devils* appears to be indicting the popular, mass appeal of
film which as a medium addresses audiences rather than the individual. Unable to embrace the movie-fed fantasies of the typical
McInnes audience, or the movie cool which is the manner Colum
affects in life as a continuation of his projected romantic temperament, Margaret brings an unyielding sense of principle and right
action to her marriage with a film star who has no identity apart
from illusion and audience adulation. Because she values the very
attributes the role-playing Colum is deficient or delinquent in,
Margaret the literalist falls in love with her husband-to-be "as a little boy of gangster propensities whom it would be her task in life to
reform." (*My Fellow Devils*, p. 77) Consequently, she indulges in
her own fantasy far more delusive with respect to Colum McInnes
than the response of his large audience, which simply finds the
gangster trash entertaining.

Colum McInnes, like the outlaw hero of Jean Luc Godard's
*Breathless*, seems to think that living in a movie dream world makes
him guiltless, even as he cannot quite believe in the plots of his own
films. Throughout *My Fellow Devils* Hartley summarizes the plots
of a number of mawkish McInnes films and his one successful play
which the actor himself authored: the typical formula calls for the
reformation of the anti-social hero usually as a result of the interces-
sion of an innocent woman. In his most recent film, triumphantly
released at the end of the novel, the charming villain of *The Devil
Is So Distinguished*, who exploits women or their husbands through
blackmail, does not reform. Everyone is finally implicated in the
evil portrayed in this film, including the little boy, the accomplice
of his duped mother, who closes the film standing on the threshold
of the latest house the "devil" is to wreck and giving the "passers-
by a little wave and a very naughty smile." (*My Fellow Devils*, p.
384) Audiences love Colum McInnes unrepentant, and the film is a
huge success except to Margaret who cannot toast the devil.

It might be conjectured that Mr. Pennefather's views about the
effect of films on the moral impulse of the modern world closely
parallel Hartley's own attitude about the popular arts and mass
culture. "You may say what you want," Mr. Pennefather cautions
his daughter after she displays new affection for the film actor, "but
the gangster films, or whatever they are called, do have a bad effect
on the minds and morals of young people. Only this morning I was

reading a letter in the *Times* to the effect that juvenile delinquency is enormously encouraged by the glamour attached to crime in films of the type we have been discussing. You, as a Justice of the Peace, should know that." (*My Fellow Devils*, p. 74) Although Margaret rejoins that no very reliable statistics exist on the causal connection between films and crimes of violence, Hartley implies that such entertainment helps to spread a moral vacuum throughout the land by heightening the cult of the criminal, even the devil, or at the very least pandering to what he considers the besetting sin of the twentieth century, dishonesty. Mass cultural commonplaces, when they serve the devil, endanger the survival of the soul.

## V   *Margaret's Conversion Experience*

Against the meretricious values of gangster films and the thievery of her actor-husband, Margaret takes refuge as a convert in the Roman Catholic Church. Originally Colum, himself a "bad Catholic," as he almost boasts, had asked Margaret to convert to his faith in order for their marriage to be truly sacramental within Holy Church. Through a friend she learns of Father McBane to whom she goes for counsel regarding the advisability of her conversion. He represents absolute integrity in the face of moral compromise; he is unimpressed with her secular attitude toward conversion comparable to the notion that Paris is worth a mass. Love of husband rather than love of God is not sufficient for entering the Roman Church, and Father McBane discourages Margaret not only from conversion but also from marriage with Colum McInnes.

Without benefit of conversion, Margaret marries Colum in the sacristy of the Salute in Venice. Immediately she begins to keep an extensive diary recording her thought-processes and moral pulse-taking. The civilized protagonists in L.P. Hartley frequently take recourse in letter-writing and diary-keeping as gauge to their morals and as structural unifying devices in the novels. During the nine months she lives with her husband the diary helps her to gain perspective and sufficient distancing to break with Colum. Likewise, very shortly after her marriage, Margaret discovers items missing from their flat and soon finds herself a "darling accessory" protecting her purloining Colum, with lie and alibi. Hartley provides an especially penetrating analysis of Margaret's plight:

Because Colum was such a successful illusionist on the screen, because he could make a foolish and improbable story so real to people's imaginations that their own lives seemed colourless and unreal by contrast, he believed no doubt, that he could perform this miracle on her, make her mistrust the evidence of her mind and senses, and accept his version of what had happened. And just as on the screen he was used to falsifying values, and presenting crime as something glamorous and romantic, so he thought he would woo her from her incredulity by clothing the episode and all that had preceded it in the charms and graces of his personality. She would cease to wonder whether his story was true; she would take it from him as unquestioningly as she took his other gifts, his looks, his kindness, his love. It would cease to be a question of right and wrong—it would be just an attribute of Colum, to be swallowed whole, as he was. (*My Fellow Devils*, pp. 191-192)

At another interview with Father McBane following her marriage to Colum and discovery of her pregnancy Margaret is aghast when the candid priest tells her that her immortal soul and the soul of her unborn child are in peril so long as she persists in staying with her husband as his accesory in sin. "Your love is of little value to him," the priest admonishes her, "if it comes from a heart as perverted as his own. Do not imagine that love is a substitute for behaving well." (*My Fellow Devils*, p. 242) This exchange harks back to the novel's epigraph taken from Proverbs: "Whoso is partner with a thief hateth his own soul." Father McBane shows her that the conflict is not simply between love and justice, as she supposes perhaps as a former magistrate; but the issue is between definitions and realities of love. He reads to her what John Henry Newman termed the "mere preamble in the formal credentials of the Catholic Church":[2]

The Catholic Church holds it better for the sun and moon to drop from heaven, for the earth to fail, and for all the many millions on it to die of starvation in extremest agony, so far as temporal affliction goes, than that one soul, I will not say, should be lost, but should commit one single venial sin, should tell one wilful untruth, or should steal one poor farthing without excuse. (*My Fellow Devils*, p. 245)

Since lying and stealing had been the very conditions which had been worrying her, Margaret responds to the awe in Father McBane's voice and the testimony of the great nineteenth-century convert. Faced with the transcendent morality, the eternal welfare of mother and her unborn child, she re-thinks her attitude toward the child whom she had formerly considered as a future bond between her and Colum, "a fount at which they would renew their innocence, a pledge of good behaviour." (*MFD*, p. 247) Suddenly the thought of corrupting their child by their shared evil becomes linked with an earlier indicent. Margaret had retrieved at an auction a Renaissance child's head which had once been in Colum's collection. She discovers that her husband had disposed of the head initially; now with the object back in their possession, he promptly breaks it. The symbolic connection between the statuary and her child, however contrived and artificial, is underscored:

> That the dishonesty of the parents might be handed on, that their punishment might be to watch their child grow up in dishonesty, had not occurred to her. She tried to adjust herself to it; and as she did so there slid into her harassed, undefended mind the image that still terrified her; Colum's hand on the smiling alabaster head, and his face as he jerked it off the mantelpiece: and it seemed to her this might not mean what she once thought it might, that she would have a miscarriage, or that the child would be born dead, but that its spiritual life would be destroyed, that it would grow up a criminal as its father was—as both its parents were. (*My Fellow Devils*, p. 247)

Their marriage collapses after Colum participates in a staged robbery during which his old friend and benefactress, the American Mrs. Belmore (the intended victim of the ruse), dies from shock, and the actor, recognized despite his mask, is faced with criminal charges. Margaret obtains Nick's services to defend her husband. However, the police drop the charges against Colum, because Nick Burden together with the actor's former girlfriend, Lauriol, fabricate an alibi removing Colum from the vicinity of Mrs. Belmore's boudoir at the time of her death. Notwithstanding Colum's claim that he disengaged himself from this masked charade before the tragic completion of the holdup, Margaret does not believe him; to her he seems guilty—the "illusion" of his participation being wholly plausible.

Margaret had planned that once the case had been settled in Colum's favor she would divorce her husband and marry her former fiancé, Nick, the successful and, in her opinion, ethical barrister, who surprises her by urging that she remain with Colum. Nick insists that she has reformed the little devil, as he had known Colum McInnes to be when they had been together at the same public school. Margaret ruefully acknowledges that, as once her husband had stolen her from Nick, now he has stolen Nick from her. She stands "like a figure in an allegory, between a man she did not care for and a man who no longer cared for her. If hands and hearts were joined in the picture, they were Nick's and Colum's." (*My Fellow Devils*, p. 366) Thus very covertly L. P. Hartley introduces a curious turn of the plot toward homosexuality without relating it specifically, as might be expected, to the infantilism which Colum McInnes demonstrates throughout the novel. As metaphor and for dramatic irony, as Peter Bien remarks,[3] homosexuality would seem to have neglected potential in *My Fellow Devils*. It is a devastating rebuke to the novel's heroine, the implications of which Hartley ignores by showing Margaret's reach for the transcendent *caritas* of Holy Church.

If the two men in her life have used the language of love to banish her, Margaret resents the vulgarization of the concept of love which is manifested in the way Nick and Colum bandy the term about in conversation and letters to her. Further, she objects to the role they in their homosexual alliance cast her in—"the prig's position of not believing what it would be for her own happiness to believe, chaining herself to a barren rock of principle while the warm tide of humanity flowed by her." (*My Fellow Devils*, p. 376) She tells Father Grantham, her new instructor following the sudden death of Father McBane, that only in the Church can she love something which is eternally true, but emotionally the former loves would seem to exert some claims upon her.

Margaret's conversion is not without its perils, but Hartley does not parody her conversion experience as he earlier seemed to in the wet initiation of Timothy Casson in *The Boat*.[4] Father Grantham reminds her to beware of ecstasy which is for saints as she returns to an imperfect world following her conversion. She is, after all, not a nun. Nonetheless, Margaret fulfills at least momentarily the transcendence sought by so many Hartley protagonists when at the end of *My Fellow Devils* her heart shouts and sings with recognition of the significance of the spire on St. Saviour's Church. And she runs toward the sacraments promised the faithful in the Roman Church, in the shadow of more than the architecture of humanism. For once the private soul in relation to divinity seems less guilt-inducing than mysteriously inviolable. As a convert, Margaret is developing a new faith different in kind from the legalisms of Nick and the irresponsibility of Colum; and, in time, perhaps the Church will serve as a bridge between her past and the future, extending even to finding some means to reconcile her with her husband. While separated from him, she is forever joined to him in marriage within the Church; thus, her marriage and her religious faith partake of a decision once and for all. Perhaps something like a marriage, viable if not mystical, between Heaven and Hell is still possible.

### VI   My Fellow Devils: *A Stillborn* *Theological Comedy of Manners*

Hartley's attempt to deal with adult problems in the postwar world is somewhat impeded by an uncertainty of tone, far more noticeable in *My Fellow Devils*, in my opinion, than in *The Boat*. His omniscience is stretched too thin, and the reliance on analysis and exposition seems extreme. Nevertheless, *My Fellow Devils* poses adult moral questions in a distinctive way against the rather adolescent terms of popular films, representing the illusory nature of modern life; and Hartley hints at an alternative model of reality in and through the Roman Church which fulfills, in truth, what it promises. On the other hand, unless she becomes a nun, an option not seriously considered in the novel, Margaret must live in the world without becoming a debased worldling; and her potential for priggishness survives and may even be strengthened by her conversion. Hartley casts some doubt on her reliability as moral paragon and perhaps some irony with respect to himself as a crypto-symbolist in the following passages which appear far along in the novel:

She had lived so long her problem, wrestling with it, that Colum had become an abstraction to her, a mere symbol of his own dishonesty. That he should still exist as a man with feelings to be hurt after she had exorcised him hardly crossed her mind. (*My Fellow Devils*, p. 396)

Why was she finding it so difficult to write [a letter to Colum]? Not because she really thought that Colum was the Devil, but because she did not want to admit that he was a husband with claims on her, or even a man. She could not re-open relations with him: he must remain an abstraction, the X in an equation, that had been solved. (*My Fellow Devils*, p. 409)

Having reduced her husband and their life together to the condition of a morality play, Margaret's scheme appears almost as false and facile as the typical premise and promise of Colum's films; both approaches present too simple an externalization of the conflicts within man, to say nothing of the world and the devil. Margaret, while more adult in her understanding of choices and responsibility than her strangely adolescent husband, is nearly as insensitive as he to human complexity in her embrace of the institutional absolute of the Roman Church, remote from its power of forgiveness. Her conversion is, therefore, strongly puritan. True to form, L. P. Hartley takes a slightly ironic, profoundly human view in the portrayal of his heroine in acknowledgement of the incongruity and paradox which affect all moral choices, even religious ones.

Margaret's child, a boy named Anthony for his mother's patron saint, is born and offered to his father nearly as a sacrifice from his mother. Colum who never wants what he has been offered (which may explain why he steals), of course, declines. Colum's or the Devil's playfellow, Lauriol, writes to Margaret inviting her to join Colum, Nick, and herself for a happy foursome in what promises to be a Sartrean drawing-room comedy set in hell:

> His boy-friend Burden drops in fairly often. Do you approve of that. I don't. Old Nick, Colum calls him, so now there are the two of them—three, counting me, but perhaps I don't count. It's a game, as the servants say, or isn't it. We rub along quite well, all things considered. But why not come back and make a fourth. (*My Fellow Devils, p. 410*)

The juxtaposition of inversion and conversion at the end of *My Fellow Devils* has intriguing possibilities which Hartley does not explore, although he introduces the novel pairing of the ideas. The mind behind this novel is mature, at once serious and playful, and as always civilized (in the best sense), possibly too much so to deal adequately with the recalcitrant themes brought into but underdeveloped in the novel. The description Hartley offers of his heroine has equal applicability to himself: "She was very English in that she could forgive offences against herself far more easily than she could condone offences against her moral standards." (*My Fellow Devils*, p. 317)

As for morality in *My Fellow Devils*, Hartley is sometimes reminiscent of Graham Greene, a Greene caught somewhere between his "entertainments" and the major novels; or possibly in Walter Allen's stunning analogy with Jane Austen's *Mansfield Park*, ". . . like Jane Austen's novel, it [*My Fellow Devils*] cannot make for comfort in readers who shun or do not understand a rigid morality. The problem posed is how we should behave in the presence of evil, and his [Hartley's] answer is unambiguous: we should have no truck with it." (*The Modern Novel. . .*,p. 253) Yet

evil is part of everyone, including Margaret, who finds in herself a
sense of more than original sin. Not merely a social or personal
aberration, though it may be denoted by such deviance, evil is
satanic, however trivial deceits are or however domestic the locus.
This recognition gives a serious dimension to the comedy of *My
Fellow Devils*, for it is a commonplace that the satanic predicament
is not really comic. For all his artful self-possession, Colum has been
tarnished. As for Margaret, she has exchanged the loss of self which
occurred as she willingly submitted to the pull of Colum's mass
audience for the recovery of self through celebration of the Mass
with a congregation, toward which she is running as the novel ends.
*My Fellow Devils*, to be sure is a flawed novel, marred most by the
dullness and self-righteousness of its heroine, but its power and
haunting quality cannot be denied.

## VII    A Perfect Woman: *Pious and Impious Quartets*

In *The Novelist's Responsibility* Hartley describes the way Henry
James works in his later fiction according to a scheme or pattern
which is quite apposite to Hartley's own novels of the fifties (as
Mulkeen notes, pp. 116-117), especially *A Perfect Woman* (1955):

. . . his [James's] characters only exist in virtue of their relationship to each
other, and to their general predicament, which the conclusion of the novel
is to solve . . . the tormented quartet in *The Golden Bowl* are almost unknown factors in a quadratic equation or lines in a parallelogram of forces,
so interdependent are they. (*The Novelist's Responsibility*, p. 180)

Such an apparatus dominates *A Perfect Woman*. Isabel Eastwood, a
suburban housewife with two children, is married to Harold, a
serious-minded and successful accountant, who is extremely con-
ventional and relishes the comfortable bourgeois pattern of his
married life. Into their household comes Alec Goodrich, a novelist
of some reputation. Harold has met him by accident on a train and
quickly becomes the novelist's tax accountant. Restless with her
own conventionality, Isabel, having once aspired before her
marriage to idealism and intellectual accomplishment, is much
taken with Alec when he visits their home as a figure of and for fantasy / romance. She, like others before and after her in L. P.
Hartley's work, longs to be his Egeria; and ironically she becomes a
kind of muse.

Alec, however, on his visit to the Eastwoods of Marshport,

another Hartleian seaside town, is smitten with an Austrian barmaid, and he asks Harold to act as his go-between to ascertain the
availability of Irma, the barmaid, for him. Isabel supports this
scheme, and on her own she helps to procure Irma for the novelist.
Not so coincidentally, Alec had recommended Laclos's *Les Liaisons
Dangereuses* to Isabel, and this French masterpiece is obviously an
antecedent of *A Perfect Woman*. Harold, himself, of course, falls in
love with Irma and she with him, releasing a suppressed imaginative strain in him. At one point Harold imagines how his wife
would explain his role of go-between to the children in a fantasia
which novelist Alec Goodrich might properly envy:

> Yes, darlings, Daddy has a friend, a new friend, and I'm very glad about
> it and I hope you will be too. . . . She doesn't belong to Daddy, you know,
> darlings, not as you and I do, she isn't one of the family, so to speak: she's
> just someone we're all very fond of. She really belongs to another
> gentleman; well, you know him, too, he's Mr. Goodrich, the novelist, who
> once paid us a visit. You remember him, Janice, you showed him your dol-
> ly, Pamela, or Pamelia, as you call her. Well, she belongs to him, just as
> Pamelia does to you. Daddy's just keeping her warm for Mr. Goodrich; no,
> I don't quite mean that—it's like this. Daddy bought Pamelia, but Pamelia
> doesn't belong to Daddy, she belongs to you. Well, Daddy bought the
> Austrian young lady but really she belongs to Mr. Goodrich: Mr. Goodrich
> gave Daddy the money to buy her with. She's Mr. Goodrich's dolly, really,
> his Pamelia, but he keeps her here and sometimes he lets Daddy play with
> her. (*A Perfect Woman*, p. 168)

To all appearances Alec gives up any thought of Irma when he
learns of Harold's interest in her. Isabel becomes his mistress instead, and through her love she imagines he will be able to write a
novel with a female character who is supportive rather than destructive, as Alec's women in his fiction usually are. With her, Isabel supposes Alec can exorcise once and for all the witch-woman, Elspeth
Elworthy, who has dominated his life and art for most of his
adulthood. Unobliging in her refusal to step down from her former
privileged position with Alec, Elspeth turns up at Marshport with
the completed manuscript of Alec's new novel which Isabel inspired. Here in the pages of the unpublished novel Isabel discovers
that Alec has transposed her into a sort of nymphomaniac who is
only the intermediary whereby the protagonist hopes to gain his
true desire, the Italian maid (or as Isabel readily comprehends, Irma, the Austrian barmaid).

Wishing revenge for being jilted, Elspeth learns from Isabel the name of Irma's German suitor, a jealous and bull-headed farm laborer, residing in a nearby town. She goes to Blastwick to report to Otto Killian, the symbolically named German, that his girl-friend is having an affair with Alec, an affair which at that time exists only as art in the manuscript. The meeting with Killian takes place during a hellish kind of fair at Blastwick where Elspeth's first sight of Killian is of him grotesquely posing as Lady Godiva. Crazy Otto immediately embarks for Marshport, and he kills both Irma and Alec. Isabel, disillusioned with Alec but more respectful of her husband because she has learned from Irma quite accidentally that Harold has been loved by another woman, and Harold, bereft of his mistress but comfortable with his old bourgeois pattern of wife and family, are reconciled as a result of their independent but curiously shared experience. Alec's posthumous novel is critically well-received and destined for financial success. The proceeds from the novel, entitled by his executors, *The Italian Maid*, are slated according to Alec's wishes to be settled on the Eastwoods' children, Jeremy and Janice. This bequest implies the novelist's guilt and desire for expiation arising from his exploitation of the Eastwood family for his art.

As Harold reads to his wife the first review of Alec's novel, Isabel hears Monica, her persona in *The Italian Maid*, described as "one of the most touching and beautiful creations in modern fiction, a pelican who feeds her loved one with her own blood. Monica is someone with whom we can all sympathize." (*A Perfect Woman*, p. 332) The supposed reviewer remarks that Mr. Goodrich should have let Monica commit suicide instead of condemning her to live on with her tiresomely correct and forgiving husband. Such a fate also devolves to Isabel, but she takes delight, without perceiving the irony Hartley assuredly intends, in the reviewer's assessment that her fictional counterpart represents a perfect woman, nobly planned. The uncannily wise child, Janice, immediately responds to her father's reading, saying the lady in the book reminds her of Mummy; however, the male contingent in the family experiences no shock of recognition. Isabel wonders whether Alec really thought of her that way—"Would she now *want* to live in the pages of his book?" (*A Perfect Woman*, p. 333) The old confusion between art and life is more exacerbated for Isabel at the end of the novel than at any other time, but the "pious quartet" of Eastwoods appears safe and secure as they carefully close their front door on a Sunday morning and make their way to church. They embody bourgeois security against the evil of Elspeth and her kind still at large in the

world. Indirectly the Eastwoods have been responsible for two
deaths, but Harold remains rather dissociated from his former affair
with the late Austrian barmaid, and Isabel gives in to the luxury of
concept she was reluctant to accord Alec—to live transposed in art
as a perfect woman, while muddling through actual life without
much claim to perfection.

## VIII   Janice and Jeremy: Hartleian Children of Mid-Century

The children in A Perfect Woman are assigned a choral and unifying function. They are perhaps more credible as devices than as
characters, since often Janice and Jeremy appear rather tendentious.
On the other hand, Hartley's treatment of these modern children
who seemingly have suffered a premature loss of innocence is
different in degree and kind from the Victorian and Edwardian
childhoods he is justly famous for evoking in Leo Colson and
Eustace Cherrington, respectively. Hartley has brought youth hor-
rifyingly up-to-date. Dropping little needling remarks suggestive of
hidden layers of gamesmanship and maybe even complicity, the
children comment with remarkable accuracy on their parents' desires, actions, and moral dilemmas always from the slightly oblique
position of childhood's lack of adult experience but with persistent
interest in the mature world.

Hartley presents Isabel's moral progress (or decline) symbolically
according to a game the children play in the garden which they call
"Crossing the Farmer's Field," using the ladder-like chalk lines
their father has laid down for golf practice. In the game Janice plays
at evading the order her brother dictates just as Isabel's desires and
fantasy about embarking on a liaison with Alec violate the order of
her conscience and bourgeois respectability:

. . . each child would take up a position, one in front of the other. The one
in front, the farmer, stood with closed eyes; the one behind, the trespasser,
tiptoed forwards, to traverse the ladder which stood for the farmer's field.
But if the farmer looked back, as he might at any moment, and saw the
trespasser on the move, the latter had to go back to where he started.
Jeremy and Janice had agreed upon a bye-law, suggested by the ladder,
that once the trespasser had reached a rung, he need not go back beyond
that rung. (A Perfect Woman, p. 58)

Periodically, throughout the novel, heralding a moment of crisis or
decision for Isabel, the directive, unheeded by the mother more

often than by the not always trustworthy daughter—"Janice go back!" sounds through the window. Near the end of *A Perfect Woman* Jeremy and Janice revive their old game, but he no longer must tell his sister to go back. She goes back now of her own accord. Janice explains that she does so because her brother likes it better that way. Likewise, her mother "goes back" for similar reasons—back to her husband, the old pattern of bourgeois responsibility, to the rules of the domestic game.

Hartley uses the two children often deftly to reveal hidden motives and conflicts in their parents. Two passages illustrate particularly well the way his filial correlatives dramatize and heighten adult dilemmas. In the first instance Janice thrusts her doll, Pamelia, upon the visiting Alec, claiming she will share her with him. Hartley analyzes Isabel's consciousness in response to this scene:

Suddenly Isabel lost her temper with Janice. Usually her surface sympathy was with her daughter, who was getting all she could out of life, while Jeremy, with his insistence on rules and regulations, his instinct for decorum in all things, seemed to her a spoil-sport and a life-denier. But now she felt Janice had gone too far. What would Alec think of her? That she was hideously spoilt, no doubt. The way she monopolized the limelight, and assumed that she must always be the centre of attention! This Madonna-act was really too much. . . . it was rather disgusting that Janice, at her tender age, should be forcing upon Alec this symbol of her maternity. And beneath all these feelings, and unknown to her, something like sex-jealousy stirred in Isabel, resentment that her daughter should be free to express her feelings in a way that she, Isabel, was not. (*A Perfect Woman*), pp. 202-203)

Equally illuminating is the letter Jeremy sends his mother, while she is engaged in her liaison with Alec. The letter is forwarded from her mother's where it is assumed she is visiting. The son shows himself the temperamental offspring of his accountant father when he explains that he bet and subsequently lost to Janice his bottom dollar on the wager of his mother's imminent return home by the past Friday:

Janice has it now because I bet her you would be back by then but you weren't. She is trying to spend it but the shops won't take it, I am glad to say, as it isn't real money except in America where it is called a greenback.

It is now Tuesday as you see. I won't bet any more it is extravagant but please come back all the same. (*A Perfect Woman*, p. 257)

This reminder from her child of her place in the home determines Isabel not to seek a divorce from her husband, as she had considered. As the children seek more mature obsessions in *A Perfect Woman*, Hartley relates them as a gauge to adult responsibilities, and indeed certain actions on the part of the children seem catalytic in determining adult experience. At the end the children are the inheritors of the fortune, if not the misfortune, which the impious quartet made possible through Alec's novel, and the loss of innocence represents the price which must be paid for the legacy.

## IX   *Art and Quantification: Moral Cost-Accounting*

*A Perfect Woman* is a compelling study of a modern bourgeois marriage, an analysis of a twentiety-century woman who resolves not to succumb to the suicidal languors of her nineteenth-century antecedents like Mme. Bovary and Hedda Gabler; but perhaps most of all it is an intricate examination of the claims of art on life and relationships of art to life, and life to art, especially from the perspective of exploitation. L. P. Hartley once more chooses the characteristic symbol of money with his familiar use of investments, blackmail, and bequests. In a sense *A Perfect Woman* like James's *The Ambassadors* is about the costs and profits of art and similar acts of the imagination. As a novelist, Alec Goodrich, whose symbolic name epitomizes what Harold first notices about him—his seeming lack of employment—seems to be a taker; the artistic imagination, as Hartley implies through Alec, is necessarily exploitative of experience, the author's own and other people's. "A novelist is a wasting asset," Alec asserts, "The more of himself he puts into his books the less of him there is." (*A Perfect Woman*, p. 283) Hence he takes the life he finds at Marshport and transposes its reality into fictive art. Like his investments which against Harold's conservative estimate usually yield substantial returns quite inexplicably, Alec produces a successful novel, even a masterpiece, out of the unpromising capital of the Eastwoods themselves. If Alec has taken advantage of other people's lives for his novel, he pays the ultimate price with his own; and, in death, the novelist balances his life's account somewhat in his role as benefactor of the Eastwood children. The moral ambivalence behind the economic fact is distinctly Hartleian. Art at least can change reality into something rich and strange, as Isabel rejoices in the excellence of her persona in *The Italian Maid*.

Isabel's smart London friends have criticized the novels of Alec Goodrich as old-fashioned, since, like Hartley himself, he tried in his characters to make the individual count and often aim too high. Their ideal novel arises from criteria which Hartley scorns not only here but also in *The Novelist's Responsibility* and *Facial Justice*:

> It mustn't aim too high, because we are too tired to aim high, and it mustn't be about people wanting to get on, in any sense, because (a) there's nowhere to go, and (b) we don't *want* to get ahead of other people now, we don't *want* to jump the queue! . . . . I mean, competitiveness must be canalized. The lowest common denominator, that's your aim, if aim you must have. (*A Perfect Woman*, pp. 248-249)

Hartley's Isabel is a worthy opponent of such exaltation of the mediocre, and her final decision about what to do with the manuscript of Alec's novel in her possession vindicates her idealism as well as her honesty. Her first impulse is to wipe the slate clean by destroying the manuscript as Hedda Gabler burned the "child" of Lovborg and Thea, but Isabel is not so philistine as that. Recognizing that this book is the best thing Alec has ever written and that legally by keeping it she is a receiver of stolen goods, Isabel anonymously returns the manuscript to Alec. Unlike Margaret Pennefather, Isabel accepts the idea that Alec still has rights and feelings to be considered, "that he was still a person, and alive, though dead to her." (*A Perfect Woman*, p. 300) Hartley brings together Isabel's respect for art and her bourgeois respectability in this action. As witnessed by *My Fellow Devils*, thievery is not a slight offense.

At the trial of Otto Killian, however, Isabel is required to lie about the extent of her knowledge of the deceased Alec and Irma in order to protect herself and her family. Because she would be able to inform the court that Elspeth stole the manuscript of Alec's novel, this "blackmail" keeps Alec's old mistress from challenging her testimony. Hartley describes Isabel's alteration in consciousness in economic terms:

> She felt that anything she said came from a tainted source—as if, to borrow a simile from Harold's world, with which she was now so much more familiar, she had been a fraudulent financier asked to give his opinion on the value of an investment. Her parents had, according to their lights, maintained their respective standards of value. She had let hers down. (*A Perfect Woman*, p. 326)

98 L. P. HARTLEY

In a key passage Hartley examines the anxiety of Isabel, after her "fall," according to symptoms which apply to any number of fearful selves in his fiction and extend credibly to the author himself:

> She suffered from a form of self-dislike, and felt that if people knew more about her they would dislike her too. She would be outside and pale of normal human sympathy, and tolerated only by the understanding and the well-disposed. She was under sufferance, on probation, and anyone could catch her out. (*A Perfect Woman*, p. 327)

And, finally, in culmination of the monetary metaphor, "her spiritual account, she felt, was overdrawn, and she would never get back into the clear." (*A Perfect Woman*, p. 327) Whether this figure adequately abstracts and dramatically crystallizes the state of being Hartley desires is debatable, but, as always, his search for an organizing form is sufficiently striking to keep *A Perfect Woman* generally interesting, especially the implicit connection between morality and contemporary economic instability. As metaphor cash nexus bodes more significantly in the novels with adult protagonists and contemporary settings than in the Hartley novels set in the past with child protagonists whose larger-than-life pictures of reality are indeed inflated but relatively free of economic context and a sense of market value.

At the end of *A Perfect Woman* the Eastwoods have come to see one another more nearly according to the categorical imperative than anyone except Mrs. Purbright ever attained in *The Boat*:

> Each was conscious of the other as a person in his or her own right, a person who for a short time had meant to someone else as much as any human being can do—a sovereign with one adoring subject—no, that wasn't true, for Harold had meant much more to Irma than she, apparently, had ever meant to Alec. Still it was nearly the same thing. Each brought to their relationship, and pooled, this gift of personal sovereignty which neither had possessed before, or recognized in the other. (*A Perfect Woman*, p. 328)

No longer book-bound except as she can identify herself as Alec's "perfect woman" in *The Italian Maid*, Isabel resumes her bourgeois marriage with alacrity. Harold relishes the new prosperity which his acquaintance with Alec first brought him, unmitigated by knowledge of the novelist's malignity. Isabel knows the darker truth, but out of self-protection must withhold the truth. The children are guaranteed financial security, and the Eastwoods' bourgeois complacency is intact, notwithstanding the rupture Alec's art and life might have caused it. They have survived his mockery of them and profited by it, in economic and moral terms.

The Eastwoods may avoid the waking nightmare of the demonic fair and ludo-players which Hartley brilliantly evokes as the suitable ambience for Elspeth's evil intent, but they cannot lock out evil entirely unless they ignore their own complicity, making evil their good. The great church tower of Marshport stands sentinel as is the wont of towers in L. P. Hartley, and the family dutifully makes its way to church. Still, the faith which the Eastwoods will keep seems less religious than familial, the faith of their frailty and experience. Hartley ends *A Perfect Woman* much as he concludes *My Fellow Devils* with the approach to a church, but the tone differs markedly. The compassionate irony and gentle comedy of *A Perfect Woman* gives proof, if proof were needed, that comedy does not belie the emotions, but qualifies them in accordance to the way of the world. It is heartening to think that Isabel laughs a little at herself even as her fictional counterpart in Alec's novel brings tears to the eyes of at least one reviewer.

# Adolescent Vulnerabilities and Adult Consequences: The Go-Between, The Brickfield, The Betrayal

H ARTLEY'S investigations of childhood perceptions and the acquisition of identity begun so successfully in *The Shrimp and the Anemone* resume in his best-known and best-loved novel, *The Go-Between* (1953).[1] In the next decade, he continues this mode with the coordinate and sequential novels, *The Brickfield* (1964) and *The Betrayal* (1966). Sharing structural, symbolic, and thematic characteristics, these three novels illustrate Hartley's espousal of and contribution to Kierkegaard's assertion that life must be understood backwards as it must be lived forward.

## I   The Go-Between: *Hartleian Quintessence of Form*

Hartley seems most convincing in understanding the period of adolescence by his portrayal of innocence on its way to being corrupted. Beginning and ending in the present with a Prologue and Epilogue, Hartley's *Go-Between* frames fifty years in the life of a man, Leo Colston, and his troubled century. While concentrating on personal relationships, Hartley reflects larger historical and political issues in the process. Via a diary of events in summer 1900 and responses provoked by them, Hartley's narrator / protagonist remembers, after a prolonged lapse of memory, his visit to Brandham Hall in Norfolk where he became thirteen and unluckily discovered the traumatic reality of adulthood (especially adult sexuality), before he was sufficiently mature to cope with that discovery. A kind of fugitive nostalgia is the initial note struck in the novel's opening sentence of the evocative Prologue, "The past is a

100

foreign country: they do things differently there." (*The Go-Between*, p. 9) But after the twenty-three chapters which stand for the twenty-three days he was in residence at Brandham Hall, the aged Leo can only too painfully acknowledge that the child was lamentably father of the man. As an analysis of the perceptive and questioning innocence of a youngster, explored and destroyed, *The Go-Between* invites, and does not suffer from, comparison with Henry James's *What Maisie Knew*, Elizabeth Bowen's *Death of the Heart*, and J. D. Salinger's *Catcher in the Rye*.

Leo Colston, as a boy, is a poor, but well-brought-up, classmate of the more affluent Marcus Maudsley, who invites him to visit the family's rented estate outside Norwich. Young Leo's most notable attribute, at least in his friend's eyes, is his schoolboy success with curses. As junior necromancer, Leo is reputed to have laid curses for two bullies at school who subsequently fell off a roof. When asked whether the victims were killed, Leo modestly replies that they were just severely mutilated. By the end of *The Go-Between*, comparable mutilations abound, including Leo's own. The Edenic world of Brandham Hall, as he conceives it, does not survive the curses Leo devises to protect it.

The Maudsleys receive Leo with patronizing graciousness of the kind reserved for rather impoverished little boys. Dressed in a heavy woolen Norfolk suit, Leo is seasonally, if not geographically, out of place. Marian Maudsley, Marcus's ravishing older sister, takes pity on Leo's discomfiture and buys him a lightweight outfit of Lincoln green during a shopping expedition to Norwich. Unknown to Leo at the time, Marian uses their trip to Norwich as a way of making an additional assignation with Ted Burgess, the Lawrentian tenant of Black Farm with whom she is having a clandestine affair. Later, out of gratitude and devotion to her, Leo assumes the role of messenger for Marian, carrying notes between the Hall and the farm. Thus, without understanding the nature of the relationship between Marian and Ted, Leo becomes a pre-pubescent Pandarus, the archetypal go-between.

Out of this plot premise, Hartley constructs an elaborate symbolic structure which he uses to enrich characterization. As soon as Leo is attired in his Lincoln green suit, he experiences a more complete and corporeal union with summer than he had earlier imagined possible. Moreover, green also introduces the motif of Robin Hood which permits Leo to see Marian as Robin's "Maid." The fact of Leo's "greenness," in the sense of naïveté figures significantly in the outcome of the novel and extends the resonance of Hartley's color symbolism. The green of the vegetative world figures prominently in Leo's ambivalent attraction and revulsion which he experiences in the presence of the Deadly Nightshade that encloses the outbuildings of Brandham Hall. At his first encounter with the plant, *atropa belladonna*, Leo's ambivalence is immediate:

> I knew that every part of it was poisonous, I knew too that it was beautiful, for did not my mother's botany book say so? I stood on the threshold, not daring to go in, staring at the button-bright berries and the dull, purplish, hairy, bell-shaped flowers reaching out towards me. I felt that the plant could poison me, even if I didn't touch it, and that if I didn't eat it, it would eat me, it looked so hungry, in spite of all the nourishment it was getting. (*The Go-Between*, pp. 42 - 43)

In addition, Hartley deftly shows the symbolic proximity, which exists in Leo's mind, between Marian and her vegetable equivalent, the "beautiful lady," as the Latin botanical name of the plant suggests.

Inasmuch as Leo's diary sports zodiacal decoration, another grandiose symbolic system finds its way into *The Go-Between*. While the aged Leo admits to his disastrous identification with the zodiac, the young Leo relishes its possibilities. He attempts to make the hierarchy of the zodiacal company conform to the high hopes he has for the new century, the dawn of a Golden Age. His own name suggests the Lion, "imperious manhood," and Marian seems ideally available for the apex of the whole structure, the Virgin. At Brandham Hall, amid a cast he sees as larger than life, minimized Leo assigns maximal, even celestial, roles to the adults around him. Prior to his visit, Leo had been torn between identification with the Archer and the Water-carrier for his persona. But Sagittarius, Marslike, violated his commitment to pacifism which he abides by as tribute to his late father's belief, and Aquarius seemed to the curiously snobbish Leo too much like a farm laborer or gardener for him to desire identification with this sign. Once at Brandham Hall Leo can make specific attributions of persons to zodiacal roles (or at least Hartley assumes the reader will): the Archer is represented by Hugh, the Ninth Viscount Trimingham, a disfigured veteran of the Boer War and ancestral owner of the Hall itself; the Water-carrier, appropriately enough, can be easily identified with Ted Burgess, the virile farmer.

Trimingham supplies Leo with a forging link between the boy's imaginative constructs and his social role when the Viscount names him Mercury, not only the smallest planet but also messenger of the gods. Leo, accordingly, rises to new heights in the service of the god-like adults, as he conceives the denizens of Brandham Hall to be. Likewise, during the unusually hot Norfolk summer, the mercury in the thermometer rises to new highs. The mercurial Leo alternates in his own extremes of mood, as the long-held scientific view of the planet Mercury, operative at the time Hartley wrote *The Go-Between*, postulated that only one hemisphere was ever illuminated, with extreme hot-and-cold conditions therefore prevailing on the planet. Metaphorically, in the course of the novel, Leo becomes drawn to the warmth of physical love, but he is scorched by the heat of passion. The aged Leo, in the cold hinterlands of life, opens the novel as the victim of turn-of-the-century extremes. The heat withers all things in summer 1900 except the deadly nightshade which flourishes.

Leo's first experience in perceiving the physical reality of adult maleness is, however, without mythological or symbolic trappings, although subliminal association with the Water-Carrier and Ted may serve as subtext in Hartley's description. Leo watches, unobserved, as Ted emerges from the river after a swim—"I retreated almost in fear before that powerful body, which spoke to me of something I did not know." His combined fascination and fear in the physical presence of Ted parallels Leo's earlier ambivalence toward the belladonna plant, all of which is indicative of the boy's response to the masculine and feminine components of the life-force which as yet he can neither comprehend nor articulate. Perhaps it is not too fanciful to take the Latin word, *fascinum*, the source of *fascinate*—as it often meant a charm, something one is compelled to look at, something that could draw away the attention, and so the effect, of the evil eye; and frequently it meant an amulet shaped like a phallus—and apply it to Leo's perception of Ted:

> Believing himself to be unseen by the other bathers, he gave himself up to being alone with his body. He wiggled his toes, breathed hard through his nose, twisted his brown moustache where some drops of water still clung, and looked himself critically all over. The scrutiny seemed to satisfy him, as well it might. I, whose only acquaintance was with bodies and minds developing, was suddenly confronted by maturity in its most undeniable form; and I wondered, what must it feel like to be him, master of those limbs which have passed beyond the need of gym and playing field, and exist for their own strength and beauty? What can they do, I thought, to be conscious of themselves? (*The Go-Between*, p. 63)

The specific nature of one kind of adult pursuit which reaffirms the body Leo does discover in consequence of his acting as go-between for Marian and Ted. Prior to this traumatic epiphany, however, Leo instinctively turns to the tenant of Black Farm in hope of obtaining an explanation from him of the mystery of man / woman relationships which the boy can only identify uncomprehendingly as "spooning":

I still conceived the act of spooning visually, comic postcard fashion; an affront to the eye and through the eye to the mind. Silliness, silliness, a kind of clowning that made people absurd, soft, soppy. . . . Pitiful at best, but who wanted pity? It was a way of looking down on people and I wanted to look up. (*The Go-Between*, p. 121)

Hartley skillfully contrasts Leo's numinous exultations of his ideal projections with the earth-bound reality which soon will overtake him. The former is often portrayed with a covert nod in the direction of Sir Thomas Browne's "O altitudo"; it is by the statue of Browne in Norwich that Leo meets Marian after his visit to the cathedral. Although Leo never does learn who Sir Thomas Browne was, Hartley engages him in rhapsodic associations which are very reminiscent of the prose of the seventeenth-century Norwich physician and his habit of mind. Indeed, the frequent periodic sentences of *The Go-Between* serve as oblique pastiche of Browne's distinctive prose style, as in the following passage:

The expenditure [of money for Leo's suit] had been godlike; it belonged to another, ampler phase of being than the one I was accustomed to. My mind could not grasp it but my imagination could make play with it, and unlike my mind, which could dismiss what it did not understand, my imagination loved to contemplate the incomprehensible and try to express my sense of it by an analogy. And I had one ready-made. From those resplendent beings, golden with sovereigns (and, I suspected, guineas), arriving, staying, leaving, apparently unaffected by any restrictions of work or family ties, citizens of the world who made the world their playground, who had it in their power (for I did not forget that) to make me miserable with a laugh and happy with a smile—from them it was but a short step to the hardly more august and legendary figures of the zodiac. (*The Go-Between*, p. 57)

Ted, only, escapes the distortions of Leo's fantasies: "He [the tenant of Black Farm] was, I felt, what a man ought to be, what I should like to be when I grew up." (*The Go-Between*, p. 164) On the other hand, Leo feels that Ted is his greatest rival as well as

Trimingham's in the courtship of Marian. Somehow Leo deduces that his service to Marian and Ted jeopardizes the decorum of the Hall. During a cricket match Leo manages to catch out Ted, winning victory for the Hall over the village—he becomes the young David who slays the Goliath of Black Farm, not with a sling but with a catch. Leo as temporary hero soon discovers that he is really like the element mercury, a nonconductor, emblematic of the "registering" characters in Hartley who always seem somewhat removed from involvement in life. Leo suffers a severe blow to his self-esteem when he learns that Marian has befriended him principally for what he can do for her as go-between rather than for what he is himself. Vainly he tries to have his mother recall him to his own home in order to abandon his Mercury role. The mythology Leo desires fulfilled entails Marian's marriage to Trimingham, but she confesses to him that however much circumstances require such a marriage her love remains with Ted. With surprisingly mature analysis, Leo deduces the moral and non-symbolic calculus applicable to each of the adults in this love triangle:

> I knew exactly what Lord Trimingham wanted. He was a constant: he wanted to marry Marian. I knew what Marian wanted, or what she intended which was not the same thing; to marry Lord Trimingham and keep Ted by her. And what did Ted want?. . . .
> I feared for Lord Trimingham, I wept with Marian, but for Ted I grieved. Only he, it seemed to me, had a real life outside the problem, a life unconnected with it to which he was always reaching. Into that other life he admitted me as a real person, not only as an errand boy who must be petted or scolded to make him function. Perhaps this was unfair to Marian and Lord Trimingham, who had both treated me with signal kindness. But to them, I knew, I was a go-between, they thought of me in terms of another person. When Lord Trimingham wanted Marian, when Marian wanted Ted, they turned to me. The confidence that Marian had made me had been forced out of her. With Ted it was different. He felt he owed me something—me, Leo: the tribute of one nature to another. (*The Go-Between*, pp. 245 - 246).

Unconsciously Leo may be abandoning his own mythology when he falsifies the next meeting time between Ted and Marian, thus betraying his trust as Mercury but perhaps witnessing to a new-found realism. Yet in childlike fashion once more he resorts to casting another spell to exorcise the devil from his former Eden at Brandham Hall. His material medium is the belladonna plant enshrouding the outbuildings:

It was like a lady standing in her doorway looking out for someone; . . .
In some way it wanted me, I felt, just as I wanted it, . . . There was no
room for me inside, but if I went outside into the unhallowed darkness
where it lurked, that springing mass of vegetable force, I should learn its
secret and it would learn mine. And in I went. (*The Go-Between*, pp. 254 -
255).

But the poisonous weed ripped from the ground and incanted over
in Leo's bedroom is not so easily destroyed in its metaphoric and
symbolic extension.

On his birthday, unluckily to turn thirteen, Leo reappears in his
Norfolk suit, as if to assert his original identity apart from the distortions it has suffered at Brandham Hall. However, the aged Leo confesses that this strategy was also a mistake:

I did not realize that this attempt to discard my dual or multiple vision
and achieve a single self was the greatest pretence that I had embarked on.
It was indeed a self-denying ordinance to cut out of my consciousness the
half I most enjoyed. To see things as they really were—what an im-
poverishment! (*The Go-Between*, pp. 265 - 266)

Marian's present to him, the bicycle, is not delivered because Leo's
discovery of sexual reality intervenes. Dragged into the garden by
Mrs. Maudsley, who is sure her daughter is not visiting Nannie
Robson, as announced, Leo discovers the "serpent" in his Eden.
Marian and Ted are found making love in the outbuilding which
formerly had been protected by the deadly nightshade. And Leo
must now look down upon them, literally, on the floor of the
building. Unwittingly Ted has fulfilled his promise to Leo to inform
him about the facts of life but in demonstration rather than explanation. How subtly and lyrically, though, does Hartley convey the
scene, from the smell of rain in the air (the continuing leitmotif of
Aquarius?) to Leo's epiphany:

. . . it was then that we saw them, together on the ground, the Virgin
and the Water-Carrier, two bodies moving like one. I think I was more
mystified than horrified; it was Mrs. Maudsley's repeated screams that
frightened me, and a shadow on the wall that opened and closed like an
umbrella. (*The Go-Between*, p. 277)

Leo, as is characterisitic in Hartley's fiction, suffers a nervous
breakdown as a result of his traumatic encounter. While still at
Brandham Hall, he vaguely recalls that somehow he learned of the

self-inflicted death of Ted Burgess. Perhaps Marian had, indeed, been the heat, and Leo became the embodiment of Icarus, flying too near the sun. Ted, who once seemed to the boy like a cornfield ripe for reaping, had been cut down and left in the sun.

Although Hartley has maintained a double articulation of time throughout the first-person narrative, Leo reminiscing about events in 1900 and retrospectively judging them from a much later date, the Epilogue catches up with the aged Leo who puts together the final pieces of the puzzle. Celibate Leo, a bibliographer working on other people's books, has committed himself to the truth of facts, finding, as Hartley brilliantly expresses it, "facts that existed independently of me, facts that my private wishes could not add to or subtract from. . . . Indeed, the life of facts proved no bad substitute for the facts of life." (*The Go-Between*, p. 280). After what he observed in the exposed outbuilding during the summer of his thirteenth year, Leo notes that the activity of spooning held no more interest for him. To be sure, his formula of seeking only the life of facts has proved as inadequate as his earlier romantic fantasies vis-à-vis an abundant life.

Dispassionately, the aged Leo opens the last piece of evidence he has retained from that fateful summer—the remaining unopened letter from Marian to Ted in which she wrote that she would be at their rendezvous at six, "and wait till seven or eight or nine or Doomsday—darling, darling." (*The Go-Between*, p. 283). No longer able to detach the "facts" of that summer from a current emotional response, Leo, now in his middle sixties, breaks down and cries as he has not cried since his thirteenth year. He understands now how Marian had used both himself and Ted.

He takes a room at the Maid's Head back in Norfolk and resumes the "life" he disengaged himself from in 1900. The Norfolk village has changed, indicative of the alterations of the most changeful half century in history. From two fairly new-looking mural tablets in the village church, Leo discovers that Hugh Francis Winlove, Ninth Viscount Trimingham, and the Saggitarius of summer 1900, had died in 1910. Leo wonders whether Trimingham's scarred face may not have represented the full extent of damage he had suffered in the Boer War, as his early death suggests. The second tablet commemorates the birth of the Tenth Viscount, born 12 February 1901 and his death in action 15 June 1944 fighting in France. His wife, it is learned, had preceded him in death during a 1941 air-raid. Leo the factualist has difficulty explaining how Trimingham contrived to get married and have a son in less than seven months after the sad events at Brandham Hall. In truth, the child, of course, was not his but the son of Ted Burgess. Subsequently, Leo becomes acquainted with the Eleventh Viscount Trimingham, whose coloring is like a wheat field in May—a proper descendant of the tenant of Black Farm. Like Leo himself, the present Lord Trimingham has eschewed the vision of imperious manhood, feeling as if he were under a curse and afraid to marry a Winlove cousin, lest he pass on the curse. These *déjà vu* details tend to become rather obtrusive and planted in the Epilogue, although they contribute to the delicate formal symmetry of the novel.

Out of his desire to please Marian once again, Leo finds himself cajoled into carrying a final message, this time to grandson Edward. Marian assumes no responsibility for the tragedy surrounding her family; she places the blame entirely on "this hideous century we live in, which has denatured humanity and planted death and hate where love and living were." (*The Go-Between*, p. 295). Perhaps she believes her late husband's conviction that nothing was ever a lady's fault, out of which sentiment presumably Trimingham had married the pregnant Marian. She now views Ted's suicide as a sign of his latent weakness, although it may well be a corollary to Trimingham's gallantry. Because Grandmother Marian cannot understand why Edward is unable to rejoice in his inheritance of love and passion, she asks Leo to carry the simple message—"there's no spell or curse except an unloving heart." (*The Go-Between*, p. 296).

Poignant as Marian's dictum seems, it is not without its special irony. That Leo notices her self-deception indicates the extent of his new-found awareness, even as he is moved by what she has said. For Marian, and, to a degree, Leo have survived to mid-century because they, too, have exploited some of the hardness and indifference of the twentieth century. In a 1957 lecture delivered at the Aldeburgh Festival, L. P. Hartley explained that his original intention for the Epilogue in *The Go-Between* was to reveal Marian as an evildoer who had utterly demoralized Leo and ruined at least seven lives, her own, Ted's, Trimingham's, her mother's, father's, Leo's, and her grandson's, but the rigorous moralist and latent misogynist fortunately did not win out in Hartley's treatment. Rather than assail Marian, Hartley restores personhood to Leo, whose life has been bereft of incidence except for summer 1900, as the brief Epilogue and briefer Prologue suggest, before letting him serve as the renewed go-between. Marian recounts the appalling history of her family since 1900 without connecting it with the idyll, as she views it, of her affair with Ted. Leo, however, understands as a survivor the cruelty which can be the uncalculated consequence of the emotions Marian celebrates.

As he turns into the lodge gates at Brandham Hall, Leo suddenly notices for the first time the much-touted south-west prospect of the Hall which he had failed to appreciate back in his youth. Having fatefully observed the dark underside of the Hall, as it were, in the outbuildings, Leo, in maturity, has mastered the moral and aesthetic distance necessary for a favorable response to the lofty facade—he can see Brandham Hall steadily and whole, as life itself. If Leo is still the go-between, he accepts the role now out of a free choice which is informed by self-knowledge and knowledge of others. He perceives the human frailty behind Marian's message of love and her curious plea to him. He responds to that plea with compassion and humanity, without zodiacal constructs, in much the same spirit as he views the south-west prospect. People are willfully vulnerable, as Leo's trauma and the body-count of those dead at Brandham Hall bear witness, and the Marian who so tenaciously has come through is especially vulnerable in her self-deception.

*The Go-Between* began in the foreign country of the Victorian past, where the cultivated upper-bourgeoise still felt secure in their privileges and tastes and where a schoolboy's education and slight experience prepared him badly for the unexpurgated realities of life. This world appeared insulated from catastrophe as long as certain restrictions were observed. Marian, as a young woman, broke out of the tidy enclosure of her privileged milieu to experience the larger and riskier emotional resources with Ted Burgess. This personal rebellion on behalf of vitality, different in kind from the Victorian propriety she came from, held a promise for the twentieth century which Marian feels was not realized. The impasse has been both personal and social. She looks back nostalgically to summer 1900 and feels understandably proud of the love which she and Ted shared. And she may be right that the hypocrisy of the Victorian period was less damaging than the nullity of the twentieth century which threatens to claim Edward. Leo has made his treaty with the century by excluding love, although he continues to understand its human meaning as well as its risk. At the end of the novel, Leo reassumes the risk of connection, accepting responsibility now because he feels (as well as knows) the facts of human existence (as opposed to his earlier fantasies). Marian is fixated on the past; however, Leo can take a message from the past to the future. He has become a go-between not only of generations but of epochs.

Leo Colston, therefore, achieves autonomy at last, while yet in Marian's service. The greatest possibility for renewal, of course, lies with Edward and the marital risk his grandmother hopes he will take. At age thirteen, Leo refused to live with and by the double-vision of good and evil, passion and quietude; young Lord Trimingham may fare better. The promise of both Hugh and Ted can yet live in Edward and his offspring. Leo remains the intermediary separated from life, but he is prepared to carry the message which endorses nature, risk, and love for one sufficiently prepared and potent to become involved in life. There is certainly no promise that Edward and his bride-to-be will live happily ever after; much in past history militates against any such optimism. Edward, nevertheless, unlike the youthful Leo, seems not so naïve in his expectations and may have the necessary preparedness (and ripeness) to meet the mysteries of life (including sex) working themselves out in a fallen but still feeling world. Edward's keen sense of moral responsibility and scruple elevates him somewhat above his grandmother, and his potential natural vitality, reminiscent of Ted's, suggests that he has the proper attributes for more than Leo's mere survival. If Edward can restore loyalty, tenderness, and honor to sexual consciousness in such a way that history need not repeat itself, the curse he feels he has inherited will be vanquished. *The Go-Between* ends, as it began, in Leo's narrative voice, but the future belongs to Edward.

In Eriksonian terms, Leo's confined and withdrawn life since his adolescent trauma has been one long "psychosocial moratorium." But at the end of the novel Leo, once more needed as a go-between, assumes concern for generativity in his willingness to guide the next generation. Leo, after all, is partly what will survive him, and *The Go-Between* ends on the threshold of the Age of Aquarius with connotations perhaps richer and more prophetic than L. P. Hartley could have imagined when the novel first appeared.

Hartley's Leo Colston comes to terms with reality through an almost Proustian imaginative relation between past and present, with the result that the plot of *The Go-Between* becomes subordinated to the method of narration and symbolic structural techniques. The symbolism is so explicit "that it may well have determined the form of the plot." (Grossvogel, p. 51) Hartley tends to employ richer symbolism in novels which look back to the more ornamented Victorian and Edwardian pasts than in novels set entirely in the present. When the time-setting and the characters are contemporary, especially when characters become more concerned with sexual passion as participants instead of observers, Hartley noticeably reduces his symbolic underpinnings. Admittedly, the real exotics in Hartley are often working-class men who, like Ted Burgess, exert their greatest appeal on boys like Leo and, inferentially, on Hartley himself because of their inherent realism which seems to place them outside the projected mythologies of reality-denying characters.

Thus Hartley's remembrances of things past, highly symbolic if less integrated into realistic situations than the later novels, belong perhaps to a convention privately chosen by the author as his particular apprbach to the tradition of the novel of education. Hartley's discipline in adhering to his chosen structure, his pleasure (and ours) in the exercise of his imagination, his bringing to life a plot which would sound banal, if baldly stated, and his gracious care with detail have given him a triumphant book. Part of that triumph rests in the way Hartley develops the symbolism of his aesthetic scheme while at the same time he assigns a very high place in his moral scheme of values to recognition of reality. In the tension and eventual collision between what Hartley envisions happening when habitual blindness to reality encounters an inescapable stroke of fate, in Leo's case symbolized by setting the zodiac against itself, *The Go-Between* vindicates the author's telling and all its intercessory means.

The late Victorian world and its millenial hopes for the twentieth century provide Hartley with forms and symbols through which he can make the imaginary real by placing it in an historical context that maintains for an imaginative little boy at Brandham Hall his own special decorum of verisimilitude even before reality overtakes him. At the same time, Hartley does not flinch from portraying Leo, even in his imaginative flights of fantasy, as a confined and imprisoned self whose dreams and curses prevent him from finding psychological fulfillment in relationships with others. Leo's movement from youth to old age takes him from symbolic distortion to ironic acceptance of modern life. Under the surface of Hartley's refined and erudite taste for symbolism, there lurks a strong, organically-affirmative, Lawrentian and even peasant-like approach to reality and survival.

In the successful film version of *The Go-Between*, winner of the Grand Prize at the Cannes Film Festival in 1971, Joseph Losey, director; Harold Pinter, author of a remarkably faithful screenplay; and Gerry Fisher, photographer, collaborate to objectify Leo's memory cinematically, evoking the ambience of Brandham Hall with its formal pleasures of tennis, cricket, and tea; the viewer, like Leo, becomes enchanted by the vistaed lawns, family deer herds, and the plenitude of silver. However, the material literalness of this visualized surface curiously obliterates the novel's richer "sub-text" of Leo's grandiose symbols which Hartley conveys indefatigably but which the film cannot show with any degree of clarity and coherence. As Hartley reveals how Leo invests the personages at Brandham Hall with larger-than-life size, considering them immortals, inheritors of the summer and progenitors of the coming glory of the twentieth century, Losey and Pinter choose rather to emphasize the absolute smallness and detachment of Leo in the midst of adults or amid the dizzying verticality of Norwich Cathedral or, as he traverses the immense horizontal expanse of the Norfolk countryside, in his role as go-between. Viewers often look down with Leo at the denizens of the Hall or down upon him from the vantage point of a large double staircase. The plentiful downward camera angles and shots throughout the film culminate in Leo's traumatic look at Marian and Ted *in flagrante delicto*. If, in the instance of Leo's mythologizing, the film reverses Hartley's perspective, cinematically the effect works generally well without doing violence to the narrative source material in the novel.

Otherwise, the film is remarkably faithful to the "look" and mood of Hartley's evocation of a special time in recent English history. Very few self-conscious cinematic devices are used which detract from this fidelity. The script is about ninety percent Hartley's, a fact which many reviewers who were not familiar with the novel did not perceive when they attributed a Pinteresque quality to dialogue taken directly from Hartley. The cast superbly captures Hartley's characterizations: Dominic Guard as the young Leo and Sir Michael Redgrave as the Old Colston; Alan Bates as Ted Burgess; beautiful, but strong, Julie Christie as Marian; and perhaps most Hartleian of all, the late Margaret Leighton, herself favored a decade earlier to play Marian in an unsuccessful project to film the novel, as Mrs. Maudsley. A mood abides with the spectator at the end of the filmed *Go-Between* which is astonishingly close to the effect generated by Hartley's graceful novel—a memory of how one felt while seeing the movie or reading the novel. The film, like the novel, captures the epistemological dilemmas which reveal the instability and subjectivity of man's grasp of external reality. Perhaps the novel should be construed, as Harvey Curtis Webster does, as "a parable of how the twentieth century deteriorated into what it has become. Leo and his experiences are a symbol of what Hartley in his darkest hours feels modern man is." (Webster, *After the Trauma*, p. 165) On the other hand, the Epilogue also adumbrates the Aquarian end of guilt and fear.

II    The Brickfield / The Betrayal: *Problematic Novels and Elusive Autobiography*

Ambitious and disturbing novels of the mid-sixties, *The Brickfield* (1964) and *The Betrayal* (1966) owe much to *The Go-Between* in their portrayal of the life of an aged man, pre- and post-trauma. However, Hartley's will seems to be trying here to do the work formerly done by his imagination. Perhaps his sense of continuity overruled the chance of change; the novels are rather programmatic, and the programs feel over-rehearsed. Because the narrator / protagonist is himself a novelist who in many ways resembles L. P. Hartley, *The Brickfield / The Betrayal* provocatively invite autobiographical speculations. Richard Mardick, a sixty-seven year old author, tells his confidential clerk and future biographer, Denys Aspin, the one guilty secret from his past which has affected his entire life: the betrayal, more imagined, as we learn in the course of the novel, than real, of the young Lucy with whom he shared his youthful initiation into love and who died in the abandoned brickfield where they held their summer trysts.

The tale which comprises *The Brickfield* is, like *The Go-Between*, a remembrance of things past, harking back to the turn of the century. Mardick relates the tale to Denys in strictest confidence, but the novelist wants his biographer to be aware of him as the product of the experience without revealing in any future memoir the full and precise details. Mardick has written only one successful novel, *The Imperfect Witness* (also, incidentally, the original working title for what became *The Brickfield*), which alone in his canon was based on his own experience and observation. His subsequent fiction has been largely invented and generally ignored, both by critics and the public. Significantly, as the aged Richard Mardick asks Denys to relay the shadow of the fact but not the fact itself, he draws others into a conspiracy of imperfect witnessing.

Denys is somewhat vaguely descended from Border chieftains of

Aspin Castle whose exploits had been celebrated in the childhood poems of the Brontës. Like Eustace and Leo before him, Richard Mardick venerates the aristocracy, even though Denys proves not only disillusioning but actually bogus in both ancestry and conduct. The narrator / protagonist especially wants to point up the ethical difference between his sense of the secret of his past, typical of one brought up to feel a kind of Victorian responsibility for his action, and the frivolous, even slothful, disregard for such rectitude demonstrated repeatedly in contemporary England. What Richard Mardick possesses is a narrative to his life as opposed to Denys Aspin whose random life lacks intelligible threads. Denys shamelessly betrays his employer and benefactor, without apparent compunction or sense of guilt, in the sequel to *The Brickfield*. In the companion volume, *The Betrayal*, Hartley seizes the opportunity to indict the English welfare state as a corollary to, if not actually the cause of, Denys's behavior. Denys Aspin of *The Betrayal* appears as Hartley's version of an irresponsible, angry young man who both reflects and finally is victimized by the circumstances of life in postwar England.

Death and emotional violence surprise and dislocate the lapidary world of Richard Mardick once in his youth, as presented in *The Brickfield*, and again in his old age, as developed in *The Betrayal*, Hartley once more exploits two chief symbols to underscore his point: the disused brickfield, where Richard experienced his postpubescent fall, and the prosperous Fordyke Fundamental Brick Company which his father had wisely invested in, thereby guaranteeing his son's financial security. To the brickfield, then, he owes his spiritual poverty, even as the brickworks supply his material prosperity. Ironically, as Richard pays ever greater blackmail to Denys in *The Betrayal* to prevent disclosure of what happened years before in the brickfield, he thinks that he has "betrayed" his father's company through the mistakes and wrongdoings of a lifetime. In the course of the second novel Richard discovers the close symbolic proximity between the two loci:

He had not connected them because the one had been a symbol of failure and the other of success. Geographically they were within a few miles of each other, but spiritually they were poles apart—life and death, truth and falsehood, day and night, were not more antithetical to each other. Yet now they seemed to have come together. Perhaps everything tended to coalesce as one grew older. Distinctions were blurred or ceased to exist with one's inability to feel them. Even wealth and poverty did not seem so different. (*The Betrayal*, p. 223)

Likewise, of key symbolic importance is Rookland Abbey, yet another ecclesiastical structure of metaphoric value in L. P. Hartley, which is transformed from *The Brickfield* to *The Betrayal*. On the north side of Rookland Abbey, called the Devil's Side, three buttresses form an *M* pattern to support the tower. Richard's mother, who overprotects her son, as mothers customarily do in Hartley, finds the structure ugly and advises him never to look at it lest he be corrupted by its ugliness. Similarly, Richard has always cultivated his detachment from the ugly and fallible except in the instance of his own boyhood "sin" from which he has figuratively averted his eyes until he reports it to Denys. Near the end of *The Betrayal* when Richard, nearly reduced to penury by Denys's blackmail, returns as an old man to the Fens of his childhood, he is surprised to discover that the unsightly *M* has been removed from the Abbey to reveal a beautiful traceries window beneath. And the brickfield itself, so persistently a memory of death and sterility throughout the two novels, has been resurrected as twelve acres of the best land possessed by descendants of Richard's earlier relatives. At this point of external convergence and symbolic renewal, Richard takes up his new life under the patronage of Aunt Carrie. She, too, once a victim of a severe nervous breakdown has been renewed through a meaningful life and the Christian faith.

In contrast to Leo Colston's role as go-between, young Richard Mardick as narrator / protagonist has participated in a love relationship of sufficient physical reality to convince his girlfriend that she might be pregnant. Consigned to his relatives' Lincolnshire farm, St. Botolph, to build up his delicate health and denied the company of his classmates, Richard becomes acquainted with Lucy Soames, the sheltered daughter of two recluses in the neighborhood. She supplants his former interest and recreation in the brickfield where he collected moths, especially *acherontia atropos*, Death's Head, a reminiscence of Hartley's lepidopterists from the short stories and of symbols like the Deadly Nightshade in *The Go-Between*.

Hartley's tender treatment of nascent young love remembered by an aging and unloved novelist achieves considerable poignance:

Yes, she clung to me, Denys, and I—well I was not the boy I had been even a few weeks ago. The doctor's verdict . . . had given me a confidence and pride in myself that I never had before, when I seemed to live only by his favour, and to know less about myself than almost everyone else knew about me. Somehow—it isn't difficult to see how—this knowledge that I was well and whole like other boys—like other men—changed my conception of myself. I felt grown up at last. It got into my consciousness and through my consciousness into my blood, that I was a free agent now and able to do what I wanted to do without asking anybody's leave, and I didn't ask it, Denys. I did ask her leave and she gave it, not knowing what it meant, not knowing in the least, as it turned out. *I* knew something, . . . but I still thought children only came with marriage. (*The Brickfield*, p. 156)

With his new sense of quasi-Lawrentian wholeness and intrepedity, Richard goes to ask Lucy's parents for their consent for his and Lucy's marriage; he claims he has fallen in love with her at first sight when he rescued her from a bad fall. Actually, they have been meeting secretly in the brickfield. Her parents withhold their consent, but they agree to let the two young people become better acquainted. However, a new governess arrives to supervise Lucy, and the girl is not so readily available to Richard. Although the prying governess does not learn about Lucy's romance with Richard, she explains to Lucy hypothetically that pregnancy is a cause of missed menstrual periods. Accordingly, the child convinces herself she is pregnant (the coroner's report states otherwise): accidentally or deliberately, Lucy drowns in the brickfield pool. Richard discovers the body, but the subsequent inquest fails to link him in any way to the tragic event. With no one suspecting his involvement, Richard becomes, indeed, an imperfect witness.

During the inquest the governess reveals the dark secret of the Soames family: namely, that Mrs. Soames is not Lucy's mother but Mr. Soames' deceased wife's sister (the pseudo-incestuous relationship, according to the Victorians, which W. S. Gilbert called "that ancient blister / marriage with deceased wife's sister"). As his narrative of the episode in the brickfield ends, Richard explains to Denys that he underwent a severe relapse and left the Fens in the loving care of his mother. Thereafter, the familiar Hartleian security of legacies and investments preserve Richard's economic future, yet emotionally he seems bankrupt except for his rather more than avuncular fondness for Denys, who at the end of *The Brickfield* affects an almost coquettish relationship with the ailing novelist.

With respect to L. P. Hartley, the autobiographical implications of *The Brickfield / The Betrayal* can only be pursued cautiously and frustratingly. While usually insisting, like Proust, that a book is the product of a self very different in habits, in society, in vices (and virtues), from the one displayed, Hartley probably does less distancing between himself and Richard Mardick than with most of his other protagonists. For example, Richard Mardick's *Who's Who* entry, which at one point Denys recites to his employer, sounds very much like Hartley's own. That his protagonist's family and his own derived their considerable financial resources from a successful brickworks increases the intriguing parallelism between author and fiction. The tragic events of Mardick's youth which occurred in the brickfield would seem to offer a clearer cause for his negative feelings toward the operations that gave him financial independence than exists in Hartley's biography. Even the designation, "Holy Family," which Uncle Austin jokingly uses in reference to Richard's relatives on his mother's side ("It was acknowledged between us, and taken for granted by me, that we stood on a pinnacle of moral worth. We did not expect other people to behave as well as we did." [*The Brickfield*, p. 108]) harks back to attitudes sometimes imputed to the Hartley family. Perhaps most fundamental of all, however, is the problem Mardick tries to face: "Trying to square the opinion people have of you with what you're really like, is quite a problem." (*The Brickfield*, p. 192) This problem is likewise an abiding one for L. P. Hartley, presumably, for whatever reason; and it constitutes, moreover, a recurring identity crisis in novel after novel.

Although *The Betrayal* lacks the economy and concision of its predecessor, it is, in some respects, the more interesting novel. Hartley absorbs much of *The Brickfield* into the sequel. Less tautological than a companion-text, *The Betrayal* gives a knowing latter-day perspective on the consequences of Richard Mardick's confession in *The Brickfield* and explores a variety of contemporary problems which exacerbate old wounds and open new ones. Instead of time flowing in reverse, as it does in *The Go-Between* and *The Brickfield*, Hartley's protagonist, though no longer narrator, confronts contemporary England and suffers distinctly modern buffets so that, at a very late date in his life, Mardick finds himself more sinned against than sinning. Unlike Denys Aspin who always feels in the right, Richard Mardick has felt in the wrong for so many years that he is unprepared psychologically for an alteration in feeling. Through this situation, Hartley continues to take measure of contemporary moral limits.

Early in *The Betrayal* Richard becomes acquainted with Lucilla Distington with whom he develops a fast and deep friendship at the expense of his former relationship with Denys:

> Richard's feeling for her was so complicated by the Lucy-Lucilla relationship, that he could not clarify it to himself. It was alternately a source of comfort and of guilt. In non-guilty moods he felt that Fate had

sent her to him, to compensate him for what he had lost: the dreary years
unfertilized by love. What was Denys? A substitute, who by nature of his
sex was not vulnerable in the way Lucy had been. Physically he could do no
harm to Denys. Morally and emotionally he might; but as for that, Denys
was old enough to look after himself. There was a limit to responsibility!
(*The Betrayal*, p. 47)

If the foregoing is somewhat reminiscent of Shakespeare's Sonnet
Twenty, Denys's reaction to his employer's friendship with Miss
Distington is characterized by petulance and jealousy, threats and
hurt feelings, as if Richard's renewed heterosexuality cannot be endured. Periodically, Denys walks out on Richard. During one such
absence, the novelist suffers a severe attack, and thereafter he is left
a semi-invalid in the care of a succession of hired help. Through his
malign neglect, Denys has indirectly been responsible for bringing
physical harm to his employer. Earlier he had sought to damage
Richard psychologically by his suggestion that the two of them not
be seen together in the square lest people suppose the young man to
be Richard's lover. Richard protests that their relationship has
always been perfectly correct, although appearances throughout the
two novels hint at secret motives on the part of both Richard and
Denys.

The perplexity in this regard is articulated very well by one of
Richard's more outspoken friends who openly encourages the
novelist to marry Lucilla:

. . . you're wedded to this idea of an arm's length relationship. If I may
say so, it's what's wrong with all your books except the first, which
everybody liked, and why? Because in it you showed people coming
together, and being together—since then, you've always shown them
hungering for each other across vast desert spaces. Your youthful self knew
something about human nature that your adult self didn't, or forgot. I don't
know what you felt for Denys Aspin—whatever it was I'm sure he wasn't
worthy of it—but whatever it was it's over, and now you have this wonder-
ful chance. We shall rejoice. We didn't like Denys Aspin—let's be
frank—and didn't very much like coming while he was here, but we *do* like
Lucilla. . . . I long to think of us as a large happy family again, presided
over by you and your . . . your consort. Haven't you proposed to her yet?"
(*The Betrayal*, p. 204)

The incipient love affair between Richard and Lucilla gains a
bittersweet quality (if not exactly credibility) with the gradual,
though inevitable, revelation that she is the late Lucy's half-sister

born after her family's sad departure from the Lincolnshire fens. As
he discovers more about her past, Richard is unable to disclose to
her the role he played as a young man in the tragic life of her family. Denys, on the other hand, is not oblivious to the blackmail
potential in Richard's situation. Denys assumes that posterity would
doubtless forgive Richard his past, but he questions Lucilla's
willingness to excuse and forget. Suddenly Richard must face up to
another ugly *M*, standing for the money he must pay out in
blackmail to his former employee and friend, Denys, in order to
keep his secret from Lucilla.

At a cocktail party Denys lets slip to two of Richard's old friends
that he has something to say about the novelist which might surprise them. Significantly, when these friends tell Richard what they
have heard, it is with new respect for him. They find in him a
precious measure of the anti-heroic and, in turn, recommend to him
that he write a new novel about Denys who himself is most assuredly anti-heroic:

> Everyone, except a few old stagers, will think the better of you, because
> you're somebody to whom something has really happened. Why don't you
> write a book about it? It's what the public wants, the raw stuff of ex-
> perience, and the rawer the better. Experience doesn't need
> justifying. . . . And you'll find that everybody will feel as we do: they'll
> hail you, not as a purveyor of old-fashioned literary wares but as a real, live,
> gay seducer—an archangel a little damaged, as someone said of Coleridge.
> (*The Betrayal*, pp. 217-218)

Neither L. P. Hartley nor his protagonist in *The Betrayal* can
accept such permissiveness. And Lucilla's response is as disastrous
as Richard had feared, she too being dedicated to standards and
moral principles which antedate the general loosening of behavior
of the post-war years. To her, Richard is nothing less than the
seducer and destroyer of her half-sister, and she cannot view the
long ago event in the brickfield as a feather in his cap contrary to
the hedonistic, anti-heroic morality of contemporary England. In
particular, Lucilla holds against Richard the stealth he employed to
find out she was Lucy's half-sister instead of directly asking her:

> He watched her changed face, shrouded in worry and it reminded him of
> Lucy's face at their last meeting when they had nothing to say to each other
> and could only, across a widening gulf, exchange signals of farewell. Lucilla
> and he were friends, not lovers, parting, and they knew what they were

about, which he and Lucy hadn't known; but did it seriously signify—was
friendship so much less precious than love that it could be renounced
without a sigh—a sigh for him and perhaps a tear for her, to mark the ine-
quality of sacrifice? (*The Betrayal*, pp. 246-247)

Once again, Richard finds himself put in the wrong, fated to bear
the guilt of loneliness. The victim of a series of calamities (and
betrayals) in youth and old age, Richard reconsiders his life and its
motives. All he has left is the consolation of Sir Thomas Browne's
advice, "Be able to be alone," which offers only slightly more comfort than the novel's epigraph, also from Browne:

'Tis onely the mischief of diseases, and the villany of poysons that make an
end of us; we vainly accuse the fury of Guns, and the new inventions of
death; it is in the power of every hand to destroy us, and we are beholding
unto every one we meet, he doth not kill us. (*The Betrayal*, p. ii)

Hartley exploits the chanciness of things, in the manner of Browne,
which permits him at the same time to manipulate a whole skein of
coincidence, even if such events point to no system beyond that of
authorial control.

The long middle portion of *The Betrayal* is given over to satire on
the chaos of modern life as it affects the ailing Richard Mardick, for
whom dying is a métier, as it is for other Hartley characters. The
parade of irresponsible servants who faithlessly discharge their
duties of caring for a sick man offers a comic variation on the larger
betrayal theme concentrated in Denys. It was Denys's departure, of
course, which necessitated employment of these surrogates. Confined to his flat, Richard embarks on an extensive correspondence,
principally with Lucilla, narrating his vicissitudes and describing
the daily women and men-servants who comprise his ever-changing
staff. The portrayal of household muddle is thoroughly familiar in
Hartley, although his satiric thrusts against the welfare state as contributor to the overall degeneracy of service have never been so
caustic.

Eccentricity becomes its own system here and demands that
every character be somehow peculiar and particular. To be sure,
they are, and Hartley has Richard Mardick record his impressions of
them with Dickensian glee, if to rather attentuated length, in letters
to Lucilla. One such exchange over insurance stamps, an attribute
of the welfare state Hartley repeatedly castigates, is representative
of the tone and effect of this section of the novel:

"Did you pay your share of his insurance stamps?" [asks a government investigator].

I searched my memory, which isn't very good now.

"Oh yes, I'm sure I did. I always paid their stamps—my share and their share, too. The whole boiling."

"You shouldn't have done that," said the Inspector. "The upkeep of the Welfare State is their concern as well as yours. By your thoughtless, though excusable generosity, you undermine their sense of civic responsibility."

"I didn't know they had any," I retorted, . . . (*The Betrayal*, p. 155)

Ironically the benefits of the welfare state do not ease the suffering of Richard Mardick but actually increase it. From his rehearsal of these daily particulars, Hartley contributes deft strokes to a portrait of domestic life in post-war England.

Richard's betrayer, too, becomes a victim of contemporary mores and "diminished responsibility," as formerly he had embodied them. A friend sends the still confined Richard newspaper clippings which report on a fight in a Soho restaurant. A building laborer had attacked and severely injured Denys. Another clipping gives the proceedings of the Magistrate's Court where the assailant had pleaded not guilty by virtue of his having construed Denys's stares in a bar as a homosexual overture. Hartley's treatment of the testimony is extended but deserves generous quotation:

Here the solicitor explained to the Court that Baker [the laborer] stated that in his early youth an infamous proposal of this kind had been made to him, which left a lasting scar on his subconscious mind. His home life had been unhappy. . ., and he suffered from an acute sense of social inferiority, which was inflamed by the sight of Aspin's flashily expensive clothes and arrogant manner. "We live in a democratic age," said the solicitor, "but unfortunately some of the more privileged members of the community do not always respect the feelings of those less fortunately placed than themselves."

Hartley obviously enjoys jabbing at popular psychoanalytic jargon and the dangers of envy, the latter reminiscent of *Facial Justice*. The trial continues:

"I submit," said the lawyer, "that the accused acted under intolerable provocation, and only did what any young man of his age and social group might have done. Violence is always regrettable but it is, unfortunately, much more prevalent than it used to be. It is also better understood by psychologists, and in a young man of Baker's type can almost be accepted as a

normal pattern of behaviour. Baker would have lost face with his
fellows—he would have forfeited their respect—if he had acted otherwise.
Unfortunately he went too far, but he did it in defence of his honour. It
must not be forgotten, either, that he has a wife and child." (*The Betrayal*,
pp. 236-237)

That Denys, rather gratuitously by this time, has also become a
husband and father is conveniently forgotten. The Chairman of the
Bench accepts the laborer's defense that he was protecting himself
against something "wholly unnatural and un-English and
abominable and ought to be stamped out or kicked out." (*The
Betrayal*, p. 238) As a satire on homophobia the foregoing has more
potential than Hartley allows to be developed. In reading the account, Richard no longer feels sorry for the blackmailer Denys, but
he remembers his former secretary's unseeing stares vividly.

Unable to testify because of his severe wounds, Denys Aspin consequently becomes the victim of testimony from an imperfect
witness whose material circumstances within the English welfare
state win him sympathy and exoneration. What begins as social
satire in Richard's letters culminates in overwhelming, if overly contrived, irony for Denys Aspin and something both more and less
than poetic justice for Richard Mardick. Hartley's purpose remains
shadowy, despite some provocative hints of possible intent. The
laborer's attack on Denys represents a violent reaction to what
Hartley has teased his readers all along into thinking must be the
confidential clerk's sexual inclination or at least exploitation. More
disturbing is the passing thought that Richard's friends and society,
in general, would not be so tolerant of, let alone enthusiastic about,
his youthful romance if it had been other than resolutely heterosex-
ual, as given the character of Richard it easily might have been. As
with *My Fellow Devils*, Hartley's introduction of homosexuality
suggests resonances which are not pursued and a tone which seems
unrelated to the novel's moral center. This particular figure in the
carpet remains mysterious in the Hartley canon.

The final scenes of *The Betrayal*, as noted earlier, return Richard
to the Fens of his youth, where he once more takes up residence at
St. Botolph, this time with his beloved Aunt Carrie. There he
delights in certain changes for the better made possible by modern
technology—changes in the Abbey, the brickfield, and the family
home. His nemesis, however, haunts him even during this idyllic
homecoming, for Denys's wife deposits on Richard's doorstep her

broken husband to die. Thus the remembered evils of the past may
have been cleared away from the Fens, but Richard sees fatalistical-
ly that there is no true escape for him: ". . . in Denys was embodied the evil principle that had tracked him down the years, and
had at last caught up with him." (*The Betrayal*, p. 293) Aunt Carrie
benevolently interprets the meaning of Denys's presence otherwise:

> Because such experiences are not under our control, they are what God
> means for us—they are His arrows, and we are His targets, they are
> messengers from Him, and whatever hits the bullseye, and gives the
> greatest pain, is the surest proof that we are chosen by Him. . . . for whom
> the Lord loveth he chasteneth, and scourgeth every son whom he receiveth.
> (*The Betrayal*, p. 309)

As he goes to assist the nurse who is to administer a narcotic sup-
pository to the suffering Denys, Richard himself, at the entrance to
the sickroom, dies. Denys will shortly follow him. L. P. Hartley has
produced yet another quietly horrific passing. Perhaps Richard, the
betrayer in his youth, has become his own deliverer, in old age; and
the mirror, as Yeats would say, has turned lamp. Role reversals
abound in *The Brickfield* / *The Betrayal*, of which, submerged, the
sexual is but one possibility, as Richard Mardick faces and
assimilates the contradictions of his entire past by caring for his own
betrayer.

Leo Colston and Richard Mardick share the Jamesian moment in
youth which Stephen Spender defines as the time when "the utmost
innocence coincided with the utmost capacity of expression,"[2] and
when their sensibilities have been heightened to a point beyond
which, as grown men, they will not be able to develop, in the tradition of James's "The Beast in the Jungle" and "The Jolly Corner."
These sensitive young men live on to become aloof old men. The
youthful identity of Leo Colson, as go-between at Brandham Hall,
and of Richard Mardick, as the lover in the brickfield, was
something born of dreams—rooted in the experience of
childhood—and the drab reality of their adulthoods is the consequence of repression and denial of what had been most vital in their
early lives. These youthful crises left unresolved come back to haunt
the aging protagonists who have spent their lives making do with
very little emotionally. Childhood might impress Hartley less, if
adulthood impressed him more. Yet if childhood lives on more conspicuously for some of his protagonists than for society at large, it is

not the energy of youth which endures but the trauma of adolescence which thereafter renders virtually impossible any integrating vision of the sexual-psychological-personal life with the political-economic-social life.

In a sense, no one ever comes of age in Hartley after seeing something nasty in the outbuildings, as Leo does, or after suffering Richard's loss when Lucy ceases to be. After the potential richness of childhood sexuality Hartley's protagonists in these novels are reduced to adult asexuality. At most, such persons finally accept, however reluctantly, the responsibility for caring for, protecting, and healing others, even a former betrayer. Herein lies the only measure of generativity which Hartley usually permits his characters. Maybe it is ultimately superior to the sexual, which Hartley persists in identifying with power and control over others rather than as love and service to others.

CHAPTER 7

# *The Novelist as Experimentalist:* Facial Justice *and* The Love-Adept

I N his essay on Jane Austen included in his critical volume, *The Novelist's Responsibility*, L. P. Hartley observes, "To experiment in fiction may be disastrous, but it may open up veins of imagination that the author did not know of."[1] At the opposing termini of the nineteen-sixties Hartley tried his own hand at experimental fiction with results which cannot be termed disastrous, if not wholly successful, in *Facial Justice* (1960) and *The Love-Adept: A Variation on a Theme* (1969).[2]

I   Facial Justice: *A Dystopian Warning or Present Shock?*

Hartley's *Facial Justice*, dedicated "with homage, acknowledgments, and apologies to the memory of Nathaniel Hawthorne," is an unusual mélange of novel, allegory, parable, and diatribe. In addition, like Aldous Huxley's *Brave New World* and George Orwell's *1984*, which preceded it, *Facial Justice* seems to owe something to Yevgeny Zamayatin's *We*, particularly the emphasis on the elimination in society of what can arouse natural passion or personal inclinations. Its imaginative vision of civilization's probable future is unique in the Hartley canon, reflecting in apocalyptic terms the author's profoundest fears about the moral direction of post-war England. As if cathartically, *Facial Justice* seems to let Hartley gain his customary control over potentially intransigent material, and the novels which follow it in his canon provide a perhaps more balanced account of what was Hartley's present than the novels of the nineteen-fifties. "Perhaps every dystopian vision," as Anthony Burgess explains in his familiar nomenclature for the anti-utopian novels of the twentieth century, "is a figure of the present, with certain features sharpened and exaggerated to point a moral and a warning."[3] Certainly the didacticism of *Facial Justice* figures conspicuously in the novel's resonance.

The setting of *Facial Justice* is England slowly recovering from the devastation of World War III, a society literally emerging from underground caverns where its few surviving members have taken refuge during atomic attacks. In such a world, evolutionary survival rather than individual freedom and dignity has become the principal value; quantity has assumed the value of quality in an economy of scarcity and a population of mere survivors. In attempting to build (and control) a moral world out of the ashes, the Darling Dictator, who alliteratively and anonymously presides over the rudimentary government, seeks to abolish personal envy and the spirit of competition. Once more the antecedents for this strategy may be found in Zamayatin's *We* where the dictator is called Benefactor and enjoys the protection of hovering Guardians. Hartley's Darling Dictator is similarly served by an Inspector Class who are named for the heavenly hosts of archangels. For the purposes of abolishing envy among women (an intriguingly sexist detail on the part of Hartley), the state has established Facial Equalization Centers where all women who feel "facially underprivileged" can avail themselves of simple plastic surgery which "betafies" them, bestowing on them a "Beta" face, an indelible, rather expressionless face neither pretty like the "Alphas" nor ugly like the "Gammas," which are other minority facial types in the society. It is a design prescribed by a committee on facial appearance, "to be suitable for all occasions, including the most intimate, although, in this respect, care should be taken not to make the design so physically alluring that the opposite sex would be impeded in the performance of its daily non-amorous duties." (*Facial Justice*, p. 124) As the novel's titles suggests, the metaphor of facial standardization of women becomes the symbolic matrix for pre-eminence of the mediocre, that systematic levelling which Hartley assumes will be at work in any future society. It is a major political theme of *Facial Justice*, as it has been a recurring idea in previous Hartley novels and will be in subsequent ones, that modern people increasingly find the right to be themselves denied them by the state.

Citizens are known as patients and delinquents in this guilt-bound society, and all are named for murderers to which numbers are appended for distinction. The heroine, for example, is Jael 97, Biblical murderers being especially popular. The Hawthornian debt may be implicit here, if it is recalled that Miriam in *The Marble*

*Faun* gives Donatello a group of her sketches, of Jael and Sisera, Judith and Holofernes, and Salome and John the Baptist. Jael 97 is born a Failed Alpha, a higher class than Beta which inspires Bad Egg (Envy) in those ladies less well-endowed facially. Yet at the moment Jael is to enter the clinic for "betafication," her friend, Judith, a Gamma who ascends the ladder of conformity and increased beauty through the same operation, talks her out of submission. Thereafter Jael becomes intent on keeping her individuality at its most conspicuous face value.

England is now a country without extremes, in weather and human personality:

> It was a relaxed and invalidish Civilization. Everything about it suggested weakness and convalescence. A sort of toadstool architecture was invented, in which circles and curves predominated; corners were allowed, though sparingly, but right angles were forbidden, [a similar avoidance of edges appears in Hartley's short story, "The Island"] and no house might be higher than two stories. Traffic was horse-drawn and whips were taboo. Any form of hurry was discouraged. Churches, casinos, and cinemas were erected in every township. The cinemas showed films of the horrors of war and attendance was compulsory twice a week, unless a doctor's certificate of exemption could be produced. (*Facial Justice*, p. 28)

The Darling Dictator has successfully reduced the gap between the ideal and the real, a strategem which not surprisingly Hartley rather respects. Indeed, much in the new state appears to implement Hartley's own ideology, even the principle that "Nature is nasty" (*Facial Justice*, p. 15), with which a number of Hartleian protagonists might agree. The Dictator recognizes that human desires according to human nature are conflicting and contradictory. They have to be sorted out, and a distinction must be made between what at any given time is, in fact, wanted or sought and what ought to be wanted or sought. The Golden Age envisioned by the Darling Dictator will emerge from the exercise of free will whereby each person will find his own private paradise without interference from others. The method for achieving this humanist end is strongly behavioristic, seeing the critical problems of man from the perspective of man's continuing evolution, as B. F. Skinner would. Similarly, Hartley himself is unsure of means and ends, values and norms, in finding a tone for dealing with the conditions of future life in the new state. He does not write in the spirit of political satire characteristic, for example, of Huxley and Orwell;

the ideal vision of the Darling Dictator is hardly norm-critical of
what Hartley most deeply espouses, individualism:

So each should have his paradise, her paradise, to be enjoyed by him or
her alone, and inaccessible to the others. And yet not inimical to the
others—oh no! Side by side, touching but not colliding, each cell enshrin-
ing a perfect individuality, that owed nothing to and took nothing from the
rest. A hive of private paradises, fashioned not by working together, or
playing together, or talking together, or thinking together, not created by
communal activity—perish the thought! But coming insensibly,
miraculously into being by the simplest of all expedients: the exercise of
free will, all your free wills, operating on their own, without reference to
others, guided by that inner light, that infallible sense of the right direction, that, as is well known, we each of us possess. (*Facial Justice*, p. 132)

On the other hand, Hartley does satirize the contingencies under
which the Dictator controls, to however benevolent an end. The
signature of official radio pronouncements from the Dictator who
exists as an unseen "Voice" in the state is "every valley shall be ex-
alted," but the prevailing view of life is strictly horizontal. Ample
precedent from the atomic holocaust indicates the danger of
height—"It was the things that stuck up that were destroyed."
(*Facial Justice*, p. 33) One former pleasure the Dictator permits his
usually horse-drawn subjects is occasional motor expeditions into
the surrounding country, all the while reminding the participants
that motorists, as they used to be called, were morally irresponsible,
consumed by envy, and possessed of egos monstrously distended
because of their motor cars. To the Dictator's surprise and horror,
these expeditions prove to be inordinately popular. In an effort to
discourage future participation in such trips but to preserve the
Voluntary Principle held essential for moral choice, the Dictator establishes a risk factor for the expeditions. One of the six vehicles
that compose the Service's fleet will meet with an accident,
although not even the drivers will know which one. After this new
contingency has been instituted, Jael joins the passengers for the expedition which has as its destination in the deciminated landscape
the solitary west tower of Ely Cathedral left in isolation after bombs
destroyed the rest of the edifice.
      Jael, who secretly deplores the flatness within and without in the
stages of nonerectness encouraged by the state (everyone takes his
daily bromide, for example, to insure domestic tranquillity), is
thrown into transport by her first view of the immense height, the

stone arrow of ineffable verticality. Despite her overpowering sense
of sin, Jael induces all the passengers to stand and look up—"they
were doing the forbidden thing, and every faculty they had
protested; but soon it established itself as something awe-inspiring
and worshipful." (*Facial Justice*, p. 48) Like R. Buckminster Fuller,
Jael concludes that vertical is to live, and horizontal is to die. As
horizontal fate on the highways would have it, Jael's group suffers
the promised accident, and her badly damaged Failed Alpha face is
"betafied" while she is unconscious. Prior to her full recovery of
consciousness in the hospital, Jael remembers, as if in a dream,
traveling with her rescuer, a member of the Inspector Class all of
whom are named for archangels, suggestive of their escape from the
opprobrium endured by Patients and Delinquents. Jael's particular
savior is appropriately named Michael, another possible tribute to
Hawthorne, considering the recurrent image of the Archangel
Michael in *The Marble Faun*.

Now begins the love story of Jael and Michael in a sterile world
where the act of love has nearly been forgotten. In the hospital Jael
is presented with a live cineraria, compliments of Michael, rather
than the standardized plastic flowers issued to every patient automatically by the Ministry of Health—the kind of detail which
would likewise loom large in the novels of Hartley's friend, C. H. B.
Kitchin, as well as Hawthorne. As Jael experiences the hitherto unfamiliar emotion of love for Michael, she harbors equal hatred for
Dr. Wainewright, the surgeon who changed her face from the Failed Alpha visage which Michael first loved to the Beta face the doctor has fallen in love with but which repels Michael. With her
metamorphosis into the Beta classification, she takes to wearing a
black veil to cover her face in another Hawthornesque tactic and
becomes the implacable foe of the identity-destroying regime. Jael
assumes leadership of the incipient rebellion against the Darling
Dictator.

Jael becomes expert at the glib sloganeering of the regime and
packages her own propoganda to undermine the Dictator, while os-
tensibly praising the levelling process in the state. What she actually does is intended as *reductio ad absurdum* of the Dictator's
strategy. In one of her essays which she blackmails Dr. Wainewright
to get published, Jael offers a review of a piano recital during which
two pianists played the Moonlight Sonata. The first performance is
flawless, and the second is dreadful. But Jael perversely singles out
the worst elements in the latter performance for praise according to
the patriotic ideals of the state:

Crash! Bang! With each deviation from the music my heart rejoiced, for this, I knew, was the way I should have played it myself; and I felt that more and more I was entering the mind of the Dictator, who had never wanted us to do anything well, for well is our highest common denominator, which excludes the many who fall by the way whereas "badly" is the lowest common denominator, and includes us all. Darling Dictator, blessed be his name, who does not require of us more than we can give, more than the least of us can give! Long may he live to make the New State safe for mediocrity! (*Facial Justice*, p. 151)

Jael successfully manages to subvert the established order and morality of the state. From Dr. Wainewright, who had once treated the Dictator, she learns that he bears a heart-shaped birthmark just below the heart itself. She, thus, organizes a massive game among the male populace to challenge one another to bare his breast to look for evidence of the telltale heart. Earlier she had inspired members of society to make deliberate mistakes as a sign of humorous, equalizing fallibility, and she recruits teams of people to pull down houses in the name of slum clearance so that everyone can have equal domestic arrangements without envy or strife. In effect, Jael invites chaos so that the Dictator will reveal himself, and then she plans to assassinate him.

The Dictator's epiphany is finally heard over the radio, but the voice of departure and benediction is not really intelligible. Only the Alpha voice of the announcer comes through with the message that everyone had been living in an elaborate play devised by the Dictator until rebellion restored a horrible reality to society's already maimed existence. Admitting that for many years the Dictator has tried to stand between his citizens and their worst desires, attempting to engineer perfectability out of human fallibility, the Dictator abdicates his power and his experiment: "In my play I tried to rob you of your identities: for who is not happier without one? But you wanted them back, you wanted them back, and now you have them." (*Facial Justice*, p. 173)

Conditions worsen in the state. Food is running out, and the only way life can continue at all is through establishment of diplomatic relations with the Underworld. To negotiate with the Underworld, the New State above ground is required to send six hostages, half of them men, half women. The Committee of Public Safety threatens to conscript six, if no volunteers come forward. "Accustomed to being treated, *en bloc*, the idea that half a dozen should be singled out for a special purpose was almost inconceivable to them." (*Facial*

*Justice*, p. 176) The people desperately look for a scapegoat, and naturally they find him in the Dictator.

In the penultimate chapter of *Facial Justice*, Jael finds herself bereft of her brother Joab and her friend Judith, both victims of the anarchy she has unleashed, and waiting for her own imminent death. She is determined to show her power of free choice by volunteering to be a hostage for the Underworld. Although her determination to assert her own individuality is unabated, her view of mankind has become distinctly misanthropic, paralleling the experience of the Dictator as she discovers subsequently. Jael has witnessed too much. The only thing she preserves affection for, since the disappearance of Michael and all those she loved, is the live cineraria which is her only reminder of her relationship with Michael. She wishes she could bequeath the flower to someone after her death who will love it as she has. She elects to leave the cineraria in her house with a message to any future inhabitants to protect the flower. Meanwhile Jael takes the flower outside in the hope the rain will help strengthen it. Jael falls asleep, concluding that "Consciousness wasn't such a blessing after all. Just close her eyes and lose it." (*Facial Justice*, p. 180)

A little old lady comes to Jael's door in the last chapter of *Facial Justice*, the same woman who visited her while she was hospitalized following plastic surgery. Because the woman is soaked, Jael urges her to change clothes, and the old lady curiously requests Permanent Sackcloth for her appropriate raiment. Identifiable by the heart-shaped birthmark, suggesting both love and mortal-weakness, the old woman turns out to be none other than the Darling Dictator. Jael, upon making this discovery, picks up Dr. Wainewright's scalpel, formerly stolen after it had been used to alter her face, to kill the Dictator. But she cannot carry out this cue for passion, which is interrupted by a knock at the door. Michael enters to be reunited with Jael. Her consciousness regained temporarily, the Darling Dictator utters "God bless you all, my children" (*Facial Justice*, p. 186), which was meant to be the final utterance on the earlier radio broadcast, but she had been unable to speak it before the microphone. The people cry for the Dictator outside, but she admits to Jael and Michael that she is dying. Her last wish is for the couple to carry on her role: " 'Say what I tried to say. . . . God bless you both,' she said mechanically." (*Facial Justice*, p. 187) Before she dies, the Dictator explains that Michael had been her Alpha announcer during her reign and enjoins her successors to give

a happy ending to whatever political play or game they devise for
the state. Finally the Darling Dictator begs Jael's forgiveness. Jael,
in turn, asks pardon of the old woman for the offenses she has committed against her. To her question of why Michael had not
appeared until now, he replies that he needed an excuse, adding
pregnantly that we all need an excuse. His particular excuse for
neglecting the facially altered Jael is the perennial Hartleian dilemma: "Mistaking the appearance for the reality." (*Facial Justice*, p.
188)

An apocalyptic fire rages around the lovers. Jael's veil is burned
where it lay on the floor, and the Dictator's anonymity will be
forever preserved, as her remains are consumed by the fire. As
Michael and Jael take their leave, they wisk up the cineraria and
depart the fallen world Jael formerly knew. She experiences new-
found power:

> She was clothed in authority, a ritual began of which she seemed to be
> the center; Michael bent his knee. Wordless they watched her but she
> recognized her mission in their eyes and knew what she must say.
> "Every valley . . . Every valley . . ."
> It was a triple summons.
> "Ladies and Gentlemen," the Voice said, "God bless you all."
> But Jael did not speak with her own voice, she spoke with Michael's.
> (*Facial Justice*, p. 189)

The plot of *Facial Justice*, even in summary, exhibits considerable
imagination, but the point of the fable remains rather obscure.
Hartley himself seems too much Mr. Facing-Both-Ways for his own
good in this most Hawthornian novel. Perhaps a better way of viewing *Facial Justice* is as predictive fabulation, to borrow and modify
the suggestive phrase coined by Robert Scholes, predicting on the
basis of current knowledge in the human sciences the nature of the
future. Hartley has moved with the times, as Scholes describes a
similar process at work in Doris Lessing, "and sees that the future is
the only lever with which we can hope to nudge the present in a
better direction."[4] Hawthorne and more recent science fiction
writers employ similar romance strategies of temporal distancing to
construct either a past or a future according to epistemological
perplexities.

But *Facial Justice* is not, I think, a good novel (romance, allegory,
or dark conceit), although it may be a worthy fictional experiment.
Hartley's originality in dealing with the future is firmly rooted in
his understanding of the past and present. The Dictator in *Facial*

*Justice* bears little resemblance to Orwell's Big Brother. Darling Dictator encourages criticisms of himself and circulates jokes about his faults, reinforcing the *mea culpa* basis of a society composed of patients and delinquents. Yet in spite of this apparent benevolence, the people are domnated as completely as the characters in *1984*, or more completely, because they are unaware of the extent to which the Dictator controls their lives.

The volte-face, so to speak, of Jael in her dealings with the Dictator at the end and in her final apotheosis does not hold out much hope for any significant change in the state under her new leadership unless she and Michael can concoct a new game which will differ from the reinforcement principles and behavior-modifications of the old Darling Dictator. Although the human environment may change radically in future shock, human nature, depressingly, will remain a constant. As the Dictator was, so Jael, erstwhile revolutionary, will be. Hartley persists in taking a narrow view of human possibility. Michael admits he has mistaken the appearance of Jael for her inner reality—presumably underneath she remains absolutely Alpha in spite of her debased Beta face. Likewise, Jael accepts the reality of the Old Woman instead of her imagined "appearance" as the hitherto unseen Dictator. Is *Facial Justice* a latter-day version of Hawthorne's *The Blithedale Romance*, illustrating that philanthropy, where it exhibits a tendency to oversimplify human nature, may be advantageous to the survival of the world, but is dangerous to the health of the individual? Yet Hawthorne has Miles Coverdale dissociate himself from Hollingsworth, whose fate shows the by-way to the pit of hell even at the very gate of heaven, whereas Hartley's Jael becomes herself the Darling Dictator.

Hartley's greatest debt to American literature generally, if not to Hawthorne specifically, in this novel resides in his devotion to a theory of individualism; but his anti-democratic stance (crystallized in the *reductio ad absurdum* device of facial standardization to remove envy) repudiates the religion of personal equality which accompanies American individualism. Hartley, like most American political theorists, cannot establish any clear connection between the individual pursuit of happiness and the common good. Instead he seems to avoid the issue by implying that happiness is not a function of society, but of the individual and his own moral and emotional integrity. As the first revolutionary of the New State Jael 97 thinks she is the revolution; Hartley's reaction to this claim is uncertain and wistful, as if he likes his spirited heroine too much to judge her. *Facial Justice*, then, is an experiment in romance or fable, quite unlike any other Hartley novel, yet dependent on them for theme and tone, and nearest in attitude and values to the essays of *The Novelist's Responsibility*. Jael's future is quite possibly now.

## II   The Love-Adept: *Pastiche and Retrospective*

Hartley's *The Love-Adept: A Variation on a Theme* continues his attempt to deal with a theory of fiction applicable to his own work and to dramatize in novel form some of the epistemological and phenomenological relationships between reader and writer, novelist and critic, which are implicit in *The Novelist's Responsibility*. The protagonist is a novelist (strikingly similar to L. P. Hartley) who, uncertain how to finish his book, also entitled *The Love-Adept*, consults four of his friends. Coincidentally, all the friends are named Elizabeth. Each favors a different ending, which makes closure almost impossible; and when pre-publication copies are ready, James Golightly, the protagonist / novelist, sends copies to his Elizabethan quartet. Each assumes the dedication "To Elizabeth" refers to herself; Hartley's own dedication is "To Elizabeth Bowen with admiration and affection." Through a series of letters between James Golightly and the Elizabeths the influence and effect of life on art and vice versa are presented as counterpoint to the fictional narrative of the internal *Love-Adept* involving Pauline, an actress; Alexy, her wealthy protector; and Jock, her chauffeur. Hartley provides certain key chapters of his protagonist's novel as part of his own *Love-Adept*, frequently with comments and asides in brackets from his Elizabethan readers or in response to them.

As a variation on the theme of truth in life and truth in the novel, as well as a study of an artist protagonist projecting both his skill and ineptitude, *The Love-Adept* invites comparison with André Gide's *The Counterfeiters* or Thomas Mann's *Tonio Kröger*, except that the moral and artistic assumptions and limitations are distinctly Hartleian. His protagonist is quite eager to please his audience, especially the Elizabeths. At the same time, James Golightly (like L. P. Hartley) is reluctant to let his morally fallible characters get off scot-free into a happy ending; but, as he concedes, these characters are not the raw material of tragedy, being deficient in the personal, moral, and emotional stature which might warrant their murdering each other, "though we read in the papers almost daily of lesser people than they who do." (*The Love Adept*, p. 2) Once more Hartley assails the permissive post-war society, and he has his protagonist satirize the claim of diminished responsibility as justification for offenses. Through the epistolary form, as James Golightly corresponds with his four Elizabeths, Hartley's protagonist is compelled to exhibit the judgment and intelligence of the critic with respect to his creation rather than rest content with the more mysterious, subjective intelligence of the artist. It is this expansion of viewpoints which provides the aesthetic and moral center of Hartley's novel about writing a novel.

Much of *The Love-Adept* is a gloss on earlier Hartley novels; and the internal novel within the novel, seen in excerpts, reads like a pastiche of familiar Hartleian scenes. After a most negative assessment of a particular chapter by the third Elizabeth, by profession a book reviewer, Hartley picks up *in medias res* his protagonist's novel. The third Elizabeth is named, with Hawthornian appropriateness, Chillingsworth; and her undermining quibbles are extensively reproduced. Her comments on James Golightly's treatment of the chauffeur's children are not actually tested against the internal *Love-Adept*, but the thrust of her remarks is patently applicable to L. P. Hartley's fiction:

> They [the children] talk like little grown-ups, each aware of the other's identity, and playing up or playing down to it as adults do, not as children would, recognizing their childhood as their own special province, in which grown-ups are seen distantly and dimly as trees walking. (*The Love Adept*, p. 44)

Moreover, rather too coyly perhaps, Elizabeth III recommends that the children, Fergus and Jean, whose mother deserted them and their father Jock for a Jamaican lover, be taken over as waifs by the state, which occasions a comment that clearly harks back to *Facial Justice* in the Hartley canon, extending even to the initials of the children, *F., J.*:

> I can see Fergus being quite happy among the male F's, if the sexes have to be discriminated, which I think would be a pity, and Jean still happier among the J's, since girls can work out their own happiness much better than boys can. Boys are competitive and emulous and brutal, whereas girls *may* be jealous and unkind, but they have a sympathy and solidarity with each other that boys don't have. The State with its aim to make our attitudes and behaviourisms acceptable to each other, would soon cut out these minor differences. (*The Love Adept*, p. 45)

Numerous comments by the third Elizabeth appear to cast light on *Facial Justice*, as Hartley's lone experiment in science fiction wherein he tenaciously held to the human values demonstrated in his other novels. Elizabeth III criticizes Pauline, Alexy, and Jock for being "exceptional," acting against a general background of happiness and reasonableness which she claims is untenable in the present world. Evil, itself, according to her view, is simply the "unpleasantness of what lies ahead for us." (*The Love Adept*, p. 43) For a novelist like L. P. Hartley (or his persona, James Golightly), such an attitude is irresponsible; and neither can accept Elizabeth's proposition which she says is derived from science fiction or recent French novels, "that the future, if there is one, is in the hands of people, not of persons." (*The Love Adept*, p. 43)

Perhaps more significantly, the fourth Elizabeth, toward whom James Golightly feels the greatest affection, raises questions about the ending of the internal *Love-Adept* which seem pertinent to the ending of *Facial Justice:*

> But the actual ending still puzzles me. Of course I know what *happened*, but what exactly do you intend by it? Is it meant to be cynical, as so much of the story is, or just *natural* and inevitable?
>
> At the end you suddenly seem to change your mind about it all. I wonder why? The volte-face has the virtue of surprise, of course, but it didn't make sense to me. (*The Love Adept*, p. 99)

Increasingly, in Hartley's late novels, he appears somewhat uncertain about moral focus and sense of an ending, as he frankly displays in the self-reference and self-distancing of *The Love-Adept*.

Allusions are made throughout *The Love-Adept* to writers who have interested and / or influenced Hartley: namely, Henry James, Jane Austen, D. H. Lawrence, and the Brontës, the latter covertly evoked in the internal novel as Alexy visits "The Brontë Bar" with its reproduction of Branwell's famous portrait of his three sisters. (*The Love Adept*, p. 144) Elizabeth III observes that James Golightly's devotion to parentheses is reminiscent of his namesake, the master, Henry James, but she notes also that the plot situation in the internal novel displays indebtedness to D. H. Lawrence, as indeed Hartley has similarly demonstrated in *The Go-Between* and *The Hireling:*

> I find the central situation dated, banal, and unoriginal to the point of being plagiaristic. The glamorous actress, the faithful swain who dogs her footsteps, and the handsome chauffeur who comes between them—'are not all these written' (as the Bible says) written, *mutatis mutandis*, once and for all in *Lady Chatterley's Lover*, which is not one of my favourite books but which is obviously one of yours, for you used the same situation, I seem to remember, in an earlier novel. This situation seems to haunt your mind, goodness knows why, like a recurring tune. (*The Love Adept*, p. 40)

These allusions and critical comments afford a kind of *roman à clef* to previous Hartley novels, and the pastiche approaches self-parody, sometimes delightfully as in the visit of Pauline and Alexy to Wharfedale Abbey in Yorkshire. The reader anticipates the typical symbolic connection which the nearly obligatory Hartleian cathedral visitations traditionally yield. But beyond Alexy assuring Pauline that she is his central tower—"Every cathedral, every life, for we are all cathedrals of a sort, however puny, and built in different styles, at different dates, needs a central tower, to pull it together. . ." (*The Love Adept*, p. 115)—little more than parody is suggested by Wharfedale Abbey. The Abbey lost its central tower, possibly during the Dissolution of the Monasteries, as Pauline will lose Alexy as a result of his own disillusionment with her at the dénouement of the internal *Love-Adept*. Hartley's stance toward his own world of fiction here is at once proud and self-deprecating, revealing the truth of what Walter Allen wrote of him and some of his contemporaries: "They approach the writing of fiction with a full knowledge of what has been done in the art before." (Allen, *The Modern Novel in Britain and the United States*, p. 257)

For all its playfulness with Hartley's *oeuvre* and some of his favorite crotchets, *The Love-Adept* becomes more than a Chinese box of self-reference. It is a tribute to historical traditions behind the genre of the novel (incidental comments are frequently made about *Don Quixote*, for example, but allusions of a more remote sort extend even to *The Portuguese Letters* and similar early antecedents of modern prose fiction). Moreover, *The Love-Adept* helps to define what might be called the phenomenology of the reading process. Much of the tension in the novel arises from the by-play between Golightly's text and his reader's or critic's response to it, as Hartley struggles to find the appropriate terms for the character and consciousness of both creation and response. Especially provocative is his handling of the area of indeterminacy between what an author thinks he is communicating and how the reader, be she a professional reviewer like Elizabeth III or the common reader, as Virginia Woolf would have it, like the other three Elizabeths, receives the novelist's signals according to her own selection process.

In the epistolary responses of the Elizabeths, for instance, Hartley surveys the degree of identification which a reader may make with a fictional character or the literary fiction itself—from the sympathetic identification of Elizabeth Prescott's, the fourth Elizabeth to whom James Golightly finally proposes marriage, perhaps partly

out of gratitude for her favorable response to his book, to frustrated
lack of identification best illustrated in the negative critique of the
third Elizabeth.[5] L. P. Hartley himself in *The Novelist's Responsibility* expressed concern about the loss of feeling authors experience toward their characters in contemporary fiction, and
Golightly admits that all the characters of the internal *Love-Adept*
are difficult to like in the sense that liking presupposes a certain
amount of moral approval: "I can't claim this for any of my
characters; they are, or are meant to be, unregenerate children of
their age." (*The Love Adept*, p. 166) By introducing this moral
problem here and elsewhere, Hartley suggests a major difficulty in
modern letters, harking back at least as far as *Madame Bovary*
which, despite Flaubert's famous statement of identification with
his heroine, was publicly censured for its lack of a norm-fulfilling
character according to society's standards: how to preserve a moral
center without audience identification, even ironic identification,
with the hero. In a very real sense, Hartley's novels are likewise
without heroes.

At the end of the internal *Love-Adept*, Jock's wife returns to
reclaim him and the children. Violence ensues with the result that
Alexy, Pauline, Jock, and now Gina, Jock's wife, end up in a
magistrate's court. The omniscient author, putatively James
Golightly, describe Alexy's thoughts after the trial:

> For the first time in this quadrilateral relationship, [*pace* this Jamesian
> paradigm observed in *The Novelist's Responsibility*] it was for him to
> decide. He didn't relish it; he didn't like power, except when modified,
> diluted, transformed, or whatever, in terms of love. Naked power, the chief
> agent in the world to-day, had never appealed to him. And decision was
> even more abhorrent to him, but the other three were waiting for him—and
> he had to make up his mind. (*The Love-Adept*, p. 141)

Alexy dispatches the women in three separate cars, while he goes
off, significantly, in the company of the chauffeur, Jock. His fantasy
regarding Pauline, in the absence of any apparent physical consummation, is shattered; "she seemed like any other woman, utterly
outside the place in his imagination that she once held." (*The Love-
Adept*, p. 158) The internal *Love-Adept* dramatizes again the theme
which Hartley had treated earlier in *Poor Clare* (1968), which immediately preceded the present novel, that whoever accepts a gift
pays a forfeit. Alexy had been the great protector / provider for all
the characters; but Pauline, in particular, was unable to fulfill the

sense of emotional obligation that her protector's generosity silently exacted. Pauline, therefore, forfeits both the protection of Alexy and the services of Jock. Golightly writes that Alexy is the luckiest of the quadrilateral group "because besides having money he had the capacity to live, emotionally, in a world of fantasy which kept the real world at bay." (*The Love Adept*, p. 165) L. P. Hartley is not usually so sanguine about his own fantasy-prone protagonists. To Elizabeth Prescott who expressed concern for the future of Jock and his children, James Golightly opts for Alexy's assuming responsibility for them in action subsequent to the completed narrative of the internal *Love-Adept*. But he stops short of a blissfully happy ending, as he explains in his last letter to the fourth Elizabeth:

> To me, a novel, and the characters who compose it, make a synthesis of three points of view. One is what the novelist *wants* to happen; the second is what he or she thinks the reader would *like* to happen; and the third is what might *really* happen, in the light of common day, regarding objectively and without *parti pris*. (*The Love Adept*, p. 165)

In the case of James Golightly, however, Hartley produces for once something like a happy ending, parallel to the internal *Love-Adept* but exceeding its felicity. As is typical of several novels during the last five years of Hartley's life, the author finally permits his characters the capacity for change and flexibility that so many earlier protagonists lacked. In an Epilogue, Hartley shows Golightly in complete social retreat following publication of his novel. He is afraid to encounter singly or in consort the Elizabeths of his dedication and his correspondence. In his letters Golightly had informed the first three Elizabeths that his dedication was not meant for any of them, but now he appears the characteristically fearful self of other Hartley novels, tormented by an over-active conscience and the possibly unfortunate consequences of his choice and action. To fortify himself against the inexorable meeting with the three Elizabeths and with them, as he views it, the strictures of the outside world, Golightly proposes marriage to Elizabeth Prescott who accepts and accompanies him to the party where indeed the fateful meeting occurs. Later, returning from the party in a cab, the couple end L. P. Hartley's novel with a kiss:

> "You said you didn't quite understand the ending of my story," James said.
> "What story?"
> "*My* story."
> "*Your* story—oh, you mean *The Love-Adept*. You mean *that?*"

"Yes," said James, a little abashed, but bearing up. "Well, *this* is how it ends."
He kissed her again. (*The Love Adept*, p. 178)

Reciprocity is attained at the end of *The Love-Adept* with one voice answering another and the culmination in the mutual non-verbal gesture of a kiss. Hartley actively seeks the "reciprocal" (the word is his) for his central characters in these late novels, an ending more often possible in art than in life. Taken together, the dénouement to Golightly's internal *Love-Adept* and Hartley's own ending to his novel with Golightly as protagonist pose questions about alternative fictions. Which is more plausible? Is the finale provided by art an escape from life, a substitute for life, or an enhancement of life? The epigraph from Shelley suggests how fully reveries and desires, not excluding the sexual, can be fulfilled fictively through art and the artist's apprehension of the physical world:

> On a poet's lips I slept
> Dreaming like a love-adept
> In the sound his breathing kept. . . .

While Alexy in Golightly's internal novel hardly seems to be a love-adept, Hartley's James Golightly can be wish-fulfilling and adept. Departure in the company of the chauffeur is doubtless truer to the circumstances of L. P. Hartley's life; marriage with Elizabeth Prescott is truer to the possibilities of art, the elsewhere world of alternatives to the familiar and real.

*The Love-Adept* permits the reader to become acquainted with the author's two selves by seeing through the fiction, participating in it, laughing at it, and finally believing it. Hartley, in a sense, becomes his own critic, as Thomas Mann once recommended every modern writer to be. As *Facial Justice* at the beginning of the sixties explored the imaginative limits of fantasy, *The Love-Adept* at the end of the same decade testifies to Hartley's continuing interest in realistic fiction and what it exacts from both the author and his audience. While marred somewhat by the author's self-consciousness, *The Love-Adept* deliberately stays as small as life, and as cold, as funny, as painful, problematic and inconsequential, but without large gestures and false notes. Human possibility, albeit fictive, and literary form are compatible and mutually fulfilling in this novel, an experiment which vindicates both the genre's and the novelist's responsibility.

## CHAPTER 8

# Emotional Education—Out-of-Class: Simonetta Perkins, The Hireling, *and* The Harness Room

*S imonetta Perkins* (1925), *The Hireling* (1957), and *The Harness Room* (1971)[1] are touchstones in Hartley's canon, embracing respectively his earliest effort in sustained prose fiction, the middle of his artistic journey, and the last years of his creativity. They also share similar thematic premises and represent, with the possible inclusion of *The Go-Between*, the largest Lawrentian admixture to his Jamesian novels, as Hartley undertakes to examine that species which D. H. Lawrence thought to be as rare as a phoenix—a man (or woman) who is emotionally educated. Hartley traces the emergence of emotional awareness and its effects on a formerly disciplined and controlled personality. That the catalyst for this emergence is always a working-class, rather Lawrentian male is of more than passing significance. Throughout his life and art L. P. Hartley, sheltered as he was by the perquisites of money, education, and social class and frightened of the modern world, turned to the working-class servants (usually male) in his bachelor household, as his characters similarly do to their gondoliers, chauffeurs, and service people, for the stimulation and involvement with mainstream reality which imagination and emotion require. With regard to these particular men, Hartley invests them with a component of sexuality which is often missing from other characterization in his fiction. They are, then, among his most appealing creations, if for no other reason than for the obvious fondness Hartley manifests toward them. At the same time, he cannot bring himself to suspend his moral rigor long enough for the potential relationships to be sustained; and, in the instance of each of these novels, Hartley's Lawrentian promise yields to separation and loss. It is as if the moment a relationship becomes even covertly

141

sexual Hartley consciously repudiates the possibilities, as he repeatedly does throughout his novels.

## I   Simonetta Perkins

Although a volume of short stories, *Night Fears*, appeared in 1924, Hartley's first sustained narrative was published the following year as *Simonetta Perkins* in what Henry James called that classical form, the novella. It was, as Hartley recognized, a technically accomplished book, perhaps owing part of its excellence to the restrictive novella form and the rest to Hartley's remarkable identification of himself with his characters. Lavinia Johnstone, the heroine of *Simonetta Perkins*, remains among the best realized women characters in his canon, as if feminine identification were easy for him in the context of this novella.

Set in Venice, the novella recounts what happens when the very wealthy, very proper Miss Lavinia Johnstone, from Boston, becomes deeply infatuated with Emilio, her handsome gondolier. Early in the novella she is described thus: "From her toes to her hair she was an incarnation of denial." (*Simonetta Perkins*, p. 4) Her thoughts while enduring a hair-dressing appointment confirm a consciousness qualified by refreshing irony:

> It was depressing, this recital of her hair's shortcomings; dry, brittle, under-nourished, split at the ends, it seemed only to stay on, as the buildings of Venice were said to stand, out of politeness. Ploughed, harrowed, sown and reaped, Lavinia's scalp felt like a battlefield. A proposal to exacerbate it further she resisted. (*Simonetta Perkins*, p. 27)

Yet, as Hartley suggests, this same talent or attitude, although it may have preserved Lavinia from much, had given her little. She is scornful of Richardson's Clarissa, the first four volumes of whose plight had brought her little but irritation. Lavinia thinks she can state categorically that there will be no Lovelaces for her. In fact, she has been steadily in retreat from a series of suitors, the last of whom she discards in Venice. No place exists in her disciplined will, cultivated by admonishments never to let any situation get the better of her, for the foolish passion which overwhelms poor Clarissa Harlowe.

However, surprised by her infatuation with Emilio, Lavinia takes recourse to the kind of epistolary exposition popularized by Samuel

Richardson. Indeed, she embarks on her own epistolary "novel," as she writes to her worldly friend, Elizabeth Templeman, who is recuperating in Rome from a chill (not fatal like James's Daisy Miller's) contracted by a nighttime visit to the Coliseum. Lavinia pretends she is concerned about her friend, "Simonetta Perkins," who has developed a romantic attachment for a gondolier. Displacement through fictional personae is not uncommon in later Hartley novels nor is projection of fantasy situations which reflect upon the protagonists's condition. Speaking allegedly for Miss Perkins, Lavinia intimates that her "friend" has talked about setting up the gondolier in the United States near her home in some attractive occupation, even possibly as footman, furnaceman, or chauffeur in the Perkins's home. The knowing Elizabeth Templeman's advice to Miss Perkins (whom she perceives immediately to be Lavinia) is to leave Venice at once.

In turn, Lavinia's mother dispatches her daughter to purchase two tickets on the Orient Express. Because she is unable to obtain them for the next day, Lavinia requests them for a week later, affirming thereby her free will over her mother's orders and permitting her to indulge her association with Emilio a bit longer. Hartley's description of the gondolier, as Lavinia views him, contrasts sharply with the way she sees herself:

> At every moment he was accessible to pleasure; at every moment, unconsciously, he could render pleasure back; it lived in his face, his movements, his whole air, where all the charms of childhood, youth and maturity without losing their identity. (*Simonetta Perkins*, p. 24)

Like her ancestors who helped to establish Puritan New England, Lavinia does not take things lightly; nor can she excuse wickedness in high places or, for that matter, in herself. She always makes up her mind against herself, as Elizabeth Templeman acknowledges in epistolary advice to her:

> But whatever you do, Lavinia, don't make your plight fifty times worse by dragging morality into it. I suspect you of examining your conscience, chalking up black marks against yourself, wearing a Scarlet Letter and generally working yourself into a state. . . . If you were anyone else you might have him as a lover. I shouldn't advise it, but with reasonable precautions it could be successfully carried through. But really, Lavinia, for you to have a *cavalier servente* of that kind would be the greatest folly; you would reproach yourself and feel you had done wrong. . . . (*Simonetta Perkins*, p. 49)

As her friend recognizes, Lavinia would place herself in the pillory, notwithstanding a fleeting thought that had Hester Prynne lived in Venice she might have escaped discovery. Nor can Lavinia be like Hester's lost child, Pearl, who became the richest heiress of her day in the New World and was rumored to have found a home abroad. Lavinia's fate is to go back to Boston and the shelter of a moral rigor inherited from ancestors who probably punished Hawthorne's Hester. Jamesian values, then, of renunciation and of passion imagined yet not enacted prevail in *Simonetta Perkins*. Although people like the honeymooning Lord and Lady Henry de Winton see Lavinia as an unlighted candle, Hartley accords his protagonist an inward illumination of conscience and consciousness.

Lavinia carefully works out the Italian grammar necessary for her declaration of love to Emilio, but her *"Ti amo"* is inwardly belied by her feelings of revulsion for the physical consequences her emotions invite. Hartley brilliantly captures her ambivalence in his description of the gondolier's straining to propel the craft—a kind of Freudian sub-text Hartley, of course, steadfastly denied existed in his work:

> She was afraid to look back, but in her mind's eye she could see, repeated again and again, the arrested rocking movement of the gondolier. The alternation of stroke and recovery became dreadful to her, suggesting no more what was useful or romantic but proclaiming a crude physical sufficiency, at once restless and unwilling. It came to her overwhelmingly that physical energy was dangerous and cruel, just in so far as it was free; it flashed across her mind the straining bodies in Tiepolo and Tintoretto, one wielding an axe, another tugging at a rope, a third heaving the Cross aloft, a fourth turning his sword upon the Innocents. And Emilio with his hands clasping the oar was such another; a minister at her martyrdom. (*Simonetta Perkins*, p. 54)

Continuing the narrative with more remarkable psychological intuition, Hartley describes how Lavinia felt, "that she was going down a tunnel that grew smaller and smaller; something was after her. She ran, she crawled; she flung herself on her face, she wiggled. . . ." (*Simonetta Perkins*, p. 55) She orders Emilio to return her to the hotel, *subito*, and with equal immediacy the story advances to the next day and its ending, as Lavinia speeds away on the Orient Express. Happiness in the sense of satisfying her passion for a prepossessing gondolier is not worth the price of moral compromise; nevertheless, contrary to what her friend, Elizabeth

Templeman, supposes, Lavinia will not forget Emilio by the time the train reaches Verona or Brescia.

Elizabeth Templeman has not acted like a non-directive therapist when queried about the course of action "Simonetta Perkins" should follow. Instead she instantly recognizes Miss Perkins's true identity and adapts her advice to Lavinia, whose moral discipline is so perfect as to seem instinctive—indeed more instinctive than either passion or love. Lavinia probably never will forget Emilio; but she must live without him—her identity and security lying in nothing beyond her own self and her relationship with the kind of life she has lived and will live. Yet a modification of consciousness has occurred; and, if nothing else, Lavinia should be able to read Samuel Richardson more sympathetically in the future, because she is no longer ignorant of passion. But this somewhat overly-Jamesian heroine attains her particular moral strength by renunciation. In this regard she differs markedly from another love-struck visitor to Venice, Thomas Mann's Aschenbach; if Lavinia seems to court a destiny similar to Aschenbach's, at the end she accepts a quite different one consistent with what she has always been.

What may seem like a failure in love for Lavinia Johnstone is partly compensated by her increased self-knowledge. As with later Hartley protagonists her feelings become cognitions. She subordinates her passion to an act of ordering which results in her choice of personhood. Such choice of one's destiny imposes limits on the kinds of freedom which subsequent Hartleian characters can choose in the face of their habitual virtue. Hartley usually seems closer to the Aristotelian position, which argues that virtue ought to be a habit, than to the Christian interpretation that virtue consists of a continuous and self-conscious triumph over temptation, although Lavinia's Puritan inheritance perhaps subsumes more of the latter Christian viewpoint than ordinarily appears explicitly in Hartley. *Simonetta Perkins*, like most of Hartley's later works, is further concerned with how the mind works both for and against emotions and the ways in which past and present intertwine in the protagonist's mental life. If Lavinia Johnstone remains rather gray as a character at the end of the novella, she establishes the fundamental detachment from the personal crisis of romantic attachment which often serves as both curse and salvation in Hartley, as the dreamer ordains in reality her own failure of romance.

Lavinia Johnstone appropriates Emilio and the sexual force he embodies into the world of "Simonetta Perkins," an artistic by-product like an epistolary novel whose fictive reality spares her the humiliation of enacting fantasy. In the impetus behind her persona, Lavinia is saved from unconsciousness, and in the anticipated literal distancing of herself from Venice and the figurative detachment of "Simonetta Perkins," she is protected from the anguish of self-consciousness. But her adventure has been limited to consciousness which confers detachment from the situation with Emilio. Her reputation and amour-propre survive unblemished despite her initiation into the alien realm of emotions and romantic love. What is romance but another possibility in one's private store of fictions? The memory of "Simonetta Perkins" and her handsome gondolier contribute to Lavinia Johnstone's emotional inheritance something which transcends the rectitude of her Puritan ancestors. She is at the mercy of the latters' temperamental limitations for her mode of existence, but the "fiction" of herself as Simonetta Perkins survives as an experiment in emotional consciousness which forever modifies what she is and has been.

## II   The Hireling: *Redemptive Fictions and*<br>*Destructive Realities*

Hartley's most unlikely "crypto-novelist," Steven Leadbitter, the car-hire driver of *The Hireling* (1957), fabricates stories of supposed married life to divert his passenger, Lady Franklin. She has suffered a nervous breakdown following the death of her ill and rather aged husband—which had occurred while she was attending a cocktail party. She resumes her activities two years later by hiring a car to drive her to Canterbury Cathedral. The ex-sergeant-major and well-ordered Leadbitter finds himself with a potentially valuable customer who, like the Ancient Mariner, begins to recount her story to the captive driver, presumably on professional advice that she find somebody as unlike herself as possible—a waiter, porter, or hireling—to act as sounding-board. Because Leadbitter tries to accommodate and gratify his customer's wishes, he fulfills her expectations by talking about his family life, inventing a wife and three children for her amusement and "therapy." Not surprisingly, the hireling creates a wife who is strikingly similar to Lady Franklin herself, the source and inspiration of his ruse. The actual women in his life from his selfish mother to the women he has occasionally lived with in the past afford the misogynistic and unmarried Leadbitter no satisfactory models suitable for a lady's ears. Pleased with the generous gratuity Lady Franklin gives him after what she calls "the Canterbury Tale," Leadbitter is disturbed to find that he dreams of being married to a woman not unlike Lady Franklin; and, despite himself, he returns to the pleasure of this memory in waking fantasy during the next day.

The implicit tragedy of *The Hireling* develops almost casually from Lady Franklin's early rhetorical question addressed to Leadbitter: "Is there anything in life that matters—really matters—except that somebody you love should know you love them?" (*The Hireling,* p. 26) Reminiscent of the "curse" of the unloving heart used in *The Go-Between,* Lady Franklin's question reflects the enormous guilt she has experienced, to the point of derangement, for not being with her husband at the time of his death. As she recounts her story to Leadbitter, he obliges with his own "fiction" purporting to be fact. Perhaps it is easier to make the daily life of poor people, even fabricated ones, more real than rich people's neurotic indulgences. Another character in *The Hireling* says of Lady Franklin," she never seemed quite real to me. Rich people never do." (*The Hireling,* p. 78) Leadbitter expands upon his fantasy wife and dream children, as Lady Franklin becomes a kind of paying guest of the family. She supplies Leadbitter with considerable amounts of money, which he acquires under false pretenses but uses, in fact, to pay off his car.

She is very responsive to his masculine competence and strength, although her reaction is not sexual. He, on the other hand, becomes more enamored of her, despite his cynical manipulation of her originally. Midway through the novel an unusual reversal occurs. Leadbitter succeeds in relieving Lady Franklin of her self-absorption through her identification with his illusory world which she thinks to be real; she resumes her social life apart from the hireling's stories at exactly the point where Leadbitter succumbs to his own illusions.

Thinking herself delivered by her chauffeur Perseus, Lady Franklin wishes to visit one last cathedral, Winchester. This time, at her entreaty, Leadbitter accompanies her on the tour of the cathedral itself. Later, when he thinks of her and remembers her, Leadbitter conceives Lady Franklin as a cathedral. It is she who instructs him on the historical cult of the Virgin Mary during their tour of Winchester, as she continues to rely on his strength and company. Acting on the impetus provided by Lady Franklin's words at Winchester about the insignificance of class distinctions,

Leadbitter seizes the moment on their return trip to London to make love to the titled lady.

Prior to his amorous advances he tells her his family does not exist; they are only "ballyhoo." But the "naked, nameless need" (*The Hireling*, p. 107) which shines in Leadbitter's eyes is genuine and honest like the action which follows from it:

> The car slowed down, turned into a side-road and stopped. Leadbitter was no bungler in the arts of love. He tried no cave-man methods, but he well knew how to make a shock delicious, and make deliciousness into a shock. The shock and the delight were there, divinely blended; and Lady Franklin had closed her eyes in rapture before she opened them in outrage. (*The Hireling*, pp. 107 - 108).

Whether or not she reciprocates—as it happens she obviously does not—Leadbitter's tragedy is that he loves Lady Franklin and must reveal the strength of his feeling—in answer through deed, if not word, to her question about what matters in life. His action is inexorable, different in degree and kind from Lavinia Johnstone's passion in *Simonetta Perkins:* at issue is not a mere misunderstanding of signals between himself and Lady Franklin. Although it may not be heroism to do what one is naturally inclined to do, Leadbitter's action betrays his own best financial interest and goes against his own instinct for resourceful and reserved self-preservation. It is to participate in the old fairy-tale theme of the peasant-and-princess sexual relationship which ordinarily would seem much too romantic for the realistic Leadbitter, and consequently he casts himself in an heroic role contrary to his entire past.

Rebuffed in and by reality, Leadbitter's honesty is less appealing to Lady Franklin than his former dishonesty was. But he is transfigured:

> The times when he was a single man, the most single of single men, absorbed in making money for himself, grew fewer; more and more frequent the times when he was breadwinner to a wife and family whose lives enriched his own, and whose personalities were as clear to him as if he had known them in the flesh. (*The Hireling*, p. 128)

The difference in class origins between Lady Franklin and Leadbitter has no relevance in his fantasy; yet it is of immense significance as he attempts to enact the dream. Lady Franklin rejects the hireling's expression of love for the self-serving illusion of love offered by the painter, Hughie Cantrip. The latter uses her and her money to maintain a continuing relationship with Constance, his mistress, even as he prepares to marry Lady Franklin.

By chance, Leadbitter becomes the driver for Hughie and Constance, who in the back of his car discuss a woman named Ernestine. Only slowly does the hireling make the connection between this name and Lady Franklin. When he comprehends the scheme which the couple plot against Lady Franklin, Leadbitter posts, in violation of his former moral code, an anonymous letter to her explaining Hughie's deception. Of course, the painter's financial motive is not so far removed from Leadbitter's own initial behavior, as the hireling more or less acknowledges subsequently:

'Corrupting,' the girl-friend [Constance] had called her, which at the time had made him laugh. Lady Franklin corrupting! Ernestine corrupting! Yet dimly he now saw what they meant; the pattern of his experience with her confirmed it. She was an indulgence, an obsession, a walking daydream, who offered for reality a fairy-tale version of life. Her gold was not fairy gold, [*pace* Hawthorne] far from it, but it didn't come through the usual channels, it had to be angled for, not worked for, with many applications of the soft flannel and a lot of blarney on both sides. (*The Hireling*, p. 184)

Leadbitter's bank account has risen with real pounds, not fairy gold, as a result of Lady Franklin's benevolence toward him and his supposed family. On impulse, the hireling takes all his capital to purchase a new limousine in order to drive Lady Franklin to her wedding. By this time he has resigned himself to Hughie's possession of her on the assumption that she will automatically disregard his anonymous warning.

Hughie Cantrip schedules the hireling for an evening drive on the Thursday before the anticipated Saturday wedding; Leadbitter supposes he will be driving the engaged couple to dinner. He decides to present the car, so to speak, to Lady Franklin in advance of the wedding day. Instead, to his dismay, he discovers Hughie is once more accompanying Constance to dinner in Richmond. She expects her lover to make his last farewells to her as a bachelor before they resume their liaison after his marriage. In fact, Hughie tells her the wedding will not take place, because Ernestine has broken their engagement after receiving the incriminating, if anonymous, letter. Furthermore, he accuses Constance of being the sender. The ensuing argument is settled only by Leadbitter's admission of responsibility for the letter.

One feature of his new limousine which Leadbitter particularly liked was the glass partition whereby he could exclude himself from overhearing his customers' conversations, but with Hughie and Constance he cannot remain aloof and impersonal. They insist they have told no one:

'You told *me*,' shouted Leadbitter. 'Do you think I'm deaf? What do you think I am? Do you think I'm just a bit of the car, or one of those bloody automatons? Do you think I can sit here without hearing all the poppycock you talk?' (*The Hireling*, p. 223)

Once more Leadbitter asserts his reality through action as well as words, notwithstanding Hughie's incredulity that it could not matter in the least what Lady Franklin thought of a hireling or vice versa:

'Oh, so I'm only a hireling, am I?' answered Leadbitter. 'Well, I shan't be much longer.' A wave of revulsion for everything his life had meant to him swept over him irresistibly. He pressed his foot on the accelerator. The car sprang forward. The street was dark; towering buildings on the right shut out what light there was. The darkness was in Leadbitter's mind too; he couldn't see to think, and when a tree suddenly loomed up half-way across the road, with a warning white blaze on it, he was never to know whether he drove into it on purpose or not. But when he saw the crash coming he turned round and shouted, 'Tell Lady Franklin that I—' (*The Hireling*, p. 228)

As the sole survivor of the crash, Constance assumes the role of go-between by carrying Leadbitter's final truncated message to Lady Franklin, while she resolves to protect herself and Hughie from the infamy of discovery. Constance admits that the "accident" had been a face-saving business for everyone; nevertheless, she feels a kind of obligation to the widow of South Halkin Street, for only she knows that the event constitutes a double tragedy for Lady Franklin. Ernestine Franklin's retreat into mourning seems irreversible this time:

What is there for me in life, but to flounder for ever in these cruel uncertainties, [e.g., by breaking off her engagement to Hughie she thinks she may have indirectly caused his death], not even knowing what I want to believe? Far better not to think and not to feel but to pass the time in a kind of drowse, as I do now, making amends to Philip [her late husband] for my neglect, for not being there when he died, and wishing I had told him that I loved him. If that be madness, well, I welcome it! At any rate the past can't change or spring surprises on me. (*The Hireling*, p. 243)

Constance, of course, tells Lady Franklin something about the past which can bring about changes. She completes Leadbitter's fragmented message as a statement of love, which it was, although Constance can only surmise and improvise the specific contents. Inadvertently Constance also reveals enough about herself and Hughie to permit Lady Franklin to infer the culpability of her late fiancé. No longer in doubt about either man, Lady Franklin dismisses Constance with gratitude. Turning to the hitherto unopened wedding presents, she picks up the smallest parcel and discovers therein a St. Christopher medal—Leadbitter's wedding gift to her, offered, at the expense of his own safety, in the hope it may bring her luck. She reads the French inscription around the margin of the medallion—"Regarde Saint Christopher et va't'en rassuré." Hartley continues:

Tears filled her eyes again and dimmed the stalwart, naked figure of the giant. One hand grasped his staff, the other, too strong for its purpose, held the child, who smiled down from his shoulder. Onward he strode into the flood. She couldn't help identifying him with the giver, who had escorted her through waters deep as these and who had parted with his luck to make hers. "Behold St. Christopher, and fearless go thy way." She felt the reassurance of his presence, a promise like the dawning of another day; he had awakened her once, though into other arms than his, and had he not awakened her again? (*The Hireling*, p. 248)

Ernestine Franklin, at last, knows the hireling for what he was, not for what he pretended to be. He had been a man who loved and died for her. Having in death no claims upon him from widow or descendants, Leadbitter bequeathes to Lady Franklin the readiness to translate his message of love for her back into life. He has implemented the lesson she gave him during their first conversation: he has loved and told his beloved so in a declaration of love which reaches beyond the grave.

An acclaimed British film of *The Hireling*, like *The Go-Between* before it the Grand Prize winner at the Cannes Film Festival, was released in 1973 with Sarah Miles as Lady Franklin and Robert Shaw as Leadbitter. Wolf Mankowitz's screenplay places the story in the years following the First World War rather than the Second, as Hartley did; this alteration of time setting makes the social conditions which underlie this small historical tragedy somewhat more plausible for being set in the past of privileged, class-conscious England. Under the taut direction of Alan Bridges, which always serves Mankowitz's compact script, *The Hireling*, on film, probes human need and fulfillment, suggesting the chaos of emotions beneath the genteel surface of inter-class relationships. Hartley's self-sacrificial ending has been eliminated. The drunken hireling bursts into Lady Franklin's home to confront her and her fiancé about Hughie's affair with Constance. When he realizes that this exposure of truth will not have the effect he desires, Robert Shaw's hireling drives drunkenly to the courtyard of his garage and proceeds to smash his newly-purchased Rolls-Royce into the parked cars, thus committing a form of suicide as the picture ends. Bridge's and Mankowitz's rather free translation of Hartley's literary mode results in a cinematically valid adaptation but with obvious, and often regrettable, loss of fidelity to the Hartley source.

In summary, *The Hireling*, as novel and film, may sound unconvincing and exquisitely boring, productive of little more than reader impatience with both Lady Franklin and Leadbitter. The effect of the actual novel, however, is quite the contrary, owing to Hartley's mastery of mood and situation. Like *The Go-Between* before it, *The Hireling* implicitly questions the cruelty of the British social structure and the insensitivity of the upper classes—paradoxically in the act of seeming to vindicate them. Hartley continues his examination of the universal truths about the way people use and abuse each other, often unwittingly but no less devastatingly. What should be the experience of love becomes instead the experience of loss: Hartley's usual approach to the portrayal of sexual tension and forbidden love.

Certainly, the self-sacrificial and melodramatic ending of Hartley's *The Hireling* has not been universally admired. But given the altered character of Leadbitter as the novel progresses and the fact of his developing resentment against the consideration of himself as an extension of his car in his role as hireling, the fatal crash seems inevitable. Leadbitter has treated his body as if it were a machine, as Hartley emphasizes in frequent observations of the hireling's denial of sleep and other basic physical and human needs. With the purchase of the new limousine Leadbitter appears to bring together his myth-making and the automobile, the very means of his identity as hireling. The limousine, in the special context of Lady Franklin's wedding, is Leadbitter's mechanical bride, but he destroys this steel surrogate of Lady Franklin and, most particularly, himself as tool of the machine or symbolically its driving consort. Through his mortality Leadbitter affirms his humanity, the end toward which he has been "accelerating" throughout the novel Like Hippolytus Leadbitter becomes the victim of his situation and his fatal chariot which ineluctably destroys him. After all, the hireling has transferred his emblem of safety, the St. Christopher medal, to Lady Franklin, leaving him with nothing but the impotence of his situation, his class, and his suppressed generative force. Hartley's ending for Steve Leadbitter puts *The Hireling* in a world of essence rather than of accident. His legacy to Lady Franklin is therefore spiritual, unlike the financial legacy of her late husband. He died that she might live.

In *The Hireling* Hartley has created his most fully realized male character outside his own class. Leadbitter is perhaps covertly an affectionate tribute to Hartley's beloved man-servant and chauffeur, Charles, whose death preceded completion of the novel. Without succumbing to Freudian suppositions, it may be tenable to suggest that Hartley found an outlet for his grief at the death of Charles in a securely disguised form of identification with Lady Franklin. More than most of his novels, *The Hireling* shows how Hartley's writing grows out of ways he feels about himself and his relations with the world. Loss, perhaps even more than love, is the great equalizer, as Hartley has demonstrated before but never more forcefully than in *The Hireling*.

One unusual feature of Hartley's portrayal of Leadbitter is his imputation of a developed sense of irony to this man who seems so very mindful of his place in society where he gives and exacts respect only as a hireling should:

> But his conversation was decorative, if not always decorous; it was a game, an exercise in irony. . . . Everything must be handled with a light touch. He seldom meant what he said, though he sometimes meant the opposite of what he said. In business talks he listened not so much to the words, which were often misleading, as to the sense behind them, which was usually more apparent in what was not said than in what was said—he listened to hear if the deal was going his way, and his replies were framed accordingly. He seldom spoke his thoughts and still more rarely, and then only in anger, did he speak his feelings, because to expose them made him feel naked and worse than naked—flayed. (*The Hireling*, p. 154)

If, like Albert Camus, Leadbitter maintained that virility is a matter of what a man does not say, his detachment has been achieved through a devaluation of human possibilities and the use of irony for defense. Implicit in his irony, however, is the imagination which leads him to a more abundant identity.

As noted earlier, the hireling is surely Hartley's most unlikely artistic character; but, perhaps more credibly than any other artist in Hartley's canon, Leadbitter as an artificer of fiction shows how the "novelist" can both confess and conceal while he also demonstrates the perils attendant upon such action. Leadbitter finds himself caught between his being-for-itself, his old persona as hireling, and being-for-others, the fictive husband and father (and therapist for Lady Franklin). With no way to resolve this division Hartley once more turns to apotheosis, and the hireling emerges not as Steven Leadbitter but as Saint Christopher at the novel's end. While this ending seems intuitively right, it is not without Hartley's customary irony, which somewhat modifies the claim of salvation. Love mingles again with death, and the "saint" triumphs only because the man is first rebuffed and then killed. Still, Leadbitter's salvation resides in Lady Franklin's belated discovery of the hireling's genuine love for her together with its promise of her restoration to life.

### III   The Harness Room: *Hartleian Dislocations Eroticized*

*The Harness Room* (1971) continues Hartley's exploration of family relationships together with deeper, though still rather tentative, examination of homosexuality as a complement, if not a superior alternative, to love between the sexes (a theme begun obliquely in *My Fellow Devils,* hinted at peripherally in *The Brickfield / The Betrayal,* and surfacing in *My Sisters' Keeper*). Although Hartley was apparently concerned that some of his friends, especially his women friends, would think he was too frank in *The Harness Room,* the excerpts from the novel quoted here illustrate that the author's treatment is a model of tact and sensibility. The novel is a brave addition to the Hartley canon because of its inclusion of an explicit sexual component in his common theme and variation of servants and masters.

As in other Hartley novels, undercurrents of deep and suppressed feeling stir beneath the seemingly placid surface of English country life where another quartet of characters plays out its ambivalences to an affecting and unexpected conclusion. The chief inhabitants of this rural retreat from a London pied-à-terre are Colonel Macready, a hot-tempered, fiery-looking little man who has been a widower for twelve years, and his sensitive and quite passive son of seventeen, Fergus. Because father and son are opposites in temperament and constitution, Colonel Macready, despite all evidence to the impossibility of a successful transformation, hopes to toughen his son sufficiently for him to enter the Royal Military College at Sandhurst and follow the family tradition of being a good soldier. Incidentally, the contrast between father and son is more than moderately reminiscent of Ford Madox Ford's depiction of passive heroes and contrasting father-figures who either deliberately or inadvertently oppress or at least oppose their passive and hypersensitive sons. Colonel Macready sees in his son the reflection of his late beloved wife:

> But now her image was receding from his mind, and the image of Fergus, as a replacement of her, was growing dim too. He realized that the feminine qualities, which he so loved in her wouldn't be suitable in a son he wanted to ride and hunt and shoot. The likeness, the physical appearance, were still there, but he wasn't being unfair to Fergus when he thought they didn't become a boy on the verge of manhood. (*The Harness Room*, p. 3)

Colonel Macready marries again. His new bride, Sonia Verriden, lived with her mother "who not only remembered better days, but was always referring to them in private and in public; her reminiscences of her visits to Lord this and Lady that, caused her daughter much embarrassment." (*The Harness Room*, p. 11) Nonetheless, Sonia is accustomed to a milieu different in kind from the Colonel's. When the Colonel and his wife leave for an extended honeymoon on the Continent, he instructs Carrington, his chauffeur and ex-guardsman, to see that Fergus is toughened up and brought up to the military mark with physical training and boxing. This training was to be conducted in the estate's former harness room, now converted to a quasi-gymnasium, just outside the chauffeur's bedroom.

As Hartley emphasizes Fergus's feminine qualities, his description of Carrington is in terms of the super-male:

> He was the embodiment of the tough guy, the cinema hero (or villain) with a mustache exactly right for the position it occupied under his straight nose, his brown eyes, his dark hair, and the splendid physique, some of which could be inferred, as being in keeping with his naked muscular forearms, burnt a deep-red-brown by the sun. (*The Harness Room*, p. 26)

Even earlier in the novel Hartley presents the homosexual content of Carrington's cult of manliness with surprising candor:

He had, as he said, been in the Guards, he had boxed for them and played rugger; he was a born athlete. He had drifted from job to job, as commissionaire, security man, and other occupations. He had been married, but that was in another country and besides the wench was dead, dead to him, at any rate. He sometimes said he was, and had come to regard himself as, a single man. What would happen to him in the end he didn't know and didn't much care. He was bisexual, as he was quite ready to admit; he had had affairs with men and women, boys and girls; he preferred his own sex in these relationships, because it led to less trouble. (*The Harness Room*, p. 5)

It is to the twenty-eight year old Carrington, the *genius loci* of the harness room that the lonely Fergus goes for physical instruction and satisfaction of his need to identify with another man, what D. H. Lawrence considered an essential relationship in any man's life. In their boxing, Fergus exchanges "the dead letter of history for the living contact with another human being." (*The Harness Room*, p. 43) Like Basil Hancock in *My Sisters' Keeper*, Fergus is reading history in the hope of going to Oxford; he finds himself torn between these "idylls" in the harness room and his absorption in history.

As their physical intimacy increases, Carrington one day shows Fergus a photograph of a painting representing a nude male in a pose suggestive of Samson:

[Fergus] had never seen the original or even the picture of a man where the emphasis was laid on his nakedness, where the lights and darks, the cavities and hillocks, bone-wise or muscle-wise, in the physical structure, got their pictorial effect from contrasting and contending [with] each other, as a hill contrasts with a valley. Especially as they did here, where the triangle of the body, reaching down to its narrow inverted climax, where the darkness of the loins took possession of it, seemed a strange miracle of the skeleton enclothed in flesh—the architectonic breadth of the shoulders, for which scapular and deltoid seemed inadequate words, the ribs expanding and clutching each other, and below them what? The dark hidden secrets which the painter, for whatever reason, had concealed under a casual but ample swathe of material, colourless in the photograph. (*The Harness Room*, p. 71)

The model, of course, is Carrington with his wife, "a right bitch," as the chauffeur calls her, looking on as Delilah. Carrington divests himself of clothes in order to prove to Fergus that he was, indeed, the subject of the canvas; and he invites the boy into his bedroom for "the whole bag of tricks," without, as Carrington says, any extra charge.

At this point in *The Harness Room*, Hartley seems on the brink of developing a *Turn of the Screw* plot with the theme of servants corrupting the morals of masters through incipient homosexual dominance. Carrington conveys an aura of decadence mixed with seductive, earthy warmth, as if he were out to seduce the world and could if he tried. At the same time, Carrington as Samson engaged in a class war against his employer is partly suggested by the photograph. Does the chauffeur regard his rich masters as Philistines whose temple of morality it is his duty to destroy? The photograph might be working symbolically—after all, Matthew Arnold did identify the English country type with the Philistines. Will some *charge* be forthcoming? Such resonances for the link between sex and money Hartley does not pursue in considering the chauffeur's motives for his involvement with Fergus. Later, when Fergus reflects with Hartleian class consciousness on the implications of Carrington's phrase—"there's no extra charge" (*The Harness Room*, p. 74)—he concludes that the chauffeur's motives are entirely motives of love, the bonus of his body as a gift outright. The potentially ominous power of the relationship between Fergus and Carrington is abandoned in favor of a little sentimental romance with accompanying loss of credibility; the motivation on both sides of the Fergus-Carrington relationship is foggy and unsatisfying.

Having charged his narrative with emotional potential, Hartley decorously (or D. H. Lawrence might say obscenely) leads the two men to an asterisk near the bottom of the page. Later, Hartley describes Fergus's feeling about his encounter in the harness room and bedroom:

> He felt proud and triumphant, he did not feel guilty, but guilt was round the corner, waiting for him in the darkness behind the side-door, cutting him off from the charmed atmosphere of the harness-room, in which he was such a different person from the sex-satisfied, whisky-satisfied, poltroon whose flagging footsteps were taking him home. (*The Harness Room*, p. 75)

Throughout his fiction Hartley never described the sexual act explicitly to supply emotion for his narrative or to evoke the pleasure of the flesh and its consciousness. In this regard he remains closer to Henry James than to Lawrence. Fergus's chief perception of Fred

Carrington's sensuality until the revelation in the bedroom comes from seeing the bare-chested chauffeur "seize the Bentley in a vulnerable spot, and give it an upward heave, as if to say, 'I'll show you who is master.' " (*The Harness Room*, p. 75) Hartley seems to have constructed a romantic mystique about the way working-class men master and control vehicles of transportation—from gondolas to Bentleys:

> Fergus could not tell what secrets Fred had stored away, secrets of sex, secrets of passion, that were commonplaces to him, such as lurked under the bonnet of the car, but to Fergus were tense with mystery. He only knew that the experience, [in Carrington's bedroom adjacent to the harness room] whatever it was, had increased his capacity for loving. (*The Harness Room*, p. 78)

Hartley's customary reticence and notable understatement yield to some sentimental overwriting or at the very least a leaden prose style to suggest the newly-released feelings of both Fergus and Fred Carrington. Before long, though, Hartley produces the threat to this idyllic masculine world with the reappearance of Colonel and Sonia Macready. While Fergus had not experienced much guilt over his physical initiation into love with Fred, he feels very uneasy about his new step-mother's attention to him. Upon the return of the newlyweds, Foxton Farm assumes more of a feminine character. Sonia quickly alters the formerly all-male environment through extensive redecoration, savory continental cuisine, and the smell of bath-salts in the air. The only place exempt from her influence and the accompanying fragrance of her femininity is the harness room. Sonia responds appreciatively to the feminine component in her step-son's masculinity; for her, unlike Colonel Macready, masculinity need not always be equated with dominance, strength, and physical superiority.

The servants gossip about Sonia's supposed, and misunderstood, attraction to Fergus, and the chauffeur acts increasingly as if he were jealous of the relationship between the woman and her step-son. Surprised by his own responsiveness to this previously unknown femininity of Sonia, Fergus asks Carrington whether he thinks Sonia might be "sweet on me." (*The Harness Room*, p. 95) The chauffeur rather maliciously warns Fergus about the possibility of Sonia's seducing him, and as the boy returns to the house after a bit of sparring with Carrington, he reflects:

". . . . Is it possible," he asked himself for the hundredth time, "that she can be in love with me?" But besides the servants' tittle-tattle, which Fred, for reasons of his own, reported, and perhaps exaggerated, there were unmistakable signs of Sonia's favour, which he couldn't disregard. Welcoming she was to everyone; kind she was to everyone, including his father; but Fergus, who had grown up emotionally during the weeks of their honeymoon, knew that as far as it concerned him, her attitude was not one of general indiscriminate affability. (*The Harness Room*, p. 100)

Hartley evokes the specter of Euripides's *Hippolytus* inasmuch as Fergus becomes terrified at the prospect of breaking up his father's marriage. He resolves to leave Foxton Farm in order to avert what he fears might become a domestic tragedy.

Meanwhile, to satisfy the Colonel's curiosity about his son's progress in physical training, Carrington arranges an exhibition boxing-match between himself and Fergus in a make-shift ring set up in the harness room. Although temperamentally opposed to scenes of organized male violence and contact sports, Sonia still submits to her husband's wishes and reluctantly accompanies him to observe Fergus's demonstration of physical prowess:

And so the bout went on, and an experienced referee would have judged that Fergus was leading on points, and not only because he was consistently the aggressor, when the unexpected happened. Fred caught his toe in the tear in the carpet, stumbled forwards, and the blow that was meant to be a mere rib-tickler, caught Fergus on the point of the jaw, a blow that, in proverbial parlance, might have felled an ox. (*The Harness Room*, p. 115)

To be sure, Fergus is gratuitously killed as a result of capricious fate. The three adults who loved him in their respective ways make their separate peace with the appalling event:

They were all, more or less, in tears, beside themselves with grief, but Fred, with manslaughter in and on his mind, manslaughter of perhaps the only human being he had ever really loved, suffered more than they did. They each had each other; he had no one, except the dead boy behind him, at which he dared not look. As a soldier he had seen many dead bodies in his time, but this time was different; and under an uncontrollable impulse, he asked almost rudely:
"Can I spend the night in the house, your house? I don't much fancy spending it here."
Colonel Macready glanced at his wife.
"Of course," she said, "I'll have a bed made up for you."

And so it happened that Fergus spent what was left to spend, the night alone in the harness room. (*The Harness Room*, p. 117)

To her husband's accusations of her incestuous interests in Fergus, Sonia retorts that members of her class would not understand the Colonel's middle-class credence in the gossip of servants. But his death Fergus destroys the marriage which, alive, despite his fears to the contrary, he might have preserved. At the end of the novel, the chauffeur assures the Colonel that his late son had "pluck" (but assuredly little luck), and Macready is momentarily cheered by this unsolicited assessment of the boy, even as he sustains loss of his wife, son, and chauffeur. On the day of the inquest the Colonel re-employs his former chauffeur. Carrington does, however, request billeting somewhere other than next to the harness room. Sonia writes to her estranged husband, suggesting possible means of reconciliation; but, as Hartley notes, Colonel Macready does not follow up on them. Phaedra-like, Sonia can merely vouchsafe that no one is master of his fate. At the end of the novel, the only relationship left intact is the asexual one between the Colonel and Carrington—the usual Hartleian master-servant tie endures beyond loss of wife and son.

Although Hartley punishes Fergus, as he does most of his other protagonists, for his desires and impulses, this boy seems to have a larger measure of self-worth than is customary in the novels—"I am myself," Fergus can say with conviction early in the novel (p. 7). Hartley establishes a significant contrast between Fergus and Fred Carrington according to their respective "assets":

Fergus might have money (as Fred perhaps thought he had) but he could not show it when he took his clothes off, as Fred could and had shown his thews and sinews. Fergus's attributes, such as they were, came from money and the prestige that money brings; true, he had added to them by working hard. Fred had added to his, but they were inherent. (*The Harness Room*, p. 76)

The foregoing summarizes the high value writers of Hartley's class frequently manifest in England toward the physical virility and aggressiveness of working-class men. What is most disturbing to Fergus Macready is the inherent danger present within his own family when he directs his emotional stirrings, formerly response to the homosexually desirable male-image, Fred, toward his stepmother; and she, he imagines, channels her feelings from his father to himself. Such incestuous heterosexuality within the family generates far more anxiety and guilt than homosexuality outside it.

Whatever Hartley's intention in moving from comfortable homosexuality to taboo heterosexuality might be, the effect is audacious in its irony. In *The Harness Room* the familiar Hartleian situation of personal and familial dislocation coupled with the protagonist's need for flexibility of temperament have never before been so much eroticized. Moreover, in this novel and most of his other later novels, Hartley eschews the kind of symbolic and psychological artifice that in the past sometimes substituted rhetoric for the blows of existence. Fergus truly takes the hammerblow on the chin, with no figurative extension; but his earlier fear of female sexual power and persuasion, as embodied in the beguiling Sonia, does hold its contextually mysterious content.

In light of the author's advanced age at the time of writing it, *The Harness Room* reads remarkably like a young man's book with Fergus's affective and emotional life narrated with feeling and—for Hartley—unusually little guilt. The power of the novel, therefore, derives in the Jamesian sense from the quality and intensity of the felt life contained within it—the precise terms of which Hartley was probably unprepared to write until the decade of the seventies. Perhaps the news of E. M. Forster's *Maurice,* a novel much discussed in British literary circles in the late nineteen-sixties before its eventual posthumous publication in the same year as *The Harness Room* (1971), gave Hartley courage to embark on this novel as neither a cautionary tale nor an exercise in special pleading but with more moral authority than he could have mustered earlier in his career.

While Fergus Macready cannot live with Carrington as Forster's Maurice can with Scudder, Hartley's young gentleman does experience, before his death, the inseparability of humanity and sexuality, as few Hartley protagonists have so comprehended it. Nature does seem less nasty in *The Harness Room* than elsewhere in Hartley, despite the fate of Fergus. Politically, too, the novel hints at a new departure for Hartley as the old power structures, especially the male chauvinist and capitalist power represented by Colonel Macready, are threatened by the covert emergence of women's sexuality in the character of Sonia, children's sexuality in Fergus's loss of virginity, and finally homosexuality in the democratic relationship of Fergus and Carrington. The promise of change is greater than the realization of it in *The Harness Room,* but the

162                                    L. P. HARTLEY

stratagems which suggest repression or sublimation are less apparent in this novel than in earlier ones. Though few of Hartley's novels are explicitly about sex, an orientation gradually reveals itself from the earliest novels to the last ones which is consistent and productive, reflecting, among other things, the changing cultural conditions of the times. In Hartley's joyous portrayal of physical and emotional bonding between men, he achieves a celebration of natural and spontaneous liberation which surpasses even the "happy" endings of books like *Facial Justice*.

## CHAPTER 9

# Victors, Victims, and Spoils: Poor Clare, My Sisters' Keeper, The Collections, *and* The Will and the Way

L P. HARTLEY'S prolific final creative period, which extended until his death in December 1972, produced novels of a somewhat lighter tone and less symbolic structure, reflective of the whole shift in manners, attitudes, and life-styles that marked the end of the sixties. Although Hartley demonstrates increasing difficulty in deciding the precise theme for some of these novels, his chief interest in most of those under consideration in this chapter seems to be the various forms of human appropriation—how and why people take (or relinquish) possession of objects, money, other people, and themselves. Failing in health, the aged Hartley still had the capital of his art and imagination which he never used up, and he continued to examine the rate of exchange between material and moral values.

## I Poor Clare: *The Perils of Looking at a Gift-Horse*

*Poor Clare* (1968) [1] represents an unusual collaboration between L. P. Hartley and his friend, novelist Francis King, whose invaluable help Hartley acknowledges in his dedication, in development of the theme that gifts tend to separate friends more than bind people together. The novel is told by a narrator (not a common point of view in Hartley), the middle-aged painter, Edward, about his friend and rival in romance, Gilbert Finstock, a passionate and tortured composer. Both men must be taken together as divided protagonists, suggesting the divided self in its struggle to reconcile art and life, being and having. If the effect is not an altogether seamless web, it is perhaps a corollary of the shared dialogue and enterprise between Mr. King and L. P. Hartley with respect to this novel of remarkable mingling—realism and romance, good and ill, England and Italy.

While *Poor Clare*, like the subsequent novels, presents a recognizable and realistic social milieu of privileged English people, Hartley indulges himself here and elsewhere in suggestive names for his characters, a trait which approaches the condition of allegory, even though the tone of the novels usually sustains the relationship of character to name in a Jamesian rather than Trollopian way. Gilbert Finstock, for example, suggests the end of the line and possibly even a dying England; he is the beneficiary of his late aunt's generosity (she is named appropriately Clare Ditchworth). In her last decade of life she gave everything away in the spirit of her moral doppelgänger, Saint Clare, the founder of the order of nuns called Poor Clares which Hartley first alluded to in *My Fellow Devils*.

The influence of Aunt Clare appears to be working through Gilbert as the novel opens. He writes in a letter to Edward that he wants "to devote the rest of my few and evil days to giving." (*Poor Clare*, p. 10) To bequeath himself to his friends is Gilbert's desire, but his "heirs" characteristically misunderstand his motive, partly because of his strange behavior regarding the gifts, mainly paintings and other objets d'art, which he distributes as if he is settling accounts with friends he wishes to abandon. The response of his friends then ranges from gratitude to dread as they learn to be wary of Greeks (and Gilbert) bearing gifts. The narrator himself is a recipient of Gilbert's curiously twisted generosity. Edward, a mediocre painter, receives a small Girtin landscape from his friend. With that benison Edward expands both his life and his art to the point of taking Myra, Gilbert's inspiration, away from him. Other friends, including Edward, are disturbed that the monetary value of Gilbert's gifts seems to be in inverse proportion to his love for the recipient. To Myra, who has received nothing by way of legacy, Gilbert had covertly sought to give not merely a material gift but his love and himself.

From whatever motive, Gilbert gives until it hurts, and he loses both his art and his life in the process. He senses that relationships are often undermined and contaminated by gifts. Like other Hartley inheritors, Gilbert discovers that having something often impedes being somone, and he cites the example of Saint Clare:

"To do people good, you must exact the utmost sacrifices from them, [cf. *The Betrayal*] not try to propitiate them with pictures and chocolates, and so on." (*Poor Clare*, p. 36) In Gilbert's mind, his Aunt Clare was endeavoring to save people's bank-balances (and perhaps her own) rather than their souls, as the Poor Clares would have it.

In a secular age the artist is more likely to be acquainted with the dark night of the soul than other practitioners including priests. Gilbert seemed to be so acquainted, relying for his art on what he confesses to be his victimization. Thus, his aunt's legacy, however well-intentioned, is meant to turn him into a victor which is contrary to the source of his art. The condition of plenty proves aesthetically destructive for his particular species of modern music. Antonia, one of Gilbert's friends, advances a theory to explain his behavior in bestowing his treasures on others:

> She believed he was in flight from himself, and that was why he wanted to dispose of his aunt's possessions, if they were his to dispose of. She thought of him as desiring a state of utter spiritual nudity, like that of a Buddhist, in order that he might be more free to pursue his art. But I [the narrator Edward] was sure she was wrong; it was *us* he wanted to dispose of, not because we were an obstacle to his horrible music, but because without *us*, and his obligation to us, he wouldn't suffer from the irritation that his muse, and his music, needed. (*Poor Clare*, p. 49).

Of particular interest and intensity is the relationship between art and life as perceived and experienced in a quite opposite manner by Edward and Gilbert. As a composer Gilbert seeks unavailingly for what he calls "reciprocity" (a recurring word and idea in Hartley's last novels) in his music, and, by extension in the disclosure of the novel, also in his personal relationships. In a letter to Edward he explains this missing element:

> "I have never been able to achieve it [reciprocity] in my work," he began; and I knew what he meant. Gilbert, a man of strong feelings, rejoiced in contrasts and conflicts. It was easier for me (as he pointed out) to achieve this reciprocity than it was for him, because my pictures are painted in low tones, which don't need violent contrasts—which wouldn't, indeed, allow them. The colours lean towards each other, the forms repeat each other, with small variations (on which I love to dwell). Whereas his music demanded contrasts as violent as that between the *Allegretto* and the *Presto* of the Moonlight Sonata, and much more cacophonous: his idea of

reciprocity was the reciprocity of the boxing-ring: "You hit me, and I'll hit you"—an exchange of fisticuffs, not the magical, magnetic approach, gradual yearning, of one sort of feeling wooing another. (*Poor Clare*, p. 9)

Apart from a foretaste of *The Harness Room* in the romance and reciprocity of the boxing-ring, Edward's definition of art accords well with certain facets of Hartley's own fiction. At one point through Edward, Hartley evokes the art of Vuillard in *Poor Clare*—surely the ideal artist for the cultivated bourgeoise in a world where art, money, comfort, talent, and selective new ideas exist in untroubled harmony.

At the same time, Gilbert Finstock's fear of emotional bankruptcy, despite his comfortable financial legacy, and his indulgence in victimization have their analogues in Hartley's work. Gilbert's music is imbued with the discords of the twentieth century. However much he may admire Handel's setting for Dryden's "Ode for St. Cecilia's Day," Gilbert calls forth far more readily jarring atoms rather than heavenly harmony in the dissonant flux and rhythmic counter point of his musical bangs, rattles, and plops. As he views the present, Gilbert sees that "The architecture of humanism has broken down—it's quite flat. All we have left are the pieces" (*Poor Clare*, p. 39). Hartley, of course, has acknowledged this leveling most explicitly himself in a novel like *Facial Justice*, and he shares with Gilbert the sense of grievance and dissolution in modern art and contemporary life. In the past, Gilbert, like Alec in *A Perfect Woman*, has been a taker with his friends Edward, Myra, and Barbara deliberately subordinating themselves to his art and his demands. Barbara, for example, is the only person who can read and transcribe his musical notations over which she laboriously struggles often at great inconvenience. Aunt Clare's legacy suddenly transforms this taker into a giver, a condition thoroughly foreign both to his temper and his previous experience.

Accordingly, Edward becomes the new embodiment of the taker, as the narrator and Gilbert exchange certain characteristics. A notable description of the disruption which occurs in Edward's room when he introduces the Girtin landscape into it suggests the transference of Gilbert's musical chaos into Edward's hitherto harmonious milieu:

Nothing went with anything else. The sofa would not agree with the carpet; the chairs looked as if they hated each other and belonged to periods (as in fact they did) that had outgrown the past without looking forward to the future. And as for the pictures, which I had chosen for some common quality (I could not have said what) they were like guests at a party, ill-matched and ill-met, who had been formally and correctly introduced, but who would not speak to each other or to me, their host. (*Poor Clare*, p. 21)

As Aunt Clare's gift to Gilbert proved disruptive for him, so his gift of the Girtin to Edward continues this consequence, except that the narrator decides to leave his tiny room and expand his talent for both art and living in the sunshine of Italy. When Englishmen go to Italy in Hartley's fiction, they are usually susceptible to a significant change in their life-styles. Gilbert's gift, then, while disruptive in some respects, proves catalytic for Edward to risk acquiring life's other gifts, including a love affair with Myra. Evidently Aunt Clare had hoped her legacy would have a similar effect on Gilbert—to change him from victim to victor—but fulfillment comes instead through Edward at Gilbert's expense.

Edward withdraws to Assisi, one of whose patron saints is St. Clare, the female parallel to St. Francis, and plunges into the full experience of life. He contrives to give away his Girtin to Myra, herself so far neglected by Gilbert's gift-giving, on the pretext that this particular bequest had been made by their mutual friend, Gilbert, who had designated Edward's home as the half-way house on the way to the painting's destination in Myra's possession. Gilbert almost immediately repudiates this gesture in a letter to Edward, stating baldly that he had not given Myra anything because he did not want to be independent of her as he has now become of the other beneficiaries. Meanwhile, Myra accepts Edward's invitation by telegram to join him on the Continent, an invitation which, incidentally, had included Gilbert as well.

For Edward and Myra their tryst in Assisi becomes a love idyll: "Under the Italian sky all was plain sailing, for the artist, as it should be for the man." (*Poor Clare*, p. 88) In classic Hartleian fashion, Edward directs his new and purposeful existence according to the clarified lines and angles of the West Front of Santa Chiara's church which he successfully captures on canvas. Earlier Barbara had described Myra metaphorically as having a magnificent West Front (though no East Front, to speak of) comparable to the Peterborough Cathedral. Hartley skillfully exploits the churches, towers, and streets of Assisi as symbolic touchstones to underscore narrative and character changes. Myra, for example, anticipates her marriage to Edward by imagining the "marriage" between the churches of

Santa Chiara and San Rufino. As Edward follows an intentionally crooked path to visit the embalmed body of Saint Clare in the crypt of her church, he symbolically takes an equally devious path in his competition with Gilbert for Myra. These relationships are portrayed against the background of Assisi which, "as Nathaniel Hawthorne charmingly said, looked at night like a rosary flung against a hillside." (*Poor Clare*, p. 66) Nothing so holy can be associated with the human relationships also flung against the Assisi hillside by the end of *Poor Clare*.

In a letter to Gilbert which Edward destroys without sending, the narrator characterizes his composer friend in quite familiar Hartleian terms:

> You live in a world of fantasy in which symbols count for more than thoughts or even feeling. At least that's how I interpret it, and I think how Myra interprets it. I have loved her for many years, as I think she has loved you, but now we have both come to feel the need for a stronger and more direct relationship than can be symbolized by gifts however precious. What you have given me, and may be going to give Myra, is a challenge to gratitude that we can't accept, for it would come between us and our feelings for each other. Grateful we shall always be, and gratitude is a bond, but not so strong a bond as the ordinary natural love of one person for another. (*Poor Clare*, p. 100).

The foregoing passage suggests that here Hartley uses his narrator to ponder his typical protagonist's limitations with a critical, even parodistic, awareness, foreshadowing perhaps *The Love-Adept* which appeared the following year. Moreover, through Edward, who is a reasonably reliable narrator (and possible mouthpiece for the author), Hartley declares his disaffection for the Edwardian symbolizing characteristic of earlier novels and their protagonists. Critics may argue that if such an alteration in narrative technique does occur in Hartley it is an aesthetic mistake, but it also represents the author's willingness to take risks and vary his method of storytelling. Hartley's trademarks remain metaphors, perhaps, yet direct relationships (even happy-endings) become significant in and of themselves in his final novels, almost like Edward's unsent rebuke to Gilbert Finstock in *Poor Clare*. With a traditionalist like Hartley, novelty lies in perception more than in what is perceived, and in the novels which follow *Poor Clare* the author alters his symbolic way of seeing in favor of noticing the obvious directly and immediately. The lineage of this changed technique would seem to be traceable to Edward and the cultural context (and syntax) of the late sixties. The Edward of *Poor Clare* is assuredly not a marooned Edwardian.

Hartley, however, cannot let Edward off the traditional moral hook, and penance will have to be done. In the Chapel of Perpetual Adoration in the Church of St. Clare, Edward sees death in the form of Gilbert's ghost, only to discover later in a newspaper that the well-known composer has disappeared from his flat in Roland Gardens. With the appearance of Barbara in Spoleto, where Edward whisked off Myra in the hope of avoiding Gilbert, the couple learn that the composer's body has been found. The confluence of the shocking manifestation of Gilbert's apparition with Barbara's simple declaration is vintage Hartley, blending the real and the surreal. Nevertheless, the fusion of image, form, and vision in the Chapel seems less convincing than similar scenes in other novels, possibly because Edward's incredulity is contagious. In his death Gilbert reestablishes a perdurable claim to Myra. As he felt abandoned when she joined Edward in Italy, she now abandons Edward in consequence of Gilbert's death. The two men continue their volley between life and eternity with the point at the end going to Gilbert. Edward experiences renewed resentment against his late friend and, in addition, against the two women to whom the narrator has become the common enemy:

> From their different angles they turned their fire on me. They kept a little of it for each other, but I, I was the villain of the piece. This I resented; for what had Gilbert done for them, or they for Gilbert, except to encourage and prolong a situation which had nothing real in it, nothing of lasting emotional value, only a dependent selfishness on his side, (for he could not manage his own life alone) and on theirs a flattered vanity, which fed on which each thought she had done for him. They didn't like each other the better for that, either. (*Poor Clare*, p. 149)

With rueful insight, Edward notes in the looks of ill-concealed hostility passing back and forth between the two women and himself the germ of a *trio antipatico* which Gilbert might well have written:

> Mild-mannered as he was, soft-hearted as he seemed to be, he [Gilbert] had set us by the ears; we should never again see eye to eye as we once had. Could it be that his music was an instinctive expression of his deepest nature, which was always at odds with itself, and that his final bequest to us was to live out, in our now discordant lives, the symphony he had not been able to finish? (*Poor Clare*, p. 153)

Thus in *Poor Clare* life imitates art, and the discordant legacy of Gilbert outlives his own special needs and desires. Passionate life and art arise from reciprocity, to use Gilbert's word for what he lacked, of passive and active selfhood; and the experience of art may affect the way life is experience. Edward's imaginative involvement in life through love is partly an outgrowth of his approach to art, a triumph over the dissonance which finally overwhelms Gilbert. While Edward's loving engages his will and temporarily wins Myra to him, Gilbert's immense need masquerading as love proves in its very passivity—extending, of course, to a kind of self-sacrifice—a stronger appeal to Myra than Edward's love.

The gifts of life are finally more than a matter of goods given and received. Gilbert looks back on his aunt's possessions and her life and thinks it all seems to make a "synthesis of *something*, but Heaven knows what!" (*Poor Clare*, p. 11) A similar promise and frustration might be imputed to Hartley's novel as well; but in *Poor Clare* and most of the novels which follow love figures as a real and adult emotion, offering if not synthesis maybe something better—the presence of new resources in Hartley's art. *Poor Clare*, alas, repeats the dying fall at the end of the novel which is familiar in Hartley, as Edward spends his last day in Assisi at the Church of St. Clare reflecting on death (as opposed to life and / or love):

> Poor Clare, poor Clare! I still had a day, and I spent most of it at Assisi, in the church of Santa Chiara, with her unaltering and (I hoped) unalterable face turned towards me, meditating on her death and Gilbert's, and trying to reconcile myself to mine. (*Poor Clare*, p. 156)

Edward, as first-person narrator, comments on behavior and explains actions, especially his own, somewhat less obtrusively than Hartley's usual omniscient-author viewpoint usually can manage. *Poor Clare* pulls together a number of themes seen elsewhere in Hartley but rendered especially concrete in this novel in the characters of the divided protagonists, Edward and Gilbert. Although Hartley continues to use a fairly complex system of symbolic motifs in this novel, principally through the art and architecture of the residually vital Christian culture of Italy, his symbolism increasingly assumes a secondary or supporting function for the central concern which is action and portrayal of Edward as a man of action.

The assumption made by Edward that life is a pleasure to be

grasped contrasts sharply with the more typical Hartleian attitude manifested through Gilbert that life is a duty to be accepted. As a ghost Gilbert may triumph over Edward, but in *Poor Clare* the narrator's clear human intention to act on his feelings of love for Myra has its considerable appeal and strength. And Myra can yet return to him as she cannot to a revenant. Hartley (with the assistance of Francis King) examines the relative contribution of both poverty and plenty to love and its capacity to bring about cooperation of divine grace and human activity. What begins as a study of the estrangement between people which arises from obligations incurred through the giving and receiving of gifts ends symbolically in Assisi under the aspect of eternity. In the Hartley canon *Poor Clare* is simultaneously a summing-up and a new frontier.

II   My Sisters' Keeper: *Who, with the Best Meaning,*
*Have Incurred the Worst.*

At one point the narrator in *Poor Clare* remarks about a string of negations spoken by Gilbert as being as comprehensive, in its small way, as was King Lear's. The Lear allusions abound in the later Hartley novels; and Dr. Powell, psychiatrist to protagonist Basil Hancock in *My Sisters' Keeper* (1970), defines his patient's dilemma in a particularly apt *Lear* reference—"We are not the first Who, with best meaning, have incurred the worst." Basil does not seem to want happiness for himself; but, as his psychiatrist correctly diagnoses, he wants other people to be happy through him, at whatever cost to themselves. In particular, Basil suffers from acute sisteritis: what happened to his three sisters mattered more than what happened to himself; and, indeed, his sisters were often substitutes for his own desires. Basil's "sisteritis" is a variant of the earlier Eustace's suffering, although Hartley's tone here seems less gently ironic than in the trilogy and may even demean Eustace's memory. After *The Love-Adept*, perhaps it was inevitable that Hartley, consciously or unconsciously, would turn upon himself, as it were, and his past fiction and let his art approach parody. Or, as in *Poor Clare*, Hartley may be working toward a fresh approach to material and themes explored elsewhere. At its best *My Sisters' Keeper* offers a comic perspective on what earlier had been treated more darkly, even tragically.

Basil Hancock's parents are described as latish Victorian in age and moral attitude; however, the time-setting of the novel seems much later than would be possible with parents actually attaining adulthood in the Victorian era. Despite this basic implausibility, Hartley apparently fuses his reflections of the Edwardian past with the behavior of the sixties in *My Sisters' Keeper*. The principles of conduct which his parents enjoin Basil to follow have, to be sure, their Victorian credibility and point of origin:

> He was to do what was right, in the moral sense; he was to be fervent in business, serving the Lord; and he was to have always before his eyes, the ideal of improvement, self-improvement which would mean other people's improvement, as well as his, and enable them to be proud of him. (*My Sisters' Keeper*, p. 1)

In his initial family crisis, Basil tries to persuade his eldest sister to break off her engagement to his former school chum, the good-looking Terry O'Donovan, who had a reputation at school for his romantic attachment—as is the wont of the English public school tradition—to boys rather than girls. Basil, as an adolescent, had not succumbed to Terry's seductive ways, and now he would like to forestall his sister's desire to marry Terry but without revealing the precise nature of his reservations. Out of the strain he experiences before this moral dilemma, Basil suffers a minor nervous breakdown. Meanwhile Gwendolen and Terry do marry with largely happy consequences and mutual fidelity.

His middle sister, Evelyn, gains admittance to a woman's college at Oxenbridge during Basil's third year at the university, and much to her brother's distress she seems predisposed to extreme forms of experience. For example, she becomes involved in a nearly fatal accident while driving a male friend's sportscar. Basil himself had helped Ralph purchase the car which the latter called the Minotaur, the devourer of damsels as Basil prophetically notes. Elated at Eve's recovery, Basil rallies sufficiently to attain a First honors degree in history much to the surprise of his tutor who feared scholarly staleness would impair his performance. Eve and Ralph are likewise married, and together they pursue archeological studies, not from a sportscar but from a sturdily-built truck.

Living in comfort at his parent's home and working at banking in London, Basil is happy with his routine, although he feels somewhat incomplete. He remembers his days at public school and wonders whether he repressed his inclinations then rather excessively:

Basil knew a great many girls of course, and he liked them, but none of them gave him that expansion of the spirit and the flesh, that he had enjoyed during the few terms at Melchester when he had been Terry's unrewarding, though not ungrateful favourite. Self-denial is a good servant but a bad master, and may be a life-long handicap. "If only I had let him have his way!" he sometimes asked himself—"I should be more capable of real feelings, sexually and emotionally, than I am now. I might have been as successful as a husband as he is" (meaning Terry), "and more successful than Ralph, whom, in my opinion, Eve treats abominably." (*My Sisters' Keeper*, p. 111)

Shortly thereafter Basil learns of an incident involving his brother-in-law and a boy in a public lavatory, or "cottage," as it is called. Suspecting that Terry may be the victim of a frame-up, Basil enlists the help of his friend Hugo to stage a return engagement at the "cottage," where the boy in question steals Basil's handkerchief and tries to charge him with the same offense previously lodged against Terry. With Hugo as hidden witness, however, the boy is forced to confess his stratagem to the police, and formal charges are entered against the boy and his father for their racket. Gwendolen henceforth keeps Terry on a much shorter rein, but his brother-in-law is grateful to Basil for saving both his marriage and reputation. Basil's interference has been beneficial to others on this occasion. Predictably, though, he suffers another nervous breakdown: "The Terry incident had knocked him sideways, and further off his balance than he realized. He still hadn't understood what a severe test of personality it is to act, in important matters, against one's inclinations." (*My Sisters' Keeper*, p. 145)

Emerging from his expensive "cure," Basil turns for a new interest to that great Hartleian avocation so dear to the hearts of his "incurables," cathedral-visiting;

And Basil did go, at week-ends, where he got the chance, to visit Durham and Lincoln, and Ely, and Peterborough, and Canterbury, and the Anglican Cathedral at Liverpool; and got from them something of what he was looking for—peace of mind. But what could he offer them? Nothing except a small subscription to their repair fund. He enjoyed his sense of littleness in comparison with their greatness, and the spiritual greatness which they embodied. They were the reverse of 'cottages', but if they ministered to the spirit's occasional efflorescence, they did not help him in his daily life. (*My Sisters' Keeper*, p. 145)

Because he sees her on a daily basis, Basil now devotes himself to the future marital happiness of his youngest sister, Amabel. His can-

didate for her is Alan Walsingham who shares, as Amabel notes, the
same name as the architect of the octagon at Ely Cathedral.
Walsingham is described as *bel-laid*, and as Amabel remarks of her
brother's endorsement of him, "I believe you have a crush on him
yourself. You like that type—not exactly pock-marked, but scar-
faced, as if he had been beaten up in a Russian prison—" (*My
Sisters' Keeper*, p. 160) Perhaps both sets of associations have their
particular relevance to Basil's approval of Alan Walsingham,
although Amabel's innuendo about her brother does appear
needlessly snide.

Amabel and Alan are duly married; however, the bride's pregnancy precedes the ceremony. Shortly thereafter, her husband having at least temporarily left her, Amabel who now despises Alan asks
Basil to obtain an abortion for her. As his youngest sister's keeper
Basil once more intervenes and persuades Amabel to have the baby.
He, nevertheless, increasingly recognizes that his knowledge about
human nature came more from books than from experience. In
retrospect, he decides that his various interventions in the lives of
his sisters and their husbands have assumed something like a stage-
scene, perhaps an aesthetic but not truly a personal experience as
far as his own identity is concerned.

Unyielding in her hatred of Alan and in her grievance against
Basil for getting her involved in the first place, Amabel still goes
through with the pregnancy. Meg Marchmont, Basil's friend who
works at the Approved School for juvenile delinquents and who
earlier found something familiar about Alan, tardily remembers
Amabel's husband as an adolescent inmate of the institution. In
turn, Basil suffers another breakdown which keeps him in a nursing
home during his sister's premature confinement. Amabel dies in
childbirth, but the seven-month premature baby boy survives.
When Basil is discharged from the nursing home and returns to his
parents' house at Middlehurst, his infant nephew, Alan, has likewise
taken up residence there:

> They saw him as a baby, ill-featured, ill-natured, but are not all babies,
> except those in pictures of the Holy Family, hideous to look at? Do they not
> all howl and scream, and clench their little fists, and grow red in the face?
> Especially boy-babies; boy-babies, as is well known, are for ever angry; that
> is why we have so many wars. Girl-babies are far more civilized; they are
> anxious to please, and will smile at a male visitor who bends over their cot,
> from their earliest age. (*My Sisters' Keeper*, pp. 227-228)

Basil sees in the child's dark, wrinkled and choleric little face the physical emblem of what, along with his own interference, destroyed the life of his beloved Amabel.

When Meg Marchmont comes to visit the convalescent Basil, who has now taken to excessive drinking, she immediately determines to adopt the infant Alan. Basil is horrified at the suggestion:

> He had little sense of what life could be, compared to what life might be. But all the same, he realized the danger of Meg's idealism, and had a vision of what her life might be like, tied to this dark-browed brat, this little Heathcliff, who might be in and out (probably more in than out) of prison. (*My Sisters' Keeper*, p. 239)

Acting on his own inclination, as he insists, rather than out of sacrifice, Basil proposes marriage to Meg. He will share with his newly chosen wife the responsibility of little Alan's upbringing. Meg accepts his proposal, and the reclamation process begins not only for the child but also for the adoptive father who accepts parenting in lieu of remaining his sisters' keeper. Even possible thraldom to a delinquent child represents enlargement of Basil's sense of what life can be.

A certain stockness and roteness mar *My Sisters' Keeper*. As a novel, it is smaller, less symbolic, and curiously less self-conscious than some of the more important novels which precede it, although still recognizably tactful in the usual Hartleian mode. In the introduction of homosexuality explicitly into this novel. Hartley reveals a new openness in contrast to the covert suggestiveness of the subject in the earlier *My Fellow Devils*. Amusingly, during an exchange at the Hancocks' engagement dinner for Amabel, the company assembled discusses the identity of Adam, humanity's sire, and Meg assumes she would know him with or without fig-leaf since one man, she thinks, is very like another. Basil is delighted with this obvious remark, for some reason, because he associates it with his plain-speaking archeologist sister, Eve (appropriately), who "would not hesitate to call a phallus a phallus, whether contemporary or a thousand years old." (*My Sisters' Keeper*, p. 177) Notwithstanding the claim of candor, Meg's and Basil's inherent shyness should be observed and honored as a reflection of Hartley's own reticence: for all of them *phallus* would doubtless be the ultimate in linguistic forthrightness.

Hartley continues to demonstrate his feel for families and his faith in the development of character which takes for granted that it is possible to grow up, at whatever advanced age, and establish familial continuity. Basil ceases to be a go-between for his sisters; in that role, contrary to his good intentions, the loving brother found himself isolated and a contributor to his sisters' unhappiness. Now as a doer at the end of the novel, Basil accedes to the psychological norm and adult identity he has been reluctant to assume and measure himself by. Typically, in several of these late Hartley novels, the author's Jamesian talent for discerning possibilities of action wins out over his equally compelling Jamesian respect for caution exhibited in earlier tales. Basil Hancock eliminates his past as a source of anxiety and proves capable, in the present, of becoming husband and parent. He and Meg assure his returning parents that baby Alan, who had been left in their care, "had been very, *very* good." (*My Sisters' Keeper*, p. 242) While not quite an accurate description of the infant's behavior, this yes-saying with respect to the child, which ends the novel, constitutes an almost unnoticed rite of passage for the couple who will now be family to him. Basil, the traditional Hartleian go-between character living through and for others, opts to become, belatedly, a participant in life. What affirmation there is in *My Sisters' Keeper* may be only the affirmation of the possibilities of change or of making-do. Such small truths, without symbolic overlay, occupy Hartley in his last novels, as the facts of life (including sex) assume a less frightful character and Hartley looks affectionately on the ordinary universe—and even on human impulses. *My Sisters' Keeper* surely lacks the formal brilliance of the *Eustace and Hilda* trilogy; but its lighter tone and buoyant curiosity about brothers and sisters, especially at a time when ever larger numbers of similarly inclined but otherwise unrelated people are fraternally identifying themselves as "sisters" and "brothers," achieve an adroit sense of pertinence through comedy. Basil Hancock is finally cured of his sisteritis, not to be confused with cystitis, as the physician in Hartley's novel notes twice lest the very small joke be missed; in putting his own former mode of being into question, brother Basil emerges as husband and surrogate father to little Alan. Hartley seems here almost ready to accept an innovative and indulgent modernism regarding social and domestic roles, and that certainly affirms acceptance of new possibilities for the author.

### III   The Collections: *A Continuous Chain of Life*

*The Collections* (1972) is the last book Hartley completed before his death, but it was released before the posthumously published *The Will and the Way* (1973). It is a brief novel, almost novella-length, demonstrating through its subject that Hartley's imagination is at home with country houses and their objects of art which bear the touch of human relationships and love. In *The Collections* a country house takes the place of Hartley's usual cathedrals as the embodiment of a way of life. The genesis of the novel perhaps is a passage in *My Sisters' Keeper* explaining the nature of certain household "gods" which bring together material and human relationship:

> The objects, whether valuable in themselves or not, are valuable to their owners as representing certain persons and places. Aunt Alice gave me this; I bought that in Venice. Taken together they constitute a continuous chain of life, and more continuous than life is, because a clock that ticks the time away, long after its donor has been dead, still recalls his or her presence, and a piece of china, bought in England or in some foreign place, recalls exactly the feeling and the circumstances of that moment. We are part of you, however humble or however valuable, such objects seem to say; you won't see Aunt Alice again, you may not see Venice again, but as long as you can see *us*, that person, and that place will still be vivid to you, and you won't have lost touch with your past life, which will be all the more precious to you, the older you grow. (*My Sisters' Keeper*, p. 104)

Ambrose Cumberwell and Edwina Antrobus in *The Collections* are perplexed as to how they can preserve intact their respective valuable collections of pictures and works of art or Edwina's archaeological discoveries. Both aging people, moreover, are concerned about the destiny of their collections after their demise. Ambrose's one phobia, characteristic of other middle-aged, unmarried men of independent means in L. P. Hartley, is the State and the fear that his carefully preserved capital would fall into the greedy hands of the Inland Revenue:

> The State, forever encroaching on the claims of individuals, on the whole principle of individuality, arrogating to itself, its unworthy, greedy, impersonal, bureaucratic self, the credit for amassing collections of more or less beautiful objects, which of itself it never had the taste and judgement to collect. (*The Collections*, p. 6)

His spoils, to use the Jamesian term which Hartley appropriates, give the timorous Ambrose both his conscience and his identity as a private patron, an endangered species in recent British history owing to severe taxation imposed by the state. The circumstances of the patron have worsened in England in the years since *The Collections*, witnessing once more to Hartley's power of augury. Ambrose's treasures, as he admits, represent him more vividly and more objectively than he can represent himself. In the continuity of his collection Ambrose sees in the preservation of the past a means of encouraging the future.

At the suggestion of his doctor, Ambrose and his collecting friend, Edwina, decide to move together to a large historic house belonging to Barbara Middleworth (the symbolic names sometimes become rather overbearing), a widow whose second husband had gambled away her fortune. Barbara has been left with a son, Anthony, a posthumous child by her first husband, and a Stately Home belonging legally to her son but now bereft of most of its furnishings thanks to the extravagance of Anthony's step-father. Edwina and Ambrose come along with sufficient artifacts in their collections to fill the vacancy of Middleworth, and shortly after their move to the estate, the house is opened to the public with Edith, Barbara's stepdaughter by her second husband, at the ticket-table. The proud possessors of the new collections now housed at Middleworth, Edwina and Ambrose experience a sense of reciprocity with one another:

> They were each dilettantes, and though their presence under the same roof had brought them together as never before, it was still their non-personal interests, their interests in the civilization which had gone on so long before, and they hoped would go on so long after them, that constituted their real bond. They could clear out of Middleworth if they wanted to. And yet their fortuitous (if it was fortuitous) conjunction there had brought them closer to each other than they ever expected to be. (*The Collections*, p. 57)

These "open and visible conservations," as Hartley's favorite Sir Thomas Browne called such spoils, become invested with human history, and, in contrast to James's collectors who regard people as things to be possessed, respect and affection directed toward things draw these collectors out of self-absorption into love. Thus, their shared collections permit Edwina and Ambrose to develop affectional attachments over and above their material coupling of art and archaeological objects. *The Collections*, then, becomes an oblique and surprising love story between two unlikely collectors.

Borrowed acquisitions together with growing tourist receipts at least temporarily save Middleworth. The family itself move into the former servants' quarters behind the green baize door, leaving the grander space to the new occupants, Edwina and Ambrose. Except for Anthony who commutes daily to the City where he labors none too successfully in commercial enterprises, everyone takes his or her turn as guide to and commentator on the treasures of Middleworth. For a small additional charge tourists may visit the family's private quarters to exult, as Barbara imagines it, in how are the mighty fallen. Yet even Anthony moderately enjoys his instant recognition as lord of the manor, however reduced he is in material circumstances. Hartley records the "progression" of renewal at Middleworth with customary deft and understated strokes:

> The twenty-five pence poured in; bankruptcy was kept at bay; and a hired gardener, if not very energetic, waged war on the weeds and even planted flowers, vegetable-fashion, nine inches apart.
>
> Often they reaped a hundred pounds a week, sometimes more; and Anthony had a plan for teas to be served in the little eighteenth century pavilion beside the lake—a delectable place! Quite soon, Middleworth, instead of being a symbol of aristocratic superiority "odi profanum vulgus et arceo", as Horace might have said, had become a popular rendezvous for the neighbourhood. "Good old Middleworth, the old lady can make a go of it when she tries!" (*The Collections*, p. 54)

Middleworth had been saved, not of course in its original grandeur, but with sufficient attractiveness to justify a half-day's outing.

Then, as if symptomatic of renewed decline, a valuable object disappears. After additional thefts and growing problems over insurance, a watchman / detective, Henry Cunliffe, is hired to reside at Middleworth and protect the collections. When Hartley describes Harry simply with "Here was a man!" (*The Collections*, p. 98), it is easy to recognize the type, since the physically strong male of the working class has figured as protagonist or foil to the protagonist in so much of Hartley's fiction which precedes *The Collections*. The Harry Cunliffes sleep well in Hartley, unlike his privileged insomniacs. But in this novel, the detective deliberately deprives himself of sleep in order to learn the identity of the Middleworth thief.

The thief is none other than Edith, the step-daughter, who conceals under her dressing-gown the little della Robbia plaque of the

Virgin and Child, which is one of Ambrose's most-loved pieces. Unsure of how to proceed with his knowledge of the culprit, the
twenty-eight year old Harry finds himself, for the first time in his
life, suffering from a large moral dilemma. Typically, in dealing
with the working class, Hartley has Harry resolve his moral problem
simply and physically by inviting Miss Edith into bed with
him—"Better a little bed, than a long trial for stealing." (*The
Collections*, p. 118) From sexual blackmail Harry moves swiftly to
financial blackmail; he demands a hundred pounds for keeping
quiet about the thefts being an inside job.

Meanwhile, Ambrose and Edwina reluctantly decide to vacate
Middleworth before they are rendered any more emotionally and
spiritually impoverished by material loss of the collection they value
together. Edith, too, announces her imminent departure in light of
the future suspension of the Middleworth tours. Not aware of the
thief within the manor, the older generation inveighs against the
permissive society which they regard as indirectly responsible for
their loss of property. Barbara reports overhearing Harry say as he
put Edith's luggage into the car and a suitcase accidentally
opened—"All the whole collection / In the same direction." (*The
Collections*, p. 134) In turn, Anthony argues for Harry's dismissal
on the basis of such an impertinence, but the detective himself in-
terrupts this debate by presenting the Middleworth quartet with a
Messien figure of a shepherdess from Ambrose's collection. Oddly
enough, it was the very thing Ambrose had meant to give Edith as a
parting present. " 'She didn't wait for you to give it to her,' said
Harry, 'I waylaid it. I won't tell you how.' " (*The Collections*, p.
134) On that fillip *The Collections* ends.

This pleasing novella on the valuation of spoils can be viewed
from a double perspective: appreciative and affectional as demonstrated by Ambrose and Edwina, who enter into a love relationship
to form what they consider to be the best possible collection; or exploitative and rapacious as calculated by Edith and her accomplice
Harry. In the contrast between the two couples Hartley records a
decline of moral and aesthetic values relative to the artifacts which
measure human continuity, as the rapacity of a shabby and dis-
pirited society seems to eat away at cultural connections. But this
essentially comic novella should not be thought of as a jeremiad of
the kind Hartley might have written for his last work. His urbanity
turns *The Collections* into human comedy which obviates a grim
"sense of an ending," to borrow Frank Kermode's pungent phrase.

Like their antecedents in Hartley, Edwina and Ambrose are rather child-like, in that they do not strip the objects they have collected of their expressive properties; the collector's imagination is not very far removed from the subjective wish as Ambrose explains:

"We know that we can't take things with us, but until that time comes, everything that we have, and look at, enhances our sense of personality, because each acquisition, however cheap, represents the fulfillment of a wish, isn't it so, Edwina? And one's life is made up of the fulfillment of wishes. When the object of them, even if it's only a cup and saucer, departs, one is spiritually and emotionally the poorer." (*The Collections*, pp. 128-129)

But Ambrose does not delude himself or misunderstand his situation (he acknowledges the condition of mortality, certainly), and therefore he does not incur the immense psychological cost which other less candid and less aware people in Hartley must pay as victims of delusion and distorting fantasy. While character may be less definable than objects in *The Collections*, art made by the inspired hand of man affirms and reveals human life and character. The artistic character of a civilization would seem to be in Hartley's mind fundamentally related to its distinctive manners and morals. Enriched by the integrated heritage of their collections, Edwina and Ambrose face the autumn of their lives hand in hand, demonstrating purposefulness which can disengage itself from fixations on the past even while venerating artifacts from former ages. Unlike Harrry and Edith, they can start a life together with their integrity intact. *The Collections* is at once rich and slight, perhaps like fragile life itself, and finally happy and fulfilling for some human wishes.

IV   The Will and the Way: *Inheritors as Lions and Sheep*

*The Will and the Way* (1973), held back from publication by L. P. Hartley in order for the author to check on some points of law germane to the plot, was published posthumously. Standing as it does as his last novel, *The Will and the Way*, while not one of his more important novels, exemplifies Hartley's moral preoccupations and craftsmanship. In contrast to the two near-novellas which surround it, *The Harness Room* and *The Collections*, *The Will and the Way* chronicles the life of a family over an extended period of time.

The great solvent in the novel is once again money, principally the inheritance from old Mr. Handforth (the symbolic naming unabashedly continues), the possession of which separates lions from sheep. The recurring metaphors of these animals relate *The Will and the Way* to the symbolic texture of earlier Hartley novels.

As a novel Hartley's last published effort in that genre is an "irregular" pastoral, a provocative, though unusual, hybrid of something like Ivy Compton-Burnett's *A Family and a Fortune* and Thomas Hardy's *The Woodlanders*. Hartley's irony and his steady sense of the inevitability of historical change significantly qualify his use of pastoral attitudes. Giles (Holroyd) in *The Will and the Way* shares his Christian name with Hardy's protagonist in *The Woodlanders*; there are also similarities in the plots: both men are dispossessed or denied a rightful inheritance; and each becomes a rejected swain, taking refuge rather foolishly in pastoral pursuits. Hartley's Giles, however, demonstrates a virulently antipastoral love of money which his "darling" sheep can hardly replace or consummate.

Giles's grandfather, the dying seventy-seven year old Mr. Handforth, finds himself caught in divided loyalty between his two daughters, Judith Snape and Hestor Holroyd. Judith, married to a merchant and company director who is always in need of capital, lives near the old man and does many kind things for him. Nevertheless, as with Faulkner's Snopses, Mr. Handforth might have been on guard to discover the Snapes' incipient meanness of spirit from their very name with the generally unpleasant connotations of *sn* beginnings in English. Before his death, the old man does learn that Judith is only after his money; so he writes a second will bequeathing the bulk of his estate to his other daughter, Hester Holroyd, who lives with her family on a sheep farm in the north. But, before he can reveal the existence of this latter will, the old man dies, leaving his new will hidden in the middle volume of Gibbon's *Decline and Fall*. The old will is probated which leaves his wealth to the Snapes. Hester's husband, Jack Holroyd, also needs subsidizing quite badly, yet his wife never ingratiated herself with her father sufficiently to secure a larger inheritance, nor did her relationship with her father seem dependent on that ulterior motive. At the time of the father's death, Hester is unaware of the late Mr. Handforth's casting her as Cordelia to her sister's Goneril. The *Lear* parallel looms especially large in *The Will and the Way*, although it has been growing in the preceding novels, as has been noted, as an old man near death contemplates the effect of his legacy on his survivors.

Mr. Handforth must cope with what Erik Erikson terms the crisis of integrity: "Only he who in some way has taken care of things and people and has adapted himself to the triumphs and disappointments adherent to being, by necessity, the originator of others and the generator of things and ideas—only he may gradually grow the fruit of these seven stages [of the life-cycle]." ("Eight Stages of man," Childhood and Society, p. 231) As Hartley observes of his "Lear," Mr. Handforth "was not a man who gave way to despair" (*The Will and the Way*, p. 27), a pre-condition, according to Erikson, for surviving the crisis of old age with ego-integrity.

The Snapes now live luxuriously as a result of their large inheritance and ignore almost completely their meek Cumberland relatives. Charlotte Snape and Giles Holroyd, Mr. Handforth's grandchildren who once proclaimed before him the love they felt for each other, grow up apart, alienated one from the other not only by distance but also by financial status. When the time comes for the nubile Charlotte to wed, her mother, Judith, naturally arranges with great care a financially desirable, although loveless, marriage for her.

The Holroyds' only real regret about their lack of inheritance, as Giles's mother sees it, is that her son has consequently lost the free choice between being a lion or a sheep, a choice contingent upon money. His father on the other hand, who is always described in terms of his own leonine looks counters, "I think he will be happier as a sheep, . . . Who wouldn't be?" (*The Will and the Way*, p. 44) Hester, in turn, rebukes her husband for being a lion in sheep's clothing. Hartley's portrayal of earlier passive sheep-types in his fiction reflects his own basic ambivalence toward the two contrasting personalities of sheep and lions. Giles appears as yet another young man in Hartley victimized by the expedience of more sophisticated people around him who dictate his destiny. As always, wealth or the absence of it plays a significant part in shaping character. The widening circles of greed, jealousy, and cruelty that can spread from the fact of a legacy receive major emphasis here with the result that Giles as a character becomes reduced finally to little more than the condition or really embodiment of his monetary deficiency.

In contrast to Giles stands the young boarder and apprentice shepherd, Philip. He has temporarily taken up farming, despite his considerable independent means, on the advice of his physician.

Hartley describes the implicit trust Philip's parents have in the advice of the doctor about their son's future in such a way that this kind of trust constitutes its own form of servitude, as reminiscent of *The Brickfield* and the medical adjunct to dictatorship in *Facial Justice*:

> Illness was a stimulus that Philip's parents (protected by their carapace of hypochondria) never enjoyed: but Philip was a kind of extension of their ruling phobia. They felt his liability to instant mortality as acutely as they felt their own. (*The Will and the Way*, p. 85)

Philip, however, takes a more robust view of himself than his parents do. Indeed, he seems the most attractive character in the novel and threatens to eclipse Giles as protagonist. As if to prevent that, he is cast in the familiar role of go-between, mediating the strained relationship between Giles and Charlotte after her marriage to Marcus Neville. Moreover, by accident Philip's go-between role is enlarged through his discovery of the second Handforth will in Gibbon. Because nobody else wanted it, the Handforth library had been given to the Holroyds where it reposed unheeded in the granary until the intellectually inclined Philip picked up some of its treasures, including the second volume of *The Decline and Fall of the Roman Empire*. Philip's initial thoughts manifest his moral acuteness:

> "What difference will this Will make to them?" he asked himself. "And how desirable is it to upset arrangements which have lasted, for good or ill, for so many years? To reverse so many things that have been accepted and taken for granted by a good many people? To dash many hopes and encourage others? To make a stroke of the pen demolish lives which—for how many years?—have been accepted on a certain basis of living?" (*The Will and the Way*, pp. 89-90)

Philip recognizes, as few Hartley protagonists ever truly do, that attempts to do the "right" thing often prove corrupting—that the repercussions of goodness are often as problematical as those of evil. His response to Gibbon foreshadows the novel's ending:

> His historical and already rather misanthropical view of human nature enjoyed this onslaught [Gibbon's] on the elected representative of Christianity in this world. Why try to be good when so many much more excellent persons, chosen to give religion a good name, were bad? (*The Will and the Way*, p. 91)

Nevertheless, Philip does inform the Holroyds of his discovery and the means for restoration of their patrimony. Further, he agrees to accompany Giles on a visit to the south. The formerly sheepish Giles vows personal revenge on Aunt Judith and demands explanation from his once beloved Charlotte:

> But Giles was, and knew himself to be, from the deferential glances cast in his direction, the hero of the hour, the lost sheep returning to the fold, the pride of the flock, full of honour though not yet of years. He held them in the hollow of his hand; but it wasn't a comfortable feeling, and the new Giles, with all his power, wasn't on good terms with the old one, who had so little. (*The Will and the Way*, p. 126)

Having brought suit against the Snapes for recovery of their inheritance, the Holroyds eventually receive their fifty thousand pound legacy. Because Hester feels sorry for her sister's straitened economic condition (Judith, for example, must sell the family's Bentley), she generously offers to divide the money equally with her sister. The Holroyds' Cumberland neighbors rejoice at the news of the settlement which they view as a victory for the agriculture of the North over the sybaritic indulgence of the South—"an ancient rivalry—a victory for the people who really *worked* in the snow and the rain, come bad weather or worse weather, over the Southerners, who basked by the sea, with little on themselves or to show for themselves." (*The Will and the Way*, p. 142)

As it happens, the munificent impulses of Hester Holroyd do not inspire reciprocity on the part of the Snapes. Shortly after the Handforth estate has been equally divided, the Holroyds see announced in the newspapers that Charlotte's unloved, recently deceased husband has left a legacy of 135,000 pounds. With Charlotte now authentically an heiress and assurances that Giles no longer has any matrimonial ambitions to be attached to his cousin. Philip ceases to be a go-between and becomes himself her second husband. This change in his status also removes Philip's former contribution to the Holroyds' income. Giles, for his own part, embarks on a low-keyed romance with Rosamond, Philip's former Cumberland sweetheart. Hester who had originally married for love finds her relationship with her husband and son greatly changed as a result of her generous action toward her sister:

> At meal-times silence reigned. Jack could not forgive Hester for parting with half her patrimony; Giles could not forgive her either, nor could he

quite forgive Philip for ploughing with his heifer, when he made this clandestine arrangement with the still-married Charlotte, possibly ignorant of her affluence. (*The Will and the Way*, p. 181)

Without money, Giles retreats to the sheepfold; the life he imagines he could lead with the help of a decent income cannot come to pass. Unable to insure Rosamond a home of their own, as he had hoped—the consequence of his parents' financial setback and loss of Philip's additional money—Giles drifts away from his anticipated marriage of sexual convenience. His manliness which made him attractive initially in the novel seems impaired at the end by the poverty of his material and emotional life. Hartley's final description of Giles is devastatingly ironic, recalling almost the manner of Flaubert:

Had they been more in love, they would not have behaved in this half-hearted fashion. But Rosamond felt that lodgings with Giles's parents was not what she was looking for; she might go further and fare better, for Giles, in spite of his undoubted physical attractions—the pale skin and fair hair, in which health and vigour bloomed so unostentatiously—was not the only pebble on the beach. For Giles, with his limited acquaintance in the neighbourhood, there were no pebbles for the moment. Luckily for him, he was attached to the flock, and they gave him a feeling of warmth born of familiarity, and animal sympathy which he couldn't have defined. He could distinguish between each, though to the inexpert, they all looked alike. He had his favourites, and sometimes, when he was counting them into the fold, he would mutter under his breath, 'One, two, three, four—good night, darling—six, seven, eight.' (*The Will and the Way*, p. 184)

Although, of course, it is a commonplace of pastoral conventions for animals to be companions of their masters, Giles's companionableness with his sheep at the end of *The Will and the Way* borders on the extreme. The epigraph to *The Shrimp and the Anemone*, taken from Emily Brontë's "Were they shepherds, who sat all day," establishes a major theme which runs throughout Hartley's canon: "I've known a hundred kinds of love / All made the loved one rue." Philip takes his cue from history, Gibbon, perhaps, and rises from his friend's decline in *The Will and the Way*, but Giles's retreat to nature and sheepfold translates him out of history and into an animal continuum where at least the creatures are both darling and true.

Like the novels which precede it, *The Will and the Way* is a traditional novel with unconventional moments. Typically too shrewd and individualistic simply to imitate past masters, or even himself, Hartley here presents his distinctive and witty treatment of the very pastoral myths—the cottage away from it all and the idyllic simplicity of the rural world—to which characters in earlier novels seemed drawn. *The Will and the Way* turns some specific pastoral assumptions and motifs inside out with the meek properly inheriting the sheep but certainly not the earth. Diane Johnson, reviewing the novel for the *New Statesman* correctly defines Hartley's effect: "a sly comedy of delicious villainy, of the hopeless ineptitude of 'good' people when up against bad ones, heightened by a certain degree of moral equivocation on the part of Hartley himself, who is here content, with an engaging and deceptive appearance of guilelessness, to confuse the reader utterly."[2]

*The Will and the Way* brings together the hunger for money, power, and status which has been the given of the bourgeois novel and the pastoral ground of life which may assuage that hunger by being independent of most human intervention and machination. Suspicious of the instinctual excesses of both lions and sheep, Hartley exhibits his customary ambivalence toward both bourgeois and pastoral alternatives, and synthesis eludes the strength of *The Will and the Way*. It is, however, an appropriate terminus in the Hartley canon, the last of a distinguished line of intricate studies where the aesthetic and moral pattern of life supports and embodies the novel's sense of life. Hartley's chase had a beast in view, a sheepish lion perhaps; and without always being able to distinguish sheep from goats (unlike those moral partisans, the Victorian novelists he admires), Hartley still brings rectitude to twentieth-century moral relativism to make his *oeuvre* all of a piece.

## CHAPTER 10

# The Novelist as Critic:
# The Novelist's Responsibility

## I   *The Writer's Apologia*

WHEN Peter Bien in the early nineteen-sixties published the first book-length study of L. P. Hartley, he lamented the absence of any collection of the novelist's extensive critical writings, mainly from English periodicals where Hartley had served many years as a reviewer. Also, during the nineteen-fifties after *The Go-Between* had achieved great success, Hartley presented numerous lectures both in England and abroad, at festivals like Aldeburgh, under the auspices of the British Council, the Foreign Office, and the like. Accordingly, Professor Bien culled a varied assortment of significant extracts from these sources, supplemented by his own interpretive glosses and links, to provide a quite comprehensive introduction to Hartley's critical temper which is unavailable elsewhere as a body of material (Bien, "Mr. Hartley as Critic," pp. 229 - 266). Hartley's habit of just estimation emerges forcefully in Bien's overview. Finally Hartley did bring out his single volume of literary criticism, comprising thirteen essays, under the general title, *The Novelist's Responsibility* (1967), interestingly enough without many of the pieces Bien surveyed. As Hartley's fiction does not forget that literature is about man and his costly choices, *The Novelist's Responsibility* further clarifies the moral impulse in Hartley through his consideration of other writers whose approaches complement his own. While, in a sense, *The Novelist's Responsibility* remains in the shallows of Hartley's own sensibility, his preference of persons to patterns and themes to structures—the text considered as neither sign nor code—vindicates the critical immediacy of his volume.

Rather patrician and detached, Hartley's criticism demonstrates a degree of fastidiousness (detractors might call it boring prissiness)

188

which reflects his recognition of human limitation. Like E. M. Forster, Hartley moves from the life by time to the life by values, and he judges the purpose, direction, decency, and worth of art as it affects life.

Hartley's moral consciousness is usually informed with human warmth and grace, or at least charm, hallmarks of the gentility which has seemed increasingly anachronistic since 1914, as Hartley repeatedly observes and yet in his own criticism habitually practices. However, while he esteems verbal tact and literary criticism in the manner of Flaubert, Hartley consistently goes beyond technique and aestheticism to the moral center of art. To be sure, the essays and lectures included in *The Novelist's Responsibility* may not add materially to L. P. Hartley's reputation; but they substantiate his commitment to the moral and social function of literature and reveal through his autobiographical honesty something of his own intentions as a writer, adumbrated in the emphasis he chooses in the analysis of other artists. His criticism witnesses to what Hartley finds artistically stimulating and morally provocative in their work. His criticism is non-competitive and sympathetic. Indeed, one of the keys to these pieces seems to be to salvage distinctive authors from the collectivist trend of the twentieth century. For that reason, *The Novelist's Responsibility* is akin to much of Hartley's previous and subsequent fiction, and especially close in spirit to *Facial Justice*, his most experimental work.

The title essay to this critical collection finds Hartley defining himself as a moralist, arguing that for the novelist, as was mentioned in an earlier chapter, something must matter,

or at any rate his characters must believe that something matters. The popular catchwords of today or yesterday—"It's just too bad," or "I couldn't care less," or "You've had it"—all suggest ironic acceptance of the inevitable, with the corollary that nothing really matters. I don't think that a novel *can* be written in that frame of mind, or any art worthy of the name be born from it. (*Novelist's Responsibility*, p. 16)

Being a moralist, Hartley knew that the human will, certainly including his own, is generally masked, that intentions are usually well-hidden even from ourselves and that therefore our noblest ideals and most selfless action may well be expressions of our more perverse and depraved wishes. The novelist's responsibility discovers the paradoxes attendant upon such recognition.

As between spiritual and moral concerns L. P. Hartley chooses the moral because "morality is a fact capable of being demonstrated whereas spirituality is a matter of guesswork." (*Novelist's Responsibility*, p. 9) Hence, while admiring Dostoyevsky for his great spiritual insight, Hartley writes novels in a Jamesian rather than a Russian tradition. Although he has been called both a symbolist and a romancer, Hartley's artistic credo, like his morality, seems solidly grounded in British empiricism:

> A novelist must give the impression of a world of external reality existing outside himself: if he mentions a table it must be a real table, and not an unsubstantial dream-table. And he must create a world which the reader can accept and live in, without feeling that it would dissolve like Prospero's if the author was not somewhere behind it. It must exist independently of the author's testimony, but not of his sensibility, not of his feeling for it, which must be as strong as, or stronger than, the feeling he has for his own life. (*Novelist's Responsibility*, p. 2)

Hartley places a high value on both the reality and the responsibility of a novel, two factors which have been increasingly undermined in the twentieth century. Readers of his fiction will find quite familiar Hartley's anguish over the loss of personal responsibility and accountability as well as his regret for the devaluation of the individual. He argues, as Stephen Hilliard did in "Eustace and Hilda" (p. 122), that "different as they are, the doctrines of Marx and Freud have combined to undermine the individual sense of personal responsibility" (*Novelist's Responsibility*, p. 10), inasmuch as they served as deterministic rejectors of free will—Marx according to cultural conditioning through social class and Freud through influences, pre-natal or infantile over which there is little individual control. "As individuals," Hartley ruefully acknowledges, "we can only expect about half of the interest and sympathy that the public would have given us before the First World War." (*Novelist's Responsibility*, p. 11)

Hartley explores the effect of these changed moral circumstances on the novelist and his material, especially the alteration of sympathy for fictional characters. He explains his own dilemma in the trilogy regarding Hilda, to whom he brought paralysis, in addition to seduction and abandonment, in order to win sympathy from the reader: "With stories of the atom bomb and the concentration camp, and the appalling sufferings they involved, fresh in people's minds how can the novelist win sympathy for a character who had, say, lost his money or his job or his wife, or even his life?"

(*Novelist's Responsibility*, p 11) Certainly, in an era of cataclysm and statistical death, involving tens of thousands, even millions, the liberal humanist faith in the intrinsic value of the individual is sorely tried, as C. B. Cox has shown.[1]

Hartley is profoundly disturbed that excellence itself has become suspect, because it is likely to arouse envy; and there is some currency to the notion that the human race must be made safe from envy. His *Facial Justice* supplies Hartley's devastatingly satirical response to that proposition. Further, he assails the legal defense of "diminished responsibility," as he does in several novels, and correctly assumes that such a plea leads to the cult of the anti-hero enshrined in contemporary fiction as well as in the statute books.

A companion essay to "The Novelist's Responsibility" is "The Novelist and His Material," a brief but pithy exposition which takes up once again some familiar complaints. Hartley decries, for example, the collectivist age, finding the queue the appropriate symbol of contemporary civilization, a formation designed to keep people literally and figuratively in their places. Moreover, Hartley laments that "the sense of sin has given way to an undifferentiated, almost impersonal sense of guilt, or it has completely disappeared. And even if the word 'fault' still carried with it the implication of personal responsibility that it once had, I doubt if it can be usefully applied to a situation which is the outcome of so many forces, scientific, economic, and other, the drift of which could not be foreseen." (*Novelist's Responsibility*, p. 185) Hartley is particularly disturbed that today's novelist feels obliged to put his worst foot forward, lest he arouse what Hartley calls "public envy," the consequences of which he projects in *Facial Justice*. He imputes to H. G. Wells and subsequent authors of his species the vogue of the Little Man, "the morally underprivileged," for whom sympathy and compassion are demanded on the grounds of "There but for the grace of God go I." (*Novelist's Responsibility*, p. 187) Hartley ends these remarks with a peroration which, besides illuminating some of the devices and intentions of *Facial Justice*, offers some guarded optimism on the future of humane values in the genre of the novel:

But the main danger is lest the individual, snowed under by the mass of suggestions, directions, orders, and ready-made designs for living to which he is exposed, should be submerged and lost in the community, so that his reactions and responses will become automatic and predictable, and protective colouring will make him indistinguishable from the rest. But I cannot help believing that this will not happen, and that an awareness of other people's personalities and their right to be themselves, and of one's dependence, for the fulfillment of one's own personality, on them as individuals—not just fellow-sufferers or fellow-criminals with identical faces—will survive, and with it the novel, which thrives on that belief. (*Novelist's Responsibility*, p. 190)

The earliest essay in *The Novelist's Responsibility* is "Some Aspects of Gregariousness," which was originally a paper read to an Oxford undergraduate society called the "Pagans" just after the First World War (Bien, p. 108), and the reader familiar with the Hartley canon juxtaposes that biographical detail with Hartley's portrayal of Eustace's undergraduate society in *The Sixth Heaven* to make a seamless web of life and art. In the essay Hartley remarks that gregariousness must be "indulged in sparingly, and only between adequate periods of solitude and quasi-solitude." (*Novelist's Responsibility*, p. 197) His suspicion of the herd instinct is a *donnée* of Hartley's career, early and late. He values, of course, "personal relations," and even the aesthetic relationships possible with inanimate objects—major themes in his fiction—but the inexhaustible moral vitality of the individual is Hartley's chief concern.

A rather negligible and patronizing little essay, "In Defense of the Short Story," scarcely illuminates either the genre or Hartley's achievement in short fiction. His argument on behalf of the short story, which perhaps is meant to be taken ironically, is that collections of short stories are a better "bargain," literarily, than the average novel. If almost anyone can write a novel, Hartley thinks it takes an artist to execute a short story. Although stories in a collection are discontinuous, he submits that the mind behind them is not. Therefore, Hartley endorses the pleasure of acquaintance with the unified achievement of Maupassant and Chekhov, or, more recently, of Maugham and H. E. Bates.

## II  *Practical Criticism: Hawthorne*

The pivot of Hartley's essays on particular authors is his monographlength study of Hawthorne, originally the Clark Lecture at Trinity College, Cambridge, in 1963, which reveals nearly as much about L. P. Hartley as it does about Nathaniel Hawthorne. For example, Hartley's terms of praise for Hawthorne's being one of the most individual and recognizable of novelists are thoroughly familiar as Hartleian norms. Hartley considers Hawthorne to have been a man more "sensitive to moral issues than to personal relationships or to social grades." (*Novelist's Responsibility*, p. 136)

Hawthorne's period of solitude fascinates Hartley, as do any number of incidental features of his biography. That Hawthorne had two sisters to whom he was devoted is dutifully noted (without autobiographical asides on Hartley's own familial parallel); Hawthorne's little natural zest for life is seen compensated for by his sense of duty—"His innate puritanism looked askance on inclination, or so it seems." (*Novelist's Responsibility*, p. 13) Hartley especially likes the way Hawthorne treats money, as faery gold, not gold that has been worked for, gold that is an object of existence, as it is in Balzac." (*Novelist's Responsibility*, p. 73) For a writer like Hartley who uses legacies and inherited incomes so frequently for his "unemployed" characters, moral status symbols of the kind found in *The Scarlet Letter* are far more appealing than Balzacian material ones.

Hartley provides from his own perspective a mitigating response to the primal sin of Pride which Hawthorne concentrated upon:

> The Church—all the Churches—have been against it—partly, I feel (as a staunch individualist), because the exercise of private judgment is an offense against whatever religious body one may happen to belong to. It is an assertion of the self against the superior authority of the many.
>
> I don't think that many people nowadays suffer from the sin of pride—one almost wishes they did, for at any rate, if it took the form of proper pride, it would prevent them from doing a great many of the things they do. The prevailing sin of our day, I should say, is dishonesty: I could fill books with instances of dishonesty that have come my way: the contractual basis of society is threatened by it. And I can hardly think of one instance of the sin of pride. (*Novelist's Responsibility*, p. 74)

On the other hand, Hartley obviously discovers a resemblance between Hawthorne's view of evil and his own:

> This view of Evil as something both inside us and outside us, the human condition, in fact, is implicit in most of Hawthorne's stories. It is the theme of *The Fall of Man*, told with many variations, and leading (in *The Marble Faun*) to the unorthodox conclusion that sin is as inevitable as sorrow, and must be accepted as part of the training of the soul on its way to a higher development: it has a regenerative power. (*Novelist's Responsibility*, p. 122)

It is this shared perception of the inevitability of sin and what can
be done with it that most specifically links Hawthorne and Hartley
as moralists together with the ambiguity of Hawthorne, the barrier
of humor and irony, as Hartley terms it, which he placed between
himself and direct experience. The similarly predisposed Hartley is
attracted to Mr. Facing-Both-Ways from Hawthorne's much-loved
and much-read copy of *Pilgrim's Progress* as an ideal emblem to
represent the author of *The Scarlet Letter*.

In his conception of Hawthorne as an apocalyptic novelist "who
felt that the very fabric of the earth is as unstable as it is presented
in the Book or Revelation" (*Novelist's Responsibility*, p. 129),
Hartley finds only one comparable English counterpart, and that is
another of his favorite authors, Emily Brontë; their affinity perhaps
more noticeable in the character of the two authors than in their
work, as Hartley skilfully develops salient biographical parallels. He
supplies a valuable contrast between the extent of social isolation in
the two authors as reflected in their two masterpieces:

> But the social background of *The Scarlet Letter*, though seldom de-
> scribed, makes itself continuously felt. In fact, the scarlet letter itself, as a
> symbol of sin, gets its force from the multitude of disapproving faces round
> it. Whereas in *Wuthering Heights* the community as a body that can con-
> demn or condone, or drop in for a chat, or can exert any influence what-
> soever on the lives of the Earnshaws, the Lintons and the Heathcliffs (for
> we must include Linton Heathcliff, one of the best-drawn characters in the
> book)—that community doesn't exist. The chief characters are far too much
> occupied with their own affairs to be even aware of social pleasures or
> pressures. (*Novelist's Responsibility*, p. 132)

After some appreciative comments on Hawthorne's diction as a
"timeless, classless, means of communication, available to all in any
walk of life, at any epoch" (*Novelist's Responsibility*, p. 136),
Hartley concludes his analysis of Hawthorne by acknowledging that
the man remains baffling, "the Sphinx that he wished, or was con-
demned, to be." (*Novelist's Responsibility*, p. 141) Along the way to
this conclusion, Hartley, however, has considered any number of
details about Nathaniel Hawthorne, as man, husband, father, and
writer. Hartley has described at some length Hawthorne's physical
attractiveness over and against the churlish remarks of Henry James
Senior on the novelist's appearance, and he has recorded the im-
pressive chest size of Julian Hawthorne, the novelist's son. He has
produced a rounded portrait of Hawthorne in terms of their shared
sense of the novelist's responsibility.

III  *Practical Criticism: Henry James, Emily Brontë, Jane Austen*

Nearly as illuminating for an understanding of Hartley as his extended discussion of Hawthorne is his brief essay on Henry James wherein a similar critical focus is transferred from Hawthorne to James, especially the Jamesian attention to art as an aspect of moral sense:

> In all his stories there is, if not a moral theme, a continual reference to moral judgment, sometimes delicate and almost flippant, as in *What Maisie Knew*; sometimes a trifle ambiguous, as in *The Ambassadors*, sometimes breathing fire and brimstone, as in *The Turn of the Screw*, and as it were the final touchstone of existence, as in *The Golden Bowl*. The rules of morality might be hard to find and as hard to practice as the rules of art, but they must be found and their working illustrated. Nor were they to be found in defiance of public opinion. In this James differed from the master of his youth, Nathaniel Hawthorne, who accepted conventional society but questioned its moral judgments. Henry James would never have written a novel which seemed to mitigate the sin of adultery. (*Novelist's Responsibility*, p. 182)

Hartley concentrates on Henry James's developmental years which he passed at Lamb House in Rye; these years were coincident with the publication of two of his best-loved novels (and, parenthetically, novels most similar to Hartley's), *The Spoils of Poynton* and *What Maisie Knew*. On a principal matter of technique, and Hartley the moralist is generally not so sensitive to differences in techniques as many critics, he observes that with the Jamesian renunciation of "omniscience" in *The Awkward Age*, which leaves the characters to make their own impression and tell their own tale, comes a departure in narrative method that has influenced nearly every serious novelist of the present day (in Elizabeth Bowen no less than Ivy Compton-Burnett, to use Hartley's examples and, though unstated, himself included). Furthermore, Hartley's contrast between the characters in the early James, like Daisy Miller and the Princess Casamassima, who can be thought of apart from their fictional contexts, and the late, tormented quartet in *The Golden Bowl*, whom he describes as "almost like unknown factors in a quadratic equation or lines in a parallelogram of forces" (*Novelist's Responsibility*, p. 180), has direct significance in his own novels with adult protagonists.

In examining "Emily Brontë in 'Gondal and Gaaldine,'" originally an address to the Emily Brontë Society, Hartley attempts

to vindicate what he considers to be the genuine emotion of
Brontë's poems (notwithstanding Edith Sitwell's evaluation to the
contrary): "They are the emotions of a rather weak, fearful, clinging, mood-and nerve-ridden personality, striving for unity of outlook. Certainly they are not the emotions that dominate *Wuthering
Heights*." (*Novelist's Responsibility*, p. 39) But, of course, these
emotions are quite familiar to the wishful or fearful thinking
characters in L. P. Hartley's fiction; and Hartley recognizes in Emily Brontë a kindred spirit who helped him to unite his material with
his sensibility. His biographical speculations on the Brontës are rich
and suggestive:

> How deeply had Emily anchored her hopes in Branwell, before she
> anchored them in Eternity? In her poems she speaks as as if he were
> dead—as indeed he was, the Branwell in whom all their hopes were
> centered. He was dead and the living Branwell was a monster whom the
> virtuous soul must shun. (*Novelist's Responsibility*, p. 52)

In the last analysis, Emily Brontë, even more than Hawthorne,
eludes definitive characterization; but Hartley shares with her an
ultimate conviction that human beings are more interesting by
themselves than in association or in relation to society.

Besides the foregoing remarks to the Emily Brontë Society,
Hartley includes in *The Novelist's Responsibility* comments on Jane
Austen, originally presented to the Jane Austen Society. When as a
schoolboy in 1913 he first read Austen, Hartley admits to having
been most impressed by her humor, "for I felt it was a kind of universal solvent, that could be applied to any experience and, by making it comic, could make it comprehensible and even enjoyable."
(*Novelist's Responsibility*, p. 21) Then during the First World War,
when civilized living of the sort embodied in Jane Austen had
seemingly vanished, his confidence in Jane Austen as an interpreter
of life was shaken. After the war Hartley returned to the romantic
mode of the Brontës; perhaps his enthusiasm for the sisters of
Haworth accounts partly for his criticism of Jane Austen's failure to
consider the irrational as a factor in human behavior. However, in
re-reading Jane Austen, Hartley writes, "what struck me most (and
this brings me back to the edge of the Abyss), is the sadness to be
found in all the novels, except perhaps in *Emma*. There is more
sunshine than shadow, of course, but there is more shadow than I
remembered from my confident pre-war days." (*Novelist's Responsibility*, p. 26)

Hartley persuasively argues that at least one Austen novel, *Sense and Sensibility*, has a tragic element (notably in the character of Marianne Dashwood) missing in some of the other novels. Once more Hartley is drawn to Marianne's "determination to go her own way and be herself" (*Novelist's Responsibility*, p. 32), matched with a sensibility for falling leaves nearly the equal of Emily Brontë's. It seems apparent, to L. P. Hartley, that Jane Austen was acquainted with the night, and possibly the Abyss, after all.

IV   *Practical Criticism: L. H. Myers, C. H. B. Kitchin,*
*The Sitwells*

Hartley's narrowness of focus in literary criticism works best in the essays dealing with minor authors of the twentieth century who resembled him artistically in some ways and who often were his friends, although this autobiographical fact is rarely included.

On L. H. Myers's tetralogy, *The Near and the Far*, Hartley identifies the singularity of another distinctive and complex writer in terms which mirror himself also: "Very seldom does Myers present emotions, even those of love and hate, in the raw: they are remembered in tranquility, softened by the author's enfolding sensibility, and dimmed by veils of ambiguity and doubt: for in this book things are seldom what they seem." (*Novelist's Responsibility*, p. 146) Hartley takes note of L. H. Myers's chronic hypochrondia and the fact that many of his characters reflect his preoccupation with ill health, a condition not unknown in Hartley's own novels. Yet what he considers the great moral strength of Myers is that out of fictitious events supposedly taking place in India during the sixteenth century, L. H. Myers illuminates the fundamental problems of good and evil, which are equally relevant to the twentieth century. Hartley, however, prefers the visionary and mystical Myers of the first three novels of the tetralogy where "we could not easily say on whose side the author is" (*Novelist's Responsibility*, p. 147) to the revolutionary and crypto-Communist Myers of the last volume, *The Pool of Vishnu*. The exotic and romantic settings of L. H. Myers's fiction obviously appeal to Hartley more compellingly than the conflicting creeds and philosophies embodied in the character in the novels.

The tribute to the neglected novels of Hartley's friend, Clifford Kitchin, whose work very much resembles his own, is a kind of watershed for a number of themes developed throughout the essays in *The Novelist's Responsibility*, as in the following quotation:

This interplay of gregariousness and isolation is central to Mr. Kitchin's thought and it becomes increasingly marked in *Olive E* and *Birthday Party*. These reflect, by reaction, the political tendencies of the times. Though not a thorough-going reactionary Mr. Kitchin is a passionate individualist, and as such loathes all forms of collectivism, compulsion and state control, whether Communist, Fascist or simply bureaucratic. With these, as enemies of the spirit, he couples Science. (*Novelist's Responsibility*, p. 151)

In addition, C. H. B. Kitchin explores his characters' fantasies in a manner reminiscent of Ronald Firbank but with a degree of reasonableness probably closer to L. P. Hartley. The questions Hartley raises about Kitchin's Mr. Balcony would seem to have equal relevance for some of his own characters:

What will come of his singular experiment in self-perversion, his determination to make himself precisely what Nature had not intended him to be? And how will it affect his guests on the yacht? Which is uppermost in him, the bully or the benefactor? He is not the only character in Mr. Kitchin's novels to use his wealth to experiment with other people's lives. (*Novelist's Responsibility*, p. 150)

Hartley remarks that love of flowers is at the heart of C. H. B. Kitchin's outlook on life, and he cites the importance of flowers as symbols and motifs in his fiction. Perhaps Kitchin as well as Hawthorne inspired the cineraria used to such good effect in Hartley's *Facial Justice:*

To the collectivizing ideologies of those days (and these) with their insistence on a uniform view of life, to the anodyne of mass feeling and mass thinking, [Kitchin] opposes his belief in the spiritual restorative power of the individual's private response to his material environment. (*Novelist's Responsibility*, p. 152)

Hartley's most enthusiastic assessment is given Kitchin's *The Auction Sale* for its treatment of Art and Nature as productive of spiritual solace though not sufficient as the basis of a religion or even a philosophy. It is as a love-story that Hartley finds *The Auction Sale* most poignant and satisfying. Regrettably, this essay was written prior to publication of Kitchin's *Jumping Joan*, a collection of macabre short stories, and the four novels that appeared before Kitchin's death in 1967. The final book, *The Book of Life*, invites comparison with *The Go-Between*, and for that reason alone it is unfortunate that Hartley did not supply a postscript to "The Novels of C. H. B. Kitchin."

The transition is fairly easy from Kitchin and Myers to the noble and highly individual Sitwells, Dame Edith and Sir Osbert—the fifth holder of the hereditary baronetcy—two vast spirits of independence, fantasy, and perception who understandably appeal to L. P. Hartley. In his review of Sir Osbert Sitwell's multi-volume autobiography, beginning with *Left Hand, Right Hand!*, Hartley describes Osbert Sitwell as "the most pervasive figure in the drama of an age which reached its zenith in 1914 and has since traced a downward curve." (*Novelist's Responsibility*, p. 161) Sir Osbert was able to fly on wings of fantasy and imagination over the arid terrain of modern uniformity, as he put to use both his inherited and acquired talents and eccentricities, his left and right hands respectively. Hartley finds reason for joy in the best-selling success of Sir Osbert's autobiography, for despite the usual Sitwell disapproval of the Common Man, the readership of this volume embraces a broad spectrum of cultures and class:

> The importance of this can hardly be overestimated, for it means that the ever-widening gap between the high-brow and the low-brow—the gap that was threatening art itself with extinction—has at last been bridged. No longer need we feel that readers are divided into two nations, self-consciously aware of and hostile to each other, for here they have met on common ground. Most of the credit must go to Sir Osbert who has known how to make these incompatibles acceptable to each other, but some is due to the public too, for having learned from the author a lesson in connoisseurship which was all the harder to learn because it involved a certain amount of self-criticism. That a great imaginative writer may now hope to address himself to the many as well as to the few is surely a happy augury for the future of English literature. (*Novelist's Responsibility*, p. 166)

On Dame Edith Sitwell's achievement, Hartley establishes a provocative dichotomy between her prose and poetry. He compares her work in prose to Ronald Firbank and attempts to remove the more pejorative connotations from the adjective *artificial* often used to describe her style:

> The artificial is only to be avoided if it is a substitute for the real, and not always then. If it is used, as Miss Sitwell used it from the first, as her brothers used it and as Ronald Firbank used it to heighten the reality of an object or an idea, to surprise it into a new vividness of meaning—then there can be no objection of artificiality. (*Novelist's Responsibility*, p. 173)

Hartley appreciates Dame Edith's prose style, not for its eccentricity or frivolity, but for its individuality. Implicit in his comparison of it to Firbank's, is Hartley's view that the prose of Edith Sitwell is yet another ornament of the Edwardian period.

When he turns to her verse, however, Hartley takes a graver tone; for he considers her later poetry, heralded by "Still Falls the Rain," "Lullaby," "Street Song," and "Serenade," to offer serious interpretations of contemporary moral conditions—those very conditions which in other contexts he concludes are nearly impossible for a novelist to deal with. By indirection and example, Hartley answers Hölderlin's desperate question of what poets are for in a destitute age or time in the following tribute to Dame Edith Sitwell's later poems:

They stand up to the most terrible phenomena of the present day, the atom bomb and concentration camp; they are indeed the only poems of our time that accept the challenge of the war, that look not unmoved, but undismayed. (*Novelist's Responsibility*, p. 173)

While this judgment is doubtless too partisan on behalf of a controversial poet, Hartley persuasively credits Edith Sitwell with the recognition, without despair, of the ultimate cold within the human heart. Alas, the manifestations of that cold have been all too frequent in the twentieth century, as Hartley notes.

## V  "Remembering Venice": The Venetian Connection

The final essay in this curiously autobiographical volume of literary criticism is neither about general literary concerns nor on a specific author; it is a remembrance of Venice, the city where L. P. Hartley passed the happiest portions of his best years. He begins the reminiscence with characteristic and ingratiating perplexity, "I lived there for many years, but I doubt if even now I could find the way from the Piazza to the railway station." (*Novelist's Responsibility*, p. 209) In an earlier essay, Hartley confesses that he was once an amateur gondolier, but in "Remembering Venice" he is quick to defer to his gondolier, Giacomo.

The evocation of the special relationship between employer and chauffeur so common in Hartley assumes added panache from the scenes the author offers of himself with his gondolier:

In spring, the voluptuous nightingales shouted from the thickets all through the heat of the day. After lunch we played a Venetian card game called *briscola*, a simple digestive game less exacting than the intellectual, memory-straining *tre-sette,* or the fascinating but maddening *Gi-la-Greca,* a kind of poker—the point of which was to lose your temper and show it, otherwise the game lost its savour. Like poker it 'belonged to the bluffer', and I could generally win: but so ignobly, that all the zest went out of it. Then, after a siesta, I turned to my book and he to his newspaper—that newspaper which, with others of its kidney, has made so much bad blood between our countries. (*Novelist's Responsibility,* p. 214)

Hartley views Venice and its inhabitants as a work of art: "To the eye and the mind the streets of Venice are a perpetual refreshment." (*Novelist's Responsibility,* p. 211) From his residence on the south side of the city opposite the Church of San Sebastiano where, he notes, Paolo Veronese is buried, Hartley contrasts the cheerful bustling thoroughfare, the *Zattere,* which he compares to a noisy symphony, with the corresponding promenade on the north side of Venice, the *Fondamente Nuove,* which he sees always in the shadow, occupied by only a few people, and suggestive of a Chopin nocturne. Given the almost operatic ambience of Venice, Hartley's free association of the different arts in his remembrance of the city seems remarkably apt, if a trifle baroque.

Hartley's feelings for Venice, a city with a philosophy of sovereignty which is wholly inappropriate to her reduced place in the modern world, are similar to the sensibility he revealed toward literary favorites. Indeed, as a city where it is sometimes difficult to distinguish between truth and fantasy, Venice reflects a number of Hartley's concerns and themes; however, Hartley does not approach the city in this vein, although the reader may well make the inference. But surely Hartley would understand and probably agree with Jan Morris's description of Venice:

Venice long ago lost her way. Built for autocracy and empire, she flounders messily through the shallows of democratic purpose, confused by dissension, corruption and uncertainty. The long, long decline continues, and with each passing year, each inconclusive debate, her robust reality fades still further, and she exists simply to be.[2]

The ending of "Remembering Venice" crystallizes the city, and by extension the world of the twentieth century, in Hartley's evocation of Saint Sebastian pierced with arrows, on the marble facade of the church outside his window:

I thought that his attitude, which though operatic suggests more physical pain than do most representations of the twice-martyred saint, had no message now for the happy, kindly, easygoing throng who chattered their way beneath him. But during the few years that have passed since I saw him, he has become a symbol of mankind. (*Novelist's Responsibility*, p. 214)

That Hartley once more alludes covertly to the melancholy crises of the twentieth century (to which he has referred throughout the essays in *The Novelist's Responsibility*) relates Venice's make-believe to contemporary reality. How strangely appropriate, then, is an essay remembering Venice—a city which very well may not survive into the next century because of high tides, air pollution, and real estate speculations—as a valedictory to Hartley's collection of criticism.

## VI   *A Critical Summing-up*

Hartley as a critic brings literary sensitivity and a developed sense of moral rectitude to critical discourse. If neither in criticism nor in his fiction does Hartley's voice succumb to violence, vulgarity, or the even more unruly emotions, it is sufficient to recall that he has recognized the dislocations of contemporary history, which prevent him, as does his moral consciousness, from pursuing a purely aesthetic attitude toward life. Although some of the thirteen essays in the collection are slight, taken together (and with apparent deliberateness they are meant to be taken together), they have an accumulative power which surpasses their interest individually. Most pleasant of all is the discovery of the somewhat diffident, but still forthright, figure of L. P. Hartley himself in these essays. *The Novelist's Responsibility* becomes more than a small gathering of reviews and addresses chosen from a vast store of possible entries; it is better conceived as a memoir, however guarded, made with good art—Hartley's own and that of others who have elicited from him a critical (and personal) response. These essays offer a summary of assumptions, interests and aims of a long creative life. L. P. Hartley appears in them as a distinctive and coherent minor master of the twentieth-century English essay.

# CHAPTER 11

# *Conclusion*

L P. HARTLEY uncovers in his *oeuvre* the classic constant—the ages of man, conceived according to a holistic approach to the individual as characteristic of the Eriksonian life-cycle as it is of the Sir Thomas Browne who speaks in the following:

> Confound not the distinctions of thy Life which Nature hath divided, that is, Youth, Adolescence, Manhood, and old Age; nor in these divided Periods, wherein thou art in a manner Four, conceive thy self but One. Let every division be happy in its proper Virtues, nor one Vice run through all. Let each distinction have its salutary transition, and critically deliver thee from the imperfections of the former, so ordering the whole, that Prudence and Virtue may have the largest Section. . . . He who hath not taken leave of the follies of his Youth, and in his maturer state scarce got out of that division, disproportionately divideth his Days, crowds up the latter part of his Life, and leaves too narrow a corner for the Age of Wisdom, and so hath room to be a Man scarce longer than he hath been a Youth.[1]

Such wholeness, to be sure, is never easy; and Hartley's special sensitivity to the tentative adolescent and the unsure adult trying to attain it represents a unique achievement in modern literature. Throughout his career, Hartley's ethos offers an alternative to mass society and conformity to a life-style bereft of moral definition. The remarkably acute psychologist which he was never submerged the equally compelling Hartleian moralist who believed that happiness cannot be a function of society but the responsibility of the individual and his own moral and emotional integrity.

At his best, like E. M. Forster, Hartley brings together poignant symbolism and significant verisimilitude. "Few writers," states Michael B. Willmott, "can match his [Hartley's] integration of realism—realism of character, of society, and of emotion—with an underlying and diffusive symbolism."[2] His mingling of realism and romance enjoys a particularly rich tradition in England, of course, extending backwards at least to Shakespeare. Interestingly enough, the nearer Hartley comes to portraying adult characters in contemporary moral choices, the less he relies on the resources of symbolism, as if the burden of the adult present was, after all, lighter for him to handle than the distant childhoods of the past.

If Hartley's canon can be seriously faulted, it is that his fiction, Prufrockian-like, seems to be moving toward some overwhelming question (about love, identity, good and evil, fantasy and fact) that is never quite phrased, let alone answered. Had Hartley been a true romancer, and not a novelist, his thematic unity might have been greater. Because the novel is notoriously more resistant than the romance to neat integrating visions, Hartley cannot altogether harmonize outward institutions and inward constitutions.

Frequently, Hartley's characters, whom he treats realistically, have romantic outlooks on life; and through them the novels gain romantic effect. Nevertheless, Hartley continually tests these characters' preconceived and romantic ideas of life and usually finds them deficient for coping with reality. As a novelist Hartley sees his characters related to society and unable to escape. His characters have to adjust to society, however uncomfortable, in whatever way they can after they realize their misconceptions. At most, he uses certain romantic means, assimilating, in turn, poetic metaphors and key symbols, the melodrama and near-allegories of romance, to achieve the novelistic end of penetrating realism, establishing continuity between events and the characters' sense of them. Granted, the numerous benefactresses for Hartley's young men partake of the quality of the fairy godmother beloved in romance; yet their influence goes only so far, and eventually each one of his protagonists has to face life and reality by himself. Thus Hartley uses art derived from both the novel and romance not to copy life but to represent it.

To quibble over the applicability of major versus minor as a value judgment on Hartley's place in modern British fiction seems less germane than to echo Gilbert Phelps to the effect that Hartley, like Ivy Compton-Burnett, must be regarded as one of the few writers who came "into prominence since the war [Second World War] whom one can mention in the company of the great novelists of the past without too great a sense of incongruity."[3] The tentativeness and tone of Phelps' assessment seems wholly appropriate to describe Hartley's contribution to the continuity of the English novel.

Like his collectors in the later novels, Hartley as a writer is a kind of conservator, a custodian of the genres of fiction which he transfers to others for future guardianship after having modestly demonstrated his own trusteeship. Out of this sense of artistic continuity and possibly religious faith as well, Hartley implies guarded optimism that humanity and its culture will somehow survive. His occasional note of asperity, reminiscent of the curmudgeonly irritation of an old Tory, or maybe better a civilized Whig, yields to hope for the individual when human action allies itself with divine purpose. Neither England nor Hartley's characters can do without the historic Church, which survives, at least in a lone tower, even the dystopian mood and disillusionment of *Facial Justice*. Insofar as Hartley invokes or presupposes an overruling Power in human life, he does so most often obliquely through omnipresent cathedrals and occasional words which bear their relation to the Word. His characters, sometimes without knowing it, continue to live on the accumulated capital of the Christian centuries.

As the foregoing pages have tried to show, Hartley entertains a number of controversial undercurrents in his fiction, from incest to homosexuality, without completely facing them. Whether out of fear, natural reticence, gentility, or repugnance, his treatment of these topics remains shadowy, though provocative. That he introduces them at all suggests a willingness on his part to confront reality with candor and even some measure of daring. Indeed, as Hartley moves from symbolic showing in the early novels to more direct telling in the later ones, the distance may be charted of how Edwardian man becomes fully later twentieth-century humanity. While Hartley belongs partly by temperament to the age he came out of and, for that reason, may seem almost anachronistically Jamesian, he looks at the new order of things in middle life and old age with more readiness to change than has usually been supposed. He upholds for his characters the necessity to develop, to discover and realize the potential self, both in the core of the individual and in his culture. Rather than seeing only arbitrary and hostile social conventions in the external world beyond the self, Hartley discovers therein indispensable factors in and for individual development, analogous to Erik Erikson's discovery through the life-cycle. In the later novels, personal stability no longer appears conditional upon lack of social change; nor is it sustained by fantasy or wish-fulfillment but by the primacy of experiential insight and action. At last, Hartley manages to sound neither sarcastic about the present nor elegiac about the past. His greater novels, admittedly, are the

earlier symbolic ones—for their texture alone—yet these should not
be seen in isolation but in fruitful communion with the later, albeit
lesser, novels.

L. P. Hartley endures, then, as a worthy twentieth-century English writer of taste and tact whose sophisticated accommodation of
human nature and tolerance for eccentricity place him in a
venerable English humanist tradition but whose moral rigor
somewhat transcends that tradition. There may be better
wordsmiths who can turn a more startling phrase or invent more
jolting plots; but few contemporary writers can equal Hartley's portrayals of the romantic temperament caught in the shifting,
equivocal nature of the past vis-à-vis the present or his humor and
compassion in exploring the ironies of the English class system.
Because of the circumscription of Hartley's experience, critics have
the right to speculate as to his contact with the "world." But lest
they forget, his narrow experience is also the raw material from
which he built his aesthetic and moral methods that are so powerful
and exact; and with these methods he created his often beautiful
novels with their incisive understanding of human life and finely
drawn unity of effect of what modern man has been, is, and perhaps
will be. Most of his novels deal in one way or another with the
spiritual and material inheritance from the past as it flounders in
the present or the vanity of the human wish to find meaning in life
by forcing spirit into objects or sensations. Rarely does Hartley succumb to the overanalyzed quality that has overtaken experimental
interior novels in modern fiction, even as he remains largely a
novelist of sensibility.

In illuminating the anxiety and fear which accompany fastidious
worldliness, Hartley, who refused to do anything unbecoming simply to get attention, adroitly captures the uncertainties of the times
as they have affected even the privileged and secure. In small
domestic dilemmas is reflected the larger history of twentieth-
century nations. Hartley speaks, therefore, for many more than a
small number of similarly disposed Englishmen; his endorsement of
individuality rings true quite apart from insular caste consciousness.
That little world becomes a microcosm of contemporary attitudes
and lives, and Hartley's artistic probity attains moral force in the
truths he tells of and to his century. What more could be asked of
an unpretentious *oeuvre* which diffidently began late but cut surprisingly deep? Finally, in Hartley, there evolves more concern for
life itself than for a way of life.

L. P. Hartley belongs with those English novelists who manifest the inner strength of a dense and rooted past. Like others who come to mind—P. H. Newby, Henry Green, Elizabeth Bowen, for example, he is often underrated or classed with eccentrics. Such attitudes confirm an author's place in literary history as something less than major; however, they may also recognize the true artist who does not write for commercial success but for cultivation of a distinctive and well-wrought literary garden—and maybe a little glory. Hartley's insularity, then, his certainty of boundaries, is characteristically English like the geography of the blessed plot, England herself. Passionately devoted to Nathaniel Hawthorne though he was, Hartley's sense of reality, together with his irony and affection, remained on the English side of the Atlantic, where daily concerns are more readily seen as episodes in civilization and where the unreconciled struggle between instinctive impulses and puritanical imperatives antedated Hawthorne and even the landing on Plymouth Rock. Despite the confusion of values in contemporary society between what is and what is not worthwhile, Hartley demonstrates in novel after novel that moral choices can and must be made—for the novelist should believe that something matters, as Hartley does. And, more to the point, he makes us through the art of his fiction share that belief, principally in the significance of humanity. L. P. Hartley deserves the attention of a continuing and expanding readership.

# Notes and References

## Chapter One

1. Clifford H. B. Kitchin, "Leslie Hartley—A Personal Angle," *Adam International Review*, Nos. 294-295-296 (1961), 8. These issues of *Adam International Review* are devoted exclusively to L. P. Hartley. Subsequent references to the Kitchin essay will be included in parentheses in the text.

2. Paul Bloomfield, "L. P. H.: Short note on a great subject," *Adam International Review*, Nos. 294-295-296 (1961), 6. Subsequent references to Bloomfield's remarks will be included in parentheses in the text.

3. L. P. Hartley, autobiographical statement to "Three Wars," in *Promise of Greatness: The War of 1914 - 18*, ed. George A. Panichas (New York: The John Day Co., 1968), p. 250.

4. Millicent Bell, "Jamesian Being," *The Virginia Quarterly Review*, 52 (Winter 1976), p. 128.

5. C. M. Bowra, *Memories 1898 - 1939* (Cambridge, Mass.: Harvard University Press, 1966), pp. 116 - 117.

6. L. P. Hartley, "Three Wars," in *Promise of Greatness: The War of 1914 - 18*, ed. George A. Panichas (New York: The John Day Co., 1968), p. 255. All subsequent references are included in parentheses in the text.

7. J. W. Lambert, "L. P. Hartley: A Tribute," *The Sunday Times*, December 17, 1972. All subsequent references to the Lambert tribute are included in parentheses in the text.

8. Richard Jones, "Kensington Ghosts," *The Listener*, November 7, 1968, p. 618.

## Chapter Two

1. The "Jamesian" interpreters include: Walter Allen, *The Modern Novel in Britain and the United States* (New York: Dutton, 1964); Peter Bien, *L. P. Hartley* (University Park: The Pennsylvania State University Press, 1963); Paul Bloomfield, *L. P. Hartley*, rev. and enlarged edition, Writers and Their Work: No. 217 (London: Longmans Group Ltd. for the British Council, 1970). The "Hawthornesque" interpreters include: Anne Mulkeen, *Wild Thyme, Winter Lightning: The Symbolic Novels of L. P. Hartley* (Detroit: Wayne State University Press, 1974); Giorgio Melchiori, "The English Novelist and the American Tradition," *Sewanee Review* 68 (1960), 502 - 515; J. P. Vernier, "La Trilogie romanesque de L. P. Hartley," *Etudes anglaises*, 13 (1960), 26 - 31. All subsequent references to these works will be in parentheses in the text.

2. Richard Ellmann, "Two Faces of Edward," *Golden Codgers: Biographical Speculations* (New York and London: Oxford University Press, 1973), pp. 113 - 131. Subsequent references to this work are included in parentheses in the text.

3. Kenneth Allsop, *The Angry Decade: A Survey of the Cultural Revolt of the Nineteen Fifties* (London: Peter Owen Ltd., 1964), p. 34.

4. Lord David Cecil, "The Forms of English Fiction," *The Fine Art of Reading and Other Literary Studies* (Indianapolis: Bobbs-Merrill, 1957), pp. 127 - 146.

5. James Hall, "Games of Apprehension: L. P. Hartley," *The Tragic Comedians: Seven Modern British Novelists* (Bloomington: Indiana University Press, 1963), pp. 111 - 128. Subsequent references to this work will be included in parentheses within the text.

6. L. P. Hartley, "The Novelist's Responsibility," in *The Novelist's Responsibility: Lectures and Essays* (London: Hamish Hamilton Ltd., 1967), p. 8.

7. Henry James, *Hawthorne.* English Men of Letters, ed. John Morley. reprint of 1879 edition (New York: Macmillan and Co., 1887), p. 133.

8. See Erik H. Erikson, "The Life Cycle: Epigenesis of Identity," in *Identity: Youth and Crisis* (New York: W. W. Norton, 1968), pp. 91 - 141. The more succinct statement is found in "Eight States of Man," in *Childhood and Society* (New York: W. W. Norton, 1950), pp. 219 - 234. Subsequent references to these two works will be included in parentheses within the text.

9. William J. Bouwsma, "Christian Adulthood," *Daedalus*, 105 (Spring 1976), pp. 77 - 92. Subsequent references to this article will be included in parentheses within the text.

10. The phrase is borrowed from Harvey Curtis Webster, "L. P. Hartley: Diffident Christian," *After the Trauma: Representative British Novelists since 1920* (Lexington: The University Press of Kentucky, 1970), pp. 152 - 167.

11. Lord David Cecil, Forward to *The Collected Stories of L. P. Hartley* (London: Hamish Hamilton Ltd., 1968), p. v.

12. Northrop Frye, *The Secular Scripture: A Study of the Structure of Romance* (Cambridge, Mass.: Harvard University Press, 1976), p. 58. Subsequent references to this work will be included within parentheses in the text.

13. John Lukacs, *The Passing of the Modern Age* (New York: Harper and Row, 1970), p. 82.

14. John Bayley, "Character and Consciousness," *New Literary History*, 5 (Winter, 1974), pp. 225 - 235.

*Chapter Three*

1. All references to Hartley's short stories in this ·chapter are to the following edition with page references included in parentheses within the

text: *L. P. Hartley, The Complete Short Stories,* with an Introduction by Lord David Cecil (London: Hamish Hamilton, 1973).

2. Howard Phillips Lovecraft, *Supernatural Horror in Literature* (New York: Dover Publications, Inc., 1973), p. 15. Subsequent references to this work are included in the text with page numbers in parentheses.

3. Sigmund Freud, "The 'Uncanny,' *Collected Papers,* Vol. 4 (New York: Basic Books, Inc., 1959), p. 399.

### Chapter Four

1. The following Faber paper covered editions of the *Eustace and Hilda* trilogy have been used in this chapter with page references placed in parentheses following the quotations in the text: L. P. Hartley, *The Shrimp and the Anemone* (London: Faber and Faber, 1965); *The Sixth Heaven* (London: Faber and Faber, 1964); *Eustace and Hilda* (London: Faber and Faber, 1965).

2. The legend of St. Eustace is a popular one in England, and it has some particular relevance to the development of the character of Eustace in Hartley's trilogy. St. Eustace, originally known as Placidus, was a captain of the guards to the Emperor Trajan. According to his legend, one day, while hunting, he saw before him a white stag with a crucifix between its antlers. Placidus, hearing the words of Christ addressed to him from the cross, became a Christian, as did his family. They were all subsequently martyred. St. Eustace is usually represented as a soldier or knight on horseback, the iconographic role Eustace Cherrington assigns Dick Stavely by the end of the first volume; Stavely is an inveterate huntsman much in need of a patron saint, but young Eustace turns out to be a poor substitute for St. Eustace. See George Ferguson, *Signs and Symbols in Christian Art* (New York: Oxford University Press, 1961), pp. 117 - 118.

3. Martin Seymour-Smith, "L. P. Hartley," *Who's Who in Twentieth-Century Literature* (New York: Hold, Rinehart and Winston, 1976), p. 152.

4. See Joseph C. Pattison, "Point of View in Hawthorne," *PMLA*, 82 (October, 1967), pp. 363 - 369.

5. Iris Murdoch, "Against Dryness," *Encounter*, 16 (January, 1961), pp. 16 - 20.

6. George Eliot, "Brother and Sister," *Poems* Vol. 2 (New York: Merrill and Baker, n.d.), pp. 169 - 170.

### Chapter Five

1. The editions used in this chapter are the following: L. P. Hartley, *The Boat* (London: Putnam, 1949); *My Fellow Devils* (New York: British Book Centre, 1959); *A Perfect Woman* (London: Hamish Hamilton, 1955). Page references from these editions will be placed in parentheses following quotations within the text.

2. John Henry Cardinal Newman, *Apologia Pro Vita Sua*, ed. David J. DeLaura (New York: W. W. Norton, 1968), p. 190.

3. See Bien, Chapter VI, n.    3, p. 280, which reads, in part: "Nick is a somewhat idiosyncratic Adam, being a homosexual. Mr. Hartley keeps the barrister's inversion completely hidden at first, and when he does finally reveal 'the schoolboy attachment' between Nick and Colum. . . , he does so in an off-hand manner, almost in passing. 'All this . . . is *in* in the book.' Mr. Hartley states [Letter 7 to Mr. Bien] 'but I played it down as much as I could, because I didn't want to write a specifically 'homosexual novel', and I didn't want to suggest that Colum was wicked because of his homosexuality.' "

4. See, for example, Jerome Hamilton Buckley, "The Pattern of Conversion," *The Victorian Temper* (New York Vintage, 1964), pp. 87 - 108.

## Chapter Six

1. The editions used in this chapter are the following: L. P. Hartley, *The Go-Between* (London: Hamish Hamilton, 1953); *The Brickfield* (London: Hamish Hamilton, 1964); *The Betrayal* (London: Hamish Hamilton, 1966). Page references from these editions will be placed in parentheses following quotations in the text.

2. Stephen Spender, "The Cult of Joe," *The New York Review of Books*, 23 (September 16, 1976), p. 28.

## Chapter Seven

1. L. P. Hartley, "Jane Austen," in *The Novelist's Responsibility: Essays and Lectures* (London: Hamish Hamilton, 1967), pp. 19 - 34. All subsequent references to this collection will be within parentheses in the text.

2. The editions used in this chapter are the following: L. P. Hartley, *Facial Justice* (New York: Curtis Books, n.d.); *The Love-Adept* (London: Hamish Hamilton, 1969). Page references from these editions will be cited in parentheses within the text.

3. Anthony Burgess, *The Novel Now: A Student's Guide to Contemporary Fiction* (London: Faber and Faber, 1967), p. 45.

4. Robert Scholes, *Structural Fabulation: An Essay on Fiction of the Future* (Notre Dame, Ind.: University of Notre Dame Press, 1975), p. 24.

5. On the matter of receptional aesthetics applied to reader identification with the hero, see Hans Robert Jauss, "Levels of Identification of Hero and Audience," *New Literary History*, 5 (Winter 1974), pp. 283 - 317.

## Chapter Eight

1. The following editions were used in this chapter: L. P. Hartley, *Simonetta Perkins*, in *The Collected Short Stories of L. P. Hartley* (London: Hamish Hamilton, 1968), pp. 3 - 55; *The Hireling* (London: Hamish

Hamilton, 1957); *The Harness Room* (London: Hamish Hamilton, 1971). References to these editions are included in parentheses within the text.

### Chapter Nine

1. The editions used in this chapter are the following: L. P. Hartley, *Poor Clare* (London: Hamish Hamilton, 1969); *My Sisters' Keeper* (London: Hamish Hamilton, 1970); *The Collections* (London: Hamish Hamilton, 1972); *The Will and the Way* (London: Hamish Hamilton, 1973). References to these editions are cited in parentheses within the text.

2. Diane Johnson, "Heirs Apparent," review of *The Will and the Way*, *New Statesman*, 13 April 1973, pp. 555 - 556.

### Chapter Ten

1. On historical circumstances as they have affected English novelists, including L. P. Hartley, see C. B. Cox, *The Free Spirit: A Study of Liberal Humanism in the Novels of George Eliot, Henry James, E. M. Forster, Virginia Woolf, Angus Wilson* (London: Oxford University Press, 1963), pp. 133, 172.

2. Jan Morris, "Let Her Sink," *The New York Times Magazine* (July 20, 1975), p. 14.

### Chapter Eleven

1. Sir Thomas Browne, *Christian Morals*, Part III, Sect. 8, *The Works of Sir Thomas Browne*, ed. Geoffrey Keynes, Vol. I (London: Faber and Gwyer, 1928), p. 138.

2. Michael B. Willmott, " 'What Leo Knew', The Childhood World of L. P. Hartley," *English* [London], 24 (1975), pp. 3 - 10.

3. Gilbert Phelps, "The Novel Today," in *The Modern Age* (The Pelican Guide to English Literature, Vol. 7), ed. Boris Ford (Baltimore: Penguin Books, 1964), p. 481.

# Selected Bibliography

PRIMARY SOURCES

*Night Fears and Other Stories.* London and New York: G. P. Putnam's Sons, 1924.

*Simonetta Perkins.* London and New York: G. P. Putnam's Sons, 1925; 2nd ed. London: James Barrie, 1952; London: Hamish Hamilton, 1957.

*The Killing Bottle.* London and New York: G. P. Putnam's Sons, 1932.

*The Shrimp and the Anemone.* London: Putnam and Co. Ltd., 1944; published as *The West Window.* Garden City, New York: Doubleday Doran and Co., Inc., 1945; London: Faber paper covered Edition, 1963.

*The Sixth Heaven.* London: Putnam and Co., Ltd., 1946; New York: Doubleday, 1947; London: Faber paper covered Edition, 1964.

*Eustace and Hilda.* London: Putnam and Co., Ltd., 1947; London: Faber paper covered Edition, 1965; *Eustace and Hilda: a Trilogy*, collected ed. London: Putnam, 1958; New York: The British Book Centre, 1958.

*The Traveling Grave and Other Stories.* Sauk City, Wisconsin: Arkham House, 1948; London: James Barrie, 1951; London: Hamish Hamilton, 1957.

*The Boat.* London: Putnam and Co., 1949; Garden City, New York: Doubleday, 1950; London: Hamish Hamilton, 1961.

*My Fellow Devils.* London: James Barrie, 1951; London: Hamish Hamilton, 1957; New York: The British Book Centre, 1959.

*The Go-Between.* London: Hamish Hamilton, 1953; New York: Knopf, 1954; Harmondsworth: Penguin Books, 1958; New York: The British Book Centre, 1959; New York: Stein and Day, 1967; New York: Avon, 1968.

*The White Wand and Other Stories.* London: Hamish Hamilton, 1954.

*A Perfect Woman.* London: Hamish Hamilton, 1955; New York: Knopf, 1956; Harmondsworth: Penguin Books, 1959.

*The Hireling.* London: Hamish Hamilton, 1957; New York: Rinehart, 1958; Harmondsworth: Penguin Books, 1964.

*Facial Justice.* London: Hamish Hamilton, 1960; Toronto: Collins, 1960; Garden City, New York: Doubleday, 1961; Harmondsworth: Penguin Books, 1966; New York: Curtis Books, n.d.

*Two for the River.* London: Hamish Hamilton, 1961; Toronto: Collins, 1961.

*The Brickfield.* London: Hamish Hamilton, 1964; Toronto: Collins, 1964.

*The Betrayal.* London: Hamish Hamilton, 1966; Toronto: Collins, 1966.

214

*The Novelist's Responsibility: Lectures and Essays.* London: Hamish Hamilton, 1967; Toronto: Collins, 1967.

*The Collected Short Stories of L. P. Hartley.* London: Hamish Hamilton, 1968.

*Poor Clare.* London: Hamish Hamilton, 1968.

*The Love-Adept.* London: Hamish Hamilton, 1969.

*My Sisters' Keeper.* London: Hamish Hamilton, 1970.

*The Harness Room.* London: Hamish Hamilton, 1971.

*Mrs. Carteret Receives and Other Stories.* London: Hamish Hamilton, 1971.

*The Collections.* London: Hamish Hamilton, 1972.

*The Will and the Way.* London: Hamish Hamilton, 1973.

*The Complete Short Stories of L. P. Hartley.* London: Hamish Hamilton, 1973.

SECONDARY SOURCES

ALLEN, WALTER. *The Modern Novel in Britain and the United States.* New York: E. P. Dutton and Co., Inc., 1964, pp. 253 - 257. A brief but appreciative assessment of Hartley, especially of the *Eustace and Hilda* trilogy. Hartley is seen as one of a number of contemporary novelists who are at the center of the English tradition of the novel.

ALLSOP, KENNETH. *The Angry Decade: A Survey of the Cultural Revolt of the Nineteen-fifties.* London: Peter Owen, Ltd., 1964, p. 34, p. 204. Passing and rather dismissive reference to L. P. Hartley as "marooned Edwardian," who "looks with intense sympathy at his graceful human beings—but through the wrong end of a telescope so that they are seen at an enormous distance, bright and separate as a day-dream."

BIEN, PETER. *L. P. Hartley.* University Park: The Pennsylvania State University Press, 1963. The first book-length study of Hartley's novels ending with *Facial Justice.* It remains a well-balanced and judicious attempt to establish "readings" for the major novels which concentrate on moral and psychological significance. Of particular note is the final section on "Mr. Hartley as Critic." Book is derived from earlier Columbia University dissertation.

BLOOMFIELD, PAUL. *L. P. Hartley,* rev. and enlarged edition. *Writers and Their Work* No. 217. London: Longmans Group, Ltd. for the British Council, 1970. A valuable monograph by one of Hartley's personal friends which interprets the novelist as a chronicler of upper-middle life who is neither a moralist nor a rebel. A novelist with a piety for days gone by.

BURGESS, ANTHONY. "Utopias and Dystopias," *The Novel Now: A Student's Guide to Contemporary Fiction.* London: Faber and Faber, 1967, pp. 44 - 45. Sees the earlier Hartley in the tradition of Henry James, but finds intriguing the symbolism of the *Eustace and Hilda trilogy* and the dystopian vision coupled with moral fable in *Facial Justice.* The brief comments on the latter novel are especially cogent.

CECIL, DAVID. "Introduction," *The Collected Short Stories of L. P. Hartley*. London: Hamish Hamilton, 1968. pp. v - viii. A gracious introduction to Hartley's Gothic imagination in his short fiction by one of his earliest and principal exponents.

———. "Introduction," *Eustace and Hilda: A Trilogy*. London: Putnam, 1958, pp. 7 - 13. Calls the trilogy a masterpiece wherein Hartley has used the story of Eustace to "express his vision of the spiritual laws governing human existence."

CLOSS, A. "Leslie Poles Hartley," *Die neueren Sprachen*, January, 1957, pp. 39 - 41. Brief comment on Hartley indicative of his reputation in Germany after publication of *Der Zoll des Glucks* (1956), the German translation of *The Go-Between*.

DAVIDSON, R. A. "Graham Greene and L. P. Hartley: 'The Basement Room' and *The Go-Between*," *Notes and Queries*, 13 (March, 1966), 101 - 102. Advances possible Greene short story source for Hartley's *The Go-Between*.

GRINDEA, MIRON. "Un maître du roman anglais," *Adam International Review*, 29, Nos. 294-295-296 (1961), 2 - 4. Introduction to the Hartley issue which features a critical essay on Hartley, printed in French by M. Brion; biographical essays and memoirs by Paul Bloomfield and C. H. B. Kitchin; French translations of "The Novelist's Responsibility," and some Hartley short stories; and a bibliography of Hartley's works, compiled by Peter Bien, to 1961.

GROSSVOGEL, DAVID I. "Under the Signs of Symbols: Losey and Hartley," *Diacritics* 4 (Fall, 1974). 51-56. A perceptive study of contrasts in literary symbolism versus film symbolism as based on Hartley's method in *The Go-Between* and Joseph Losey's film version of the novel.

HALL, JAMES. "Games of Apprehension: L. P. Hartley," *The Tragic Comedians: Seven Modern British Novelists*. Bloomington: Indiana University Press, 1963, pp. 111 - 128. A brilliant, pioneering essay on Hartley, concentrating on four novels of adult life with emphasis given to *The Boat*. "Human relations are a continuing, voluntary game of hide-and-seek, with great risks and few prospects of finding."

JONES, EDWARD T. "Summer of 1900: A la récherche of *The Go-Between*," *Literature / Film Quarterly*, 1 (Spring, 1973), 154 - 160. Evaluation of Joseph Losey / Harold Pinter's success in adapting the Hartley novel to film.

KARL, FREDERICK R. "Composite," *The Contemporary English Novel*. New York: Farrar, Straus, Cudahay, 1962, pp. 277 - 278. A somewhat patronizing yet fair assessment of Hartley as a novelist of manners rather akin to the American John P. Marquand.

LAS VERGNAS, Raymond. Book VIII, "The Twentieth Century" (1914 - 1963), Legouis and Cazamian's *History of English Literature*. New York: The Macmillan Co., 1964, p. 1389. Acknowledges Hartley's skill as a psychologist but finds his moral qualms somewhat too engaging "to be taken altogether seriously. "Considers Hartley a trifle out of date and "finical": "his recourse to drawing-room supernatural" leaves Las Vergnas with a sense of effeteness.

MASON, MICHAEL, and PETER BURTON. "A Domestic Animal?: An Interview with Francis King," *Gay News*, No. 100 (July 29, 1976), 23 - 24. Some candid and revealing biographical remarks about L. P. Hartley from a close friend.

MELCHIORI, GIORGIO. "The English Novelist and the American Tradition," *Sewanee Review*, 18 (1960), 502 - 515. An early essay on Hartley, principally with respect to *The Go-Between*, which is used to illustrate Hartley's debt to Hawthorne and the American symbolic tradition of romance. A seminal essay.

MOAN, MARGARET A. "Setting and Structure: An Approach to Hartley's *The Go-Between*," *Critique* 15 (1973), 26 - 37. Ingeniously relates the three-part structure of the novel and its setting to the spiritual and psychological experiences of Leo Colston. A good essay on the thematic function of Hartley's narrative technique.

MULKEEN, ANNE. *Wild Thyme, Winter Lightning: The Symbolic Novels of L. P. Hartley*. Detroit: Wayne State University Press, 1974. The second book-length study of Hartley's fiction, including the short stories and ending in the canon with *Poor Clare*, based on a University of Wisconsin dissertation, makes an intelligent case for Hartley as an innovator in modern fiction who combined myth, symbol, and fantasy in a rather Hawthornesque way to produce metaphysical romances and mock-romances rather than psychological novels. An alternative interpretation to the earlier Bien volume.

REYNOLDS, DONALD LLOYD, JR. "The Novels of L. P. Hartley," Unpubl. Diss. University of Washington, 1967. A refreshingly straightforward survey of Hartley's fiction, distinguished for its lack of thesis-riding.

SEYMOUR-SMITH, MARTIN. "L. P. Hartley," *Who's Who in Twentieth Century Literature*. New York: Holt, Rinehart and Winston, 1976, pp. 151 - 152. Rather unflattering characterization of the man and his work, yet provocative and even persuasive, e.g., "The element of cruel stupidity in the man becomes, in the novelist, refined into a posture more subtle and imaginative and built into that posture is a rueful acknowledgement of Hartley's own sadistic interest in punishment and of his own sexual frustration." He finds Hartley hardly surpassed as a relaxed comedian of manners.

SORENSEN, KNUD. "Language and Society in L. P. Hartley's *Facial Justice*," *Orbis Litterarum* (Copenhagen), 26 (1971), 68 - 78. An essay in English which offers a rather Orwellian reading of the relationship between language and society as Hartley employs the technique in *Facial Justice* of criticizing society by satirizing its debasement of language.

VERNIER, J.-P. "La Trilogie romanesque de L. P. Hartley," *Études anglaises*, 13 (1960), 26 - 31. An examination of three levels of significance in the *Eustace and Hilda* trilogy—social, psychological, and metaphysical. Opts finally for Hartley as a visionary novelist whose characters are in search of some kind of salvation. Allied with those interpreters who see Hartley as a writer of romance.

WEBSTER, HARVEY CURTIS. "L. P. Hartley: Diffident Christian," *After the Trauma: Representative British Novelists Since 1920*. Lexington: The University Press of Kentucky, 1970, pp. 152 - 167. Comprehensive and perceptive overview of Hartley's fiction, exclusive of the short stories, from *Simonetta Perkins* to *Poor Clare*. The Christian context is especially helpful because it is not overstated.

————. "The Novels of L. P. Hartley," *Critique*, 4 (1961), 39 - 51. Earlier version of the foregoing chapter, ending with *Facial Justice*. The first introduction to Hartley published in the United States which ascribed to him a corpus of significant fiction.

WILLMOTT, MICHAEL B. " 'What Leo Knew', The Childhood World of L. P. Hartley," *English* (London), 24 (1975), 3 - 10. Introductory survey with plot summaries of three Hartleian childhoods: Leo's in *The Go-Between*; Eustace's in *The Shrimp and the Anemone*; and Richard's in *The Brickfield*. Sees *The Go-Between* as Hartley's masterpiece for its definitive evocation of youthful perceptions; allies Hartley with a Jamesian tradition, as the title suggests.

# Index